Vert.x in Action

Vert.x in Action

ASYNCHRONOUS AND REACTIVE JAVA

JULIEN PONGE

FOREWORD BY MARTIJN VERBERG

MANNING

SHELTER ISLAND

For online information and ordering of this and other Manning books, please visit
www.manning.com. The publisher offers discounts on this book when ordered in quantity.
For more information, please contact

Special Sales Department
Manning Publications Co.
20 Baldwin Road
PO Box 761
Shelter Island, NY 11964
Email: orders@manning.com

Manning Publications Co.
20 Baldwin Road
PO Box 761
Shelter Island, NY 11964

Development editor:	Leslie Trites
Technical development editor:	Raphael Villela
Review editor:	Aleksandar Dragosavljević
Production editor:	Lori Weidert
Copy editor:	Andy Carroll
Proofreader:	Melody Dolab
Technical proofreader:	Evyator Kafkafi
Typesetter:	Gordan Salinovic
Cover designer:	Marija Tudor

ISBN 9781617295621
Printed in the United States of America

To Marie and Mathieu

brief contents

contents

foreword

I first ran across Vert.x in 2014 when I was the CTO at jClarity, a start-up I'd co-founded with Ben Evans and Kirk Pepperdine. We were building a SaaS that needed to receive large amounts of telemetry data, run analytics over it, and then present tuning recommendations to the end-user. Our use case required non-blocking, asynchronous communication, multi-tenancy (cost savings!), the ability to talk to data stores, and decent support for secured WebSockets. It would need to be a distributed system that scaled. Enter Vert.x!

John Oliver, our Chief Scientist, discovered this flexible framework for building asynchronous applications. Vert.x could do it all. It had blazing performance, thanks to its Netty base, and it supported all other functional and non-functional requirements. Even better was that it was backed by a bunch of brilliant, humble, and friendly engineers, such as Julien Ponge, the author of this book.

Vert.x is deliberately a non-prescriptive framework, in that it doesn't guide you down a narrow path like, say, Spring Boot does. It's more like a toolkit of high-quality tools that are designed to work together, but you have to decide how to integrate them. That's where this book becomes your indispensable guide.

Part one of the book exposes the two main building blocks, the Verticle processing unit and the event bus, along with how the asynchronous programming model works with them. But part two is where the real value lies. Julien guides you through the best practices around designing a reactive application and plugging in Vert.x capabilities such as Data Storage and the web-stack.

Strangely, for me it's the awesome testing chapter that brings the most value; testing reactive applications is just plain hard, and you'll really appreciate this chapter!

It's an absolute privilege and pleasure to have read this book, even if it reminded me of where we'd gone wrong in a few places! Not to worry, though; we took Vert.x along with us when we got acquired by Microsoft, and this book will be the perfect companion to help us complete our story on a truly global scale.

MARTIJN VERBURG—"THE DIABOLICAL DEVELOPER"
PRINCIPAL SWE GROUP MANAGER (JAVA)—MICROSOFT

preface

I remember sitting in a comfortable cinema room at Devoxx Belgium 2012. Among the many conferences that I had planned to attend was one with Tim Fox introducing his new project called *Vert.x*. At the time, Node.js was all the hype, returning to asynchronous programming as the magic solution to all scalability problems. Through his presentation, Tim convinced me (and many other attendees) that he had just laid down a solid foundation for asynchronous programming on the JVM, embracing the strength of the Java ecosystem and picking the good ideas from Node.js. One thing that struck me at the time was that you could write simple Java code, and forget complex annotation-based frameworks and application servers. Vert.x felt like a breath of fresh air, so I kept an eye on the project. Fast-forward a few years: I am now working in the Vert.x team at Red Hat, something I wouldn't have imagined back in 2012!

Vert.x is increasingly relevant in an era when applications are deployed to virtualized environments and containers. We expect applications to scale up and down to accommodate fluctuating traffic. We expect applications to have low latency. We expect applications to be resilient when other systems fail. We expect to pack as many applications as possible onto a given server. In short, we need resource-efficient, scalable, and dependable applications.

This is what *reactive applications* are all about: latency is under control both as the workload grows and when failures happen. Vert.x is a solid foundation for building such reactive applications, but Vert.x alone is no silver bullet. You don't build reactive applications by taking a software stack off the shelf; you also need a methodology as you architect and develop a reactive application.

In this book we will explore how to write reactive applications with Vert.x. This is not just about learning Vert.x, but also the fundamentals of asynchronous programming and techniques to assess whether an application is truly reactive or not. Last but not least, Vert.x is fun, and you will see that this simplicity and forgetting about some supposed "best practices" can be liberating.

acknowledgments

My first thanks go to my partner Marie and my son Mathieu for their incredible support. Writing a book takes some time away from your family, and I am very lucky to have them by my side.

I am grateful to be working with exceptional people at Red Hat. Thanks to Mark Little, David Ingham, Rodney Russ, and Julien Viet who gave me the opportunity to first take a sabbatical to work on Vert.x with Red Hat, and then to move to a full-time position. Many thanks to my closest colleagues Julien Viet, Thomas Segismont, Clément Escoffier, Paulo Lopes, Rodney Russ, Stéphane Épardaud, and Francesco Guardiani: working with all of you is a privilege.

I started writing this book while I was still working as an Associate Professor at INSA Lyon, and I was fortunate enough to receive warm support in my career choices. Thanks to Fabrice Valois, Frédéric Le Mouël, Nicolas Stouls, Oscar Carillo, François Lesueur, and Éric Maurincomme.

It is an honor for me that Martijn Verburg wrote the foreword for this book. Martijn is a historical figure in the Vert.x project, and he showed early on that Vert.x was production-grade for building challenging services at his jClarity startup, later bought by Microsoft. Thanks a lot, Martijn.

The Manning MEAP program gave me the opportunity to receive lots of feedback as the writing progressed; thanks to everyone who contacted me with remarks, typos, and suggestions.

In fact, having written for Manning, I now understand why their books are so good. Manning is very serious about investing in authors and books. Many thanks to my development editor Lesley Trites for her always positive and constructive guidance, and to Kristen Watterson who started the book with me. Thanks to Michael Stephens for being enthusiastic about writing a book on reactive applications in Java. Many thanks to Raphael Vilella for his accurate technical feedback as I was writing chapters, and to Evyatar Kafkafi for his excellent technical proofreading. Also, thanks to Candace Gillhoolley from marketing, who I had the chance to meet at the Reactive Summit 2018 held in Montreal.

To all the reviewers: Michał Ambroziewicz, Andrew Buttery, Salvatore Campagna, Philippe Charrière, Ahmed Chicktay, John Clingan, Earl Benjamin Bingham, Arnaud Esteve, Damian Esteban, Leonardo Jose Gomes da Silva, Evyatar Kafkafi, Alexandros Koufoudakis, Sanket Naik, Eoghan O'Donnell, Dan Sheikh, Jerry Stralko, George Thomas, Evan Wallace, James Watson, and Matthew Welke, your suggestions helped make this a better book.

about this book

Asynchronous and reactive applications are an important topic in modern distributed systems, especially as the progressive shift to virtualized and containerized runtime environments emphasizes the need for resource-efficient, adaptable, and dependable application designs.

Asynchronous programming is key to maximizing hardware resource usage, as it allows us to deal with more concurrent connections than in traditional blocking I/O paradigms. Services need to cater to workloads that may drastically change from one hour to the next, so we need to design code that naturally supports horizontal scalability. Last but not least, failure is inevitable when we have services interacting with other services over the network. Embracing failure is key to designing dependable systems.

Combine asynchronous programming, horizontal scalability, and resilience, and you have what we today call *reactive applications*, which can also be summarized without marketing jargon as "scalable and dependable applications."

That being said, there is no free lunch, and the transition to writing asynchronous and reactive applications is difficult when you have a background in more traditional software stacks. Grokking asynchrony in itself is difficult, but the implications of scalability and resilience on the design of an application are anything but trivial.

This book is aimed at Java developers from all backgrounds who would like to teach themselves both the concepts and practices of building asynchronous and reactive applications. This book uses Eclipse Vert.x, a "no-magic" toolkit for writing such applications. Developers appreciate Vert.x for its simplicity, easy embedding, and field-tested performance.

Who should read this book

This book is intended for intermediate Java developers familiar with web development, networked services, and enterprise Java frameworks like Spring or Java EE. No prior experience in asynchronous or reactive programming is required.

How this book is organized: A roadmap

Vert.x in Action is split into two parts.

Part 1 covers the fundamentals of asynchronous programming and the core APIs of Vert.x:

- Chapter 1 is an introduction to Vert.x, asynchronous programming, and Vert.x. If you have never been exposed to asynchronous programming before, this chapter will take you back to the core non-blocking APIs in Java, and it will show you why Vert.x provides a more approachable programming model. This chapter also discusses the need for reactive in modern distributed systems.
- Chapter 2 introduces *verticles*, the core building blocks for writing non-blocking code in Vert.x. Since you will sometimes need to call blocking or long-running operations, this chapter also gives you tools and techniques for mixing blocking and non-blocking code.
- Chapter 3 presents the *event bus*, an eventing system verticles use to communicate. The nice thing about the event bus is that it allows verticles to communicate not just within a single process but also across a cluster, which makes it a powerful abstraction.
- Chapter 4 discusses asynchronous streams, with a focus on the notion of *backpressure* which is required to regulate the flow of events between consumers and producers.
- Chapter 5 shows you how to use other asynchronous programming models than callbacks. While callbacks are simple and efficient, there are many cases where they render the coordination of asynchronous operations difficult. Vert.x can mix and match different models: futures and promises, reactive extensions, and Kotlin coroutines.
- Chapter 6 revisits the event bus and introduces event-bus services, a component abstraction on top of the event bus. Since the event bus serves as a natural delimitation between event-processing units, this chapter also discusses how to write tests in Vert.x.

Part 2 of the book focuses on building a realistic reactive application:

- Chapter 7 presents a realistic reactive application use case that will be used throughout the chapters of part 2. The application is composed of multiple event-driven microservices that we will specify.

- Chapter 8 exposes some key elements of the Vert.x web stack: designing HTTP APIs, JSON web tokens, cross-origin resource sharing, and integrating with a modern web application frontend.
- Chapter 9 is all about messaging and event streaming. We'll cover the AMQP protocol used in message brokers, Apache Kafka, and sending emails over SMTP.
- Chapter 10 covers databases and persistent state management with Vert.x. It shows how to use MongoDB (a so-called NoSQL database) and the PostgreSQL relational database for which Vert.x offers a native reactive client.
- Chapter 11 tackles end-to-end real-time reactive event processing with RxJava and Apache Kafka. This chapter also discusses how to connect JavaScript web applications to the Vert.x event bus for a unified programming model.
- Chapter 12 is highly experimental and provides techniques to assess whether a service is actually reactive. By using load and chaos testing tools, we'll observe a service's behavior and discuss failure mitigation techniques such as circuit breakers, and their impact on the service's overall behavior.
- Chapter 13 is the final chapter, and it discusses Vert.x applications running in container environments. We'll discuss clustering, application configuration, and service discovery using simple mechanisms. You'll see how to package Vert.x services as container images, deploy them to a Kubernetes cluster, and expose health checks and metrics.

Chapters 1 to 6 are intended for all readers. Some parts can be skipped if you already have some experience with asynchronous programming.

Chapter 7 shows the decomposition of an application based on event-driven reactive services.

Chapters 8 to 11 cover the most popular pieces of the Vert.x stack and should be useful for all readers interested in becoming proficient with Vert.x.

Chapter 12 is where we consolidate everything and touch on the topic of resiliency, which is fundamental to making reactive applications. This chapter can nearly be read on its own by anyone interested in load and chaos testing. Indeed, there is less code and more hands-on content in this chapter, and you could apply the same methodology to a service written in a stack other than Vert.x.

Finally, chapter 13 can be skipped if you are not interested in containers and Kubernetes.

About the code

The source code of the book's examples can be downloaded free of charge from the GitHub repository at https://github.com/jponge/vertx-in-action or from the Manning website at www.manning.com/books/vertx-in-action.

The samples require Java 8 or 11 to compile. Maven and Gradle builds are provided. An installation of Docker is required to run the tests and examples for the chapters in part 2. The book's workflow is better in a Unix environment: Linux, macOS, or the Microsoft Windows Subsystem for Linux (WSL). I use a few command-line tools that you may have to install; details are given in the corresponding chapters.

This book contains many examples of source code, both in numbered listings and in line with normal text. In both cases, source code is formatted in a `fixed-width font like this` to separate it from ordinary text. In many cases, the original source code has been reformatted; we've added line breaks and reworked indentation to accommodate the available page space in the book. Additionally, comments in the source code have often been removed from the listings when the code is described in the text. Code annotations accompany many of the listings, highlighting important concepts.

liveBook discussion forum

Purchase of *Vert.x in Action* includes free access to a private web forum run by Manning Publications where you can make comments about the book, ask technical questions, and receive help from the author and from other users. To access the forum, go to https://livebook.manning.com/#!/book/vertx-in-action/discussion. You can also learn more about Manning's forums and the rules of conduct at https://livebook .manning.com/#!/discussion.

Manning's commitment to our readers is to provide a venue where a meaningful dialogue between individual readers and between readers and the author can take place. It is not a commitment to any specific amount of participation on the part of the author, whose contribution to the forum remains voluntary (and unpaid). We suggest you try asking the author some challenging questions lest his interest stray! The forum and the archives of previous discussions will be accessible from the publisher's website as long as the book is in print.

about the author

DR. JULIEN PONGE is a Principal Software Engineer at Red Hat, working on reactive and the Eclipse Vert.x project. He is on leave from INSA Lyon and the CITI Laboratory where he was an Associate Professor in computer science and engineering. He held various teaching, research, management, and executive positions there. He has 20 years of experience in open source ecosystems, having participated in many projects and created the likes of IzPack and the Eclipse Golo programming language. He is also a regular speaker at user groups and conferences. He is an alumni from Université Clermont Auvergne (France) and the University of New South Wales (Australia) where he obtained his PhD degrees.

about the cover illustration

The figure on the cover of *Vert.x in Action* is captioned "Femme Kourilienne," or a woman from the Kurile Islands. The illustration is taken from a collection of dress costumes from various countries by Jacques Grasset de Saint-Sauveur (1757–1810), titled *Costumes de Différents Pays,* published in France in 1797. Each illustration is finely drawn and colored by hand. The rich variety of Grasset de Saint-Sauveur's collection reminds us vividly of how culturally apart the world's towns and regions were just 200 years ago. Isolated from each other, people spoke different dialects and languages. In the streets or in the countryside, it was easy to identify where they lived and what their trade or station in life was just by their dress.

The way we dress has changed since then and the diversity by region, so rich at the time, has faded away. It is now hard to tell apart the inhabitants of different continents, let alone different towns, regions, or countries. Perhaps we have traded cultural diversity for a more varied personal life—certainly for a more varied and fast-paced technological life.

At a time when it is hard to tell one computer book from another, Manning celebrates the inventiveness and initiative of the computer business with book covers based on the rich diversity of regional life of two centuries ago, brought back to life by Grasset de Saint-Sauveur's pictures.

Part 1

Fundamentals of asynchronous programming with Vert.x

The first step toward building reactive systems is to adopt *asynchronous programming*. Traditional programming models based on blocking I/O do not scale as well as those that use non-blocking I/O. Serving more requests with fewer resources is very appealing, so where's the catch? There is indeed a *little* problem: asynchronous programming is a non-trivial paradigm shift if you have never been exposed to it!

The chapters in this part of the book will teach you the fundamental concepts of asynchronous programming by using the Vert.x toolkit. Thinking in asynchronous operations is definitely approachable (and fun!) with Vert.x, and we will explore the main building blocks of a Vert.x application.

Vert.x, asynchronous programming, and reactive systems

1

This chapter covers

- What Vert.x is
- Why distributed systems cannot be avoided
- The challenges in programming resource-efficient networked applications
- What asynchronous and non-blocking programming is
- What a reactive application is, and why asynchronous programming is not enough
- Alternatives to Vert.x

We developers live in an industry of buzzwords, technologies, and practices hype cycles. I have long taught university students the elements of designing, programming, integrating, and deploying applications, and I have witnessed first-hand how complicated it can be for newcomers to navigate the wild ocean of current technologies.

3

Asynchronous and *reactive* are important topics in modern applications, and my goal with this book is to help developers understand the core concepts behind these terms, gain practical experience, and recognize *when* there are benefits to these approaches. We will use *Eclipse Vert.x,* a toolkit for writing asynchronous applications that has the added benefit of providing solutions for the different definitions of what "reactive" means.

Ensuring that you understand the concepts is a priority for me in this book. While I want to give you a solid understanding of how to write Vert.x applications, I also want to make sure that you can translate the skills you learn here to other similar and possibly competing technologies, now or five years down the road.

1.1   *Being distributed and networked is the norm*

It was common 20 years ago to deploy business applications that could perform all operations while running isolated on a single machine. Such applications typically exhibited a graphical user interface, and they had local databases or custom file management for storing data. This is, of course, a gross exaggeration, as networking was already in use, and business applications could take advantage of database servers over the network, networked file storage, and various remote code operations.

Today, an application is more naturally exposed to end users through web and mobile interfaces. This naturally brings the network into play, and hence distributed systems. Also, *service-oriented architectures* allow the reuse of some functionality by issuing requests to other services, possibly controlled by a third-party provider. Examples would be delegating authentication in a consumer application to popular account providers like Google, Facebook, or Twitter, or delegating payment processing to Stripe or PayPal.

1.2   *Not living on an isolated island*

Figure 1.1 is a fictional depiction of what a modern application is: a set of networked services interacting with each other. Here are some of these networked services:

- A database like PostgreSQL or MongoDB stores data.
- A search engine like Elasticsearch allows finding information that was previously indexed, such as products in a catalog.
- A durable storage service like Amazon S3 provides persistent and replicated data storage of documents.
- A messaging service can be
  - An SMTP server to programmatically send emails.
  - A bot for interacting with users over messaging platforms, such as Slack, Telegram, or Facebook Messenger.
  - An integration messaging protocol for application-to-application integration, like AMQP.
- An identity management service like Keycloak provides authentication and role management for user and service interactions.
- Monitoring with libraries like Micrometer exposes health statuses, metrics, and logs so that external orchestration tools can maintain proper quality of service, possibly by starting new service instances or killing existing ones when they fail.

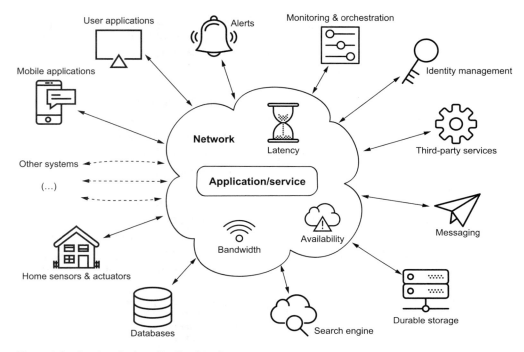

Figure 1.1 A networked application/service

Later in this book you will see examples of typical services such as API endpoints, stream processors, and edge services.[1] The preceding list is not exhaustive, of course, but the key point is that services rarely live in isolation, as they need to talk to other services over the network to function.

1.3 *There is no free lunch on the network*

The network is exactly where a number of things may go wrong in computing:

- The bandwidth can fluctuate a lot, so data-intensive interactions between services may suffer. Not all services can enjoy fast bandwidth inside the same data center, and even so, it remains slower than communications between processes on the same machine.
- The latency fluctuates a lot, and because services need to talk to services that talk to additional services to process a given request, all network-induced latency adds to the overall request-processing times.
- Availability should not be taken for granted: Networks fail. Routers fail. Proxies fail. Sometimes someone runs into a network cable and disconnects it. When the network fails, a service that sends a request to another service may not be able to determine if it is the other service or the network that is down.

---

[1]For readers already familiar with microservice patterns, "edge service" is, in my opinion, a better term than "API gateway."

In essence, modern applications are made of distributed and networked services. They are accessed over networks that themselves introduce problems, and each service needs to maintain several incoming and outgoing connections.

1.4 *The simplicity of blocking APIs*

Services need to manage connections to other services and requesters. The traditional and widespread model for managing concurrent network connections is to allocate a thread for each connection. This is the model in many technologies, such as Servlets in Jakarta EE (before additions in version 3), Spring Framework (before additions in version 5), Ruby on Rails, Python Flask, and many more. This model has the advantage of simplicity, as it is *synchronous.*

Let's look at an example where a TCP server echoes input text back to the client until it sees a /quit terminal input (shown in listing 1.3).

The server can be run using the Gradle run task from the book's full example project (./gradlew run -PmainClass=chapter1.snippets.SynchronousEcho in a terminal). By using the netcat command-line tool, we can send and receive text.

Listing 1.1 Client-side output of a `netcat` session

```
$ netcat localhost 3000        This line is the user input
Hello, Vert.x!              <—  on the command line.
Hello, Vert.x!     <—
Great                          This line is sent by
Great                          the TCP server.
/quit
/quit
$
```

TIP You may need to install netcat (or nc) on your operating system.

On the server side, we can see the following trace.

Listing 1.2 Server-side trace

```
$ ./gradlew run -PmainClass=chapter1.snippets.SynchronousEcho
(...)
~ Hello, Vert.x!
~ Great
~ /quit
```

The code in the following listing provides the TCP server implementation. It is a classical use of the java.io package that provides synchronous I/O APIs.

Listing 1.3 Synchronous echo TCP protocol

```
public class SynchronousEcho {
  public static void main(String[] args) throws Throwable {
    ServerSocket server = new ServerSocket();
```

```
    server.bind(new InetSocketAddress(3000));
    while (true) {
      Socket socket = server.accept();
      new Thread(clientHandler(socket)).start();
    }
  }

  private static Runnable clientHandler(Socket socket) {
    return () -> {
      try (
        BufferedReader reader = new BufferedReader(
          new InputStreamReader(socket.getInputStream()));
        PrintWriter writer = new PrintWriter(
          new OutputStreamWriter(socket.getOutputStream()))) {
        String line = "";
        while (!"/quit".equals(line)) {
          line = reader.readLine();
          System.out.println("~ " + line);
          writer.write(line + "\n");
          writer.flush();
        }
      } catch (IOException e) {
        e.printStackTrace();
      }
    };
  }
}
```

> The main application thread plays the role of an accepting thread, as it receives socket objects for all new connections. The operation blocks when no connection is pending. A new thread is allocated for each connection.

> Reading from a socket may block the thread allocated to the connection, such as when insufficient data is being read.

> Writing to a socket may also block, such as until the underlying TCP buffer data has been sent over the network.

The server uses the main thread for accepting connections, and each connection is allocated a new thread for processing I/O. The I/O operations are synchronous, so threads may block on I/O operations.

1.5   *Blocking APIs waste resources, increase costs*

The main problem with the code in listing 1.3 is that it allocates a new thread for each incoming connection, and threads are anything but cheap resources. A thread needs memory, and the more threads you have, the more you put pressure on the operating system kernel scheduler, as it needs to give CPU time to the threads. We could improve the code in listing 1.3 by using a thread pool to reuse threads after a connection has been closed, but we still need *n* threads for *n* connections at any given point in time.

This is illustrated in figure 1.2, where you can see the CPU usage over time of three threads for three concurrent network connections. Input/output operations such as readLine and write may *block* the thread, meaning that it is being parked by the operating system. This happens for two reasons:

- A read operation may be waiting for data to arrive from the network.
- A write operation may have to wait for buffers to be drained if they are full from a previous write operation.

A modern operating system can properly deal with a few thousand concurrent threads. Not every networked service will face loads with so many concurrent requests,

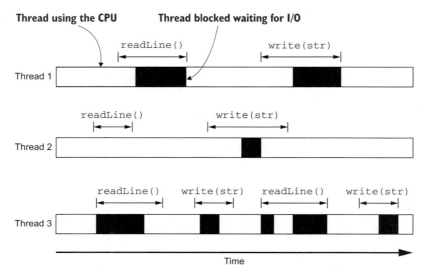

Figure 1.2   Threads and blocking I/O operations

but this model quickly shows its limits when we are talking about tens of thousands of concurrent connections.

It is also important to recall that we often need more threads than incoming network connections. To take a concrete example, suppose that we have an HTTP service that offers the best price for a given product, which it does by requesting prices from four other HTTP services, as illustrated in figure 1.3. This type of service is often

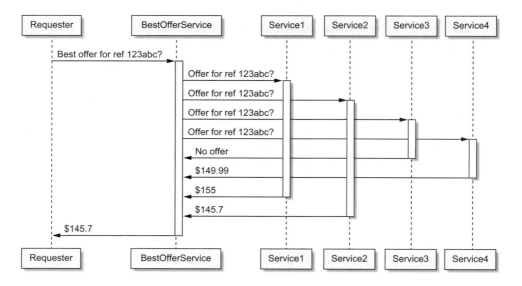

Figure 1.3   Request processing in an edge service

called an *edge service* or an *API gateway*. Requesting each service in sequence and then selecting the lowest price would render our service very slow, as each request adds to our own service's latency. The efficient way is to start four concurrent requests from our service, and then wait and gather their responses. This translates to starting four more threads; if we had 1,000 concurrent network requests, we might be using up to 5,000 threads in the worst naive case, where all requests need to be processed at the same time and we don't use thread pooling or maintain persistent connections from the edge service to the requested services.

Last, but not least, applications are often deployed to containerized or virtualized environments. This means that applications may not see all the available CPU cores, and their allocated CPU time may be limited. Available memory for processes may also be restricted, so having too many threads also eats into the memory budget. Such applications have to share CPU resources with other applications, so if all applications use blocking I/O APIs, there can quickly be too many threads to manage and schedule, which requires starting more server/container instances as traffic ramps up. This translates directly to increased operating costs.

1.6 Asynchronous programming with non-blocking I/O

Instead of waiting for I/O operations to complete, we can shift to *non-blocking* I/O. You may have already sampled this with the `select` function in C.

The idea behind non-blocking I/O is to request a (blocking) operation, and move on to doing other tasks until the operation result is ready. For example a non-blocking read may ask for up to 256 bytes over a network socket, and the execution thread does other things (like dealing with another connection) until data has been put into the buffers, ready for consumption in memory. In this model, many concurrent connections can be multiplexed on a single thread, as network latency typically exceeds the CPU time it takes to read incoming bytes.

Java has long had the `java.nio` (Java NIO) package, which offers non-blocking I/O APIs over files and networks. Going back to our previous example of a TCP service that echoes incoming data, listings 1.4 through 1.7 show a possible implementation with Java non-blocking I/O.

Listing 1.4 Asynchronous variant of the echo service: main loop

We need to put the channel into non-blocking mode.

```
public class AsynchronousEcho {
  public static void main(String[] args) throws IOException {
    Selector selector = Selector.open();

    ServerSocketChannel serverSocketChannel = ServerSocketChannel.open();
    serverSocketChannel.bind(new InetSocketAddress(3000));
    serverSocketChannel.configureBlocking(false);
    serverSocketChannel.register(selector, SelectionKey.OP_ACCEPT);

    while (true) {
      selector.select();
```

The selector will notify of incoming connections.

This collects all non-blocking I/O notifications.

```
            Iterator<SelectionKey> it = selector.selectedKeys().iterator();
We          while (it.hasNext()) {
have a new     SelectionKey key = it.next();
connection.    if (key.isAcceptable()) {
                 newConnection(selector, key);          A socket has
               } else if (key.isReadable()) {           received data.
                 echo(key);
               } else if (key.isWritable()) {          A socket is ready
                 continueEcho(selector, key);          for writing again.
               }
               it.remove();          Selection keys need to be manually
            }                         removed, or they will be available
          }                           again in the next loop iteration.
        }
        // (...)
```

Listing 1.4 shows the server socket channel preparation code. It opens the server socket channel and makes it non-blocking, then registers an NIO key selector for processing events. The main loop iterates over the selector keys that have events ready for processing and dispatches them to specialized methods depending on the event type (new connections, data has arrived, or data can be sent again).

Listing 1.5   Asynchronous variant of the echo service: accepting connections

```
private static class Context {
    private final ByteBuffer nioBuffer = ByteBuffer.allocate(512);
    private String currentLine = "";               The Context class keeps
    private boolean terminating = false;           state related to the handling
}                                                  of a TCP connection.

private static final HashMap<SocketChannel, Context> contexts =
   new HashMap<>();

private static void newConnection(Selector selector, SelectionKey key)
   throws IOException {
  ServerSocketChannel serverSocketChannel = (ServerSocketChannel)
   key.channel();
  SocketChannel socketChannel = serverSocketChannel.accept();
  socketChannel
    .configureBlocking(false)
    .register(selector, SelectionKey.OP_READ);        We set the channel
  contexts.put(socketChannel, new Context());         to non-blocking and
}                                                     declare interest in
                          We keep all connection      read operations.
                          states in a hash map.
```

Listing 1.5 shows how new TCP connections are dealt with. The socket channel that corresponds to the new connection is configured as non-blocking and then is tracked for further reference in a hash map, where it is associated to some *context object*. The context depends on the application and protocol. In our case, we track the current line and whether the connection is closing, and we maintain a connection-specific NIO buffer for reading and writing data.

**If we find a line ending with /quit,
we terminate the connection.**
```java
private static final Pattern QUIT = Pattern.compile("(\\r)?(\\n)?/quit$");

  private static void echo(SelectionKey key) throws IOException {
    SocketChannel socketChannel = (SocketChannel) key.channel();
    Context context = contexts.get(socketChannel);
    try {
      socketChannel.read(context.nioBuffer);
      context.nioBuffer.flip();
      context.currentLine = context.currentLine +
        Charset.defaultCharset().decode(context.nioBuffer);
      if (QUIT.matcher(context.currentLine).find()) {
        context.terminating = true;
      } else if (context.currentLine.length() > 16) {
        context.currentLine = context.currentLine.substring(8);
      }
      context.nioBuffer.flip();
      int count = socketChannel.write(context.nioBuffer);
      if (count < context.nioBuffer.limit()) {
        key.cancel();
        socketChannel.register(key.selector(), SelectionKey.OP_WRITE);
      } else {
        context.nioBuffer.clear();
        if (context.terminating) {
          cleanup(socketChannel);
        }
      }
    } catch (IOException err) {
      err.printStackTrace();
      cleanup(socketChannel);
    }
  }
```

Java NIO buffers need positional manipulations: the buffer has read data, so to write it back to the client, we need to flip and return to the start position.

It may happen that not all data can be written, so we stop looking for read operations and declare interest in a notification indicating when the channel can be written to again.

Listing 1.6 has the code for the echo method. The processing is very simple: we read data from the client socket, and then we attempt to write it back. If the write operation was only partial, we stop further reads, declare interest in knowing when the socket channel is writable again, and then ensure all data is written.

```java
private static void cleanup(SocketChannel socketChannel) throws IOException {
    socketChannel.close();
    contexts.remove(socketChannel);
  }
```

```
  private static vcid continueEcho(Selector selector, SelectionKey key)
➡  throws IOException {
    SocketChannel socketChannel = (SocketChannel) key.channel();
    Context context = contexts.get(socketChannel);
    try {
      int remainingBytes = context.nioBuffer.limit() -
      context.nioBuffer.position();
      int count = socketChannel.write(context.nioBuffer);
      if (count == remainingBytes) {      ◄
        context.nioBuffer.clear();
        key.cancel();
        if (context.terminating) {
          cleanup(socketChannel);
        } else {
          socketChannel.register(selector, SelectionKey.OP_READ);
        }
      }
    } catch (IOException err) {
      err.printStackTrace();
      cleanup(socketChannel);
    }
  }
}
```

We remain in this state until all data has been written back. Then we drop our write interest and declare read interest.

Finally, listing 1.7 shows the methods for closing the TCP connection and for finishing writing a buffer. When all data has been written in `continueEcho`, we register interest again in reading data.

As this example shows, using non-blocking I/O is doable, but it significantly increases the code complexity compared to the initial version that used blocking APIs. The echo protocol needs two states for reading and writing back data: reading, or finishing writing. For more elaborate TCP protocols, you can easily anticipate the need for more complicated state machines.

It is also important to note that like most JDK APIs, `java.nio` focuses solely on what it does (here, I/O APIs). It does not provide higher-level protocol-specific helpers, like for writing HTTP clients and servers. Also, `java.nio` does not prescribe a threading model, which is still important to properly utilize CPU cores, nor does it handle asynchronous I/O events or articulate the application processing logic.

> **NOTE**   This is why, in practice, developers rarely deal with Java NIO. Networking libraries like Netty and Apache MINA solve the shortcomings of Java NIO, and many toolkits and frameworks are built on top of them. As you will soon discover, Eclipse Vert.x is one of them.

1.7   *Multiplexing event-driven processing: The case of the event loop*

A popular threading model for processing asynchronous events is that of the event loop. Instead of polling for events that may have arrived, as we did in the previous Java NIO example, events are pushed to an *event loop*.

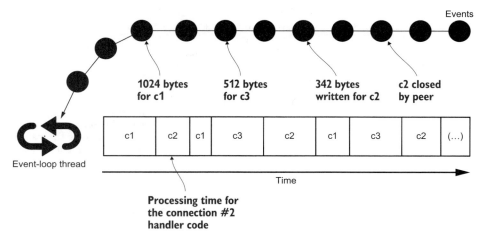

Figure 1.4   Processing events using an event loop

As you can see in figure 1.4, events are queued as they arrive. They can be I/O events, such as data being ready for consumption or a buffer having been fully written to a socket. They can also be any *other* event, such as a timer firing. A single thread is assigned to an event loop, and processing events shouldn't perform any blocking or long-running operation. Otherwise, the thread blocks, defeating the purpose of using an event loop.

Event loops are quite popular: JavaScript code running in web browsers runs on top of an event loop. Many graphical interface toolkits, such as Java Swing, also have an event loop.

Implementing an event loop is easy.

Listing 1.8   Using a simple event loop

```
public static void main(String[] args) {            A first thread that dispatches
  EventLoop eventLoop = new EventLoop();            events every second to the
  new Thread(() -> {                          ◁─── event loop
    for (int n = 0; n < 6; n++) {
      delay(1000);
      eventLoop.dispatch(new EventLoop.Event("tick", n));
    }
    eventLoop.dispatch(new EventLoop.Event("stop", null));
  }).start();
  new Thread(() -> {   ◁─┤ A second thread that dispatches two
    delay(2500);          events at 2500 ms and 3300 ms
    eventLoop.dispatch(new EventLoop.Event("hello", "beautiful world"));
    delay(800);
    eventLoop.dispatch(new EventLoop.Event("hello", "beautiful universe"));
  }).start();
  eventLoop.dispatch(new EventLoop.Event("hello", "world!"));  ◁─┤ Events
  eventLoop.dispatch(new EventLoop.Event("foo", "bar"));          │ dispatched from
  eventLoop                                                       │ the main thread
```

```
      .on("hello", s -> System.out.println("hello " + s))      ◁──────┐
      .on("tick", n -> System.out.println("tick #" + n))              │  Event handlers
      .on("stop", v -> eventLoop.stop())                              │  defined as Java
      .run();                                                         │  lambda functions
  System.out.println("Bye!");
}

private static void delay(long millis) {              ◁──────┐
  try {                                                       This method wraps a possibly *checked*
    Thread.sleep(millis);                                     exception into an *unchecked* exception
  } catch (InterruptedException e) {                          to avoid polluting the main method
    throw new RuntimeException(e);                            code with exception-handling logic.
  }
}
```

The code in listing 1.8 shows the use of an event-loop API whose execution gives the following console output.

Listing 1.9   Console output from the event-loop example

```
hello world!
No handler for key foo
tick #0
tick #1
hello beautiful world
tick #2
hello beautiful universe
tick #3
tick #4
tick #5
Bye!
```

More sophisticated event-loop implementations are possible, but the one in the following listing relies on a queue of events and a map of handlers.

Listing 1.10   A simple event-loop implementation

```
public final class EventLoop {
  private final ConcurrentLinkedDeque<Event> events = new ConcurrentLinkedDeq
      ue<>();
  private final ConcurrentHashMap<String, Consumer<Object>> handlers = new
  ➥ ConcurrentHashMap<>();

  public EventLoop on(String key, Consumer<Object> handler) {      ◁──────┐
    handlers.put(key, handler);                                           Handlers are stored in a map
    return this;                                                          where each key has a handler.
  }

  public void dispatch(Event event) { events.add(event); }  ◁──────┐
  public void stop() { Thread.currentThread().interrupt(); }        Dispatching is
                                                                    pushing events
  public void run() {                                               to a queue.
```

```
    while (!(events.isEmpty() && Thread.interrupted())) {
      if (!events.isEmpty()) {
        Event event = events.pop();
        if (handlers.containsKey(event.key)) {
          handlers.get(event.key).accept(event.data);
        } else {
          System.err.println("No handler for key " + event.key);
        }
      }
    }
  }
}
```

> The event loop looks for events and finds a handler based on event keys.

The event loop runs on the thread that calls the run method, and events can be safely sent from other threads using the dispatch method.

Last, but not least, an event is simply a pair of a key and data, as shown in the following, which is a static inner class of EventLoop.

> **Listing 1.11   A simple event-loop implementation**

```
public static final class Event {
  private final String key;
  private final Object data;

  public Event(String key, Object data) {
    this.key = key;
    this.data = data;
  }
}
```

1.8   What is a reactive system?

So far we have discussed how to do the following:

- Leverage asynchronous programming and non-blocking I/O to handle more concurrent connections and use less threads
- Use one threading model for asynchronous event processing (the event loop)

By combining these two techniques, we can build scalable and resource-efficient applications. Let's now discuss what a *reactive system* is and how it goes beyond "just" asynchronous programming.

The four properties of reactive systems are exposed in *The Reactive Manifesto*: *responsive, resilient, elastic,* and *message-driven* (www.reactivemanifesto.org/). We are not going to paraphrase the manifesto in this book, so here is a brief take on what these properties are about:

- *Elastic*—Elasticity is the ability for the application to work with a variable number of instances. This is useful, as elasticity allows the app to respond to traffic spikes by starting new instances and load-balancing traffic across instances. This has an interesting impact on the code design, as shared state across instances needs to be well identified and limited (e.g., server-side web sessions). It is useful for instances to report *metrics*, so that an orchestrator can decide when to start or stop instances based on both network traffic and reported metrics.

- *Resilient*—Resiliency is partially the flip side of elasticity. When one instance crashes in a group of elastic instances, resiliency is naturally achieved by redirecting traffic to other instances, and a new instance can be started if necessary. That being said, there is more to resiliency. When an instance cannot fulfill a request due to some conditions, it still tries to answer in *degraded mode*. Depending on the application domain, it may be possible to respond with older cached values, or even to respond with empty or default data. It may also be possible to forward a request to some other, non-error instance. In the worst case, an instance can respond with an error, but in a timely fashion.

- *Responsive*—Responsivity is the result of combining elasticity and resiliency. Consistent response times provide strong service-level agreement guarantees. This is achieved both thanks to the ability to start new instances if need be (to keep response times acceptable), and also because instances still respond quickly when errors arise. It is important to note that responsivity is not possible if one component relies on a non-scalable resource, like a single central database. Indeed, starting more instances does not solve the problem if they all issue requests to one resource that is quickly going to be overloaded.

- *Message-driven*—Using asynchronous message passing rather than blocking paradigms like remote procedure calls is the key enabler of elasticity and resiliency, which lead to responsiveness. This also enables messages to be dispatched to more instances (making the system elastic) and controls the flow between message producers and message consumers (this is *back-pressure*, and we will explore it later in this book).

A reactive system exhibits these four properties, which make for dependable and resource-efficient systems.

Does asynchronous imply reactive?

This is an important question, as being asynchronous is often presented as being a magic cure for software woes. Clearly, reactive implies asynchronous, but the converse is not necessarily true.

As a (not so) fictitious example, consider a shopping web application where users can put items in a shopping cart. This is classically done by storing items in a server-side web session. When sessions are being stored in memory or in local files, the system is not reactive, even if it internally uses non-blocking I/O and asynchronous programming. Indeed, an instance of the application cannot take over another one because sessions are application state, and in this case that state is not being replicated and shared across nodes.

A reactive variant of this example would use a memory grid service (e.g., Hazelcast, Redis, or Infinispan) to store the web sessions, so that incoming requests could be routed to any instance.

1.9   What else does reactive mean?

As *reactive* is a trendy term, it is also being used for very different purposes. You just saw what a *reactive system* is, but there are two other popular reactive definitions, summarized in table 1.1.

Table 1.1   All the reactive things

Reactive?	Description
Systems	Dependable applications that are message-driven, resilient, elastic, and responsive.
Programming	A means of reacting to changes and events. Spreadsheet programs are a great example of reactive programming: when cell data changes, cells having formulas depending on affected cells are recomputed automatically. Later in this book you will see RxJava, a popular *reactive extensions* API for Java that greatly helps coordinate asynchronous event and data processing. There is also *functional reactive programming*, a style of programming that we won't cover in this book but for which *Functional Reactive Programming* by Stephen Blackheath and Anthony Jones (Manning, 2016) is a fantastic resource.
Streams	When systems exchange continuous streams of data, the classical producer/consumer problems arise. It is especially important to provide *back-pressure* mechanisms so that a consumer can notify a producer when it is emitting too fast. With reactive streams (www.reactive-streams.org), the main goal is to reach the best throughput between systems.

1.10   What is Vert.x?

According to the Vert.x website (https://vertx.io/), "Eclipse Vert.x is a tool-kit for building reactive applications on the JVM."

Initiated by Tim Fox in 2012, Vert.x is a project now fostered at the vendor-neutral Eclipse Foundation. While the first project iterations were aimed at being a "Node.js for the JVM," Vert.x has since significantly deviated toward providing an asynchronous programming foundation tailored for the specifics of the JVM.

> **The essence of Vert.x**
>
> As you may have guessed from the previous sections of this chapter, the focus of Vert.x is processing asynchronous events, mostly coming from non-blocking I/O, and the threading model processes events in an event loop.

It is very important to understand that Vert.x is a *toolkit* and not a *framework*: it does not provide a predefined foundation for your application, so you are free to use Vert.x as a library inside a larger code base. Vert.x is largely unopinionated on the build tools that you should be using, how you want to structure your code, how you intend to package and deploy it, and so on. A Vert.x application is an assembly of modules providing exactly what you need, and nothing more. If you don't need to access a database, then your project does not need to depend on database-related APIs.

The Vert.x project is organized in composable modules, with figure 1.5 showing the structure of a random Vert.x application:

- A core project, called `vertx-core`, provides the APIs for asynchronous programming, non-blocking I/O, streaming, and convenient access to networked protocols such as TCP, UDP, DNS, HTTP, or WebSockets.
- A set of modules that are part of the community-supported Vert.x stack, such as a better web API (`vertx-web`) or data clients (`vertx-kafka-client`, `vertx-redis`, `vertx-mongo`, etc.) provide functionality for building all kinds of applications.
- A wider ecosystem of projects provides even more functionality, such as connecting with Apache Cassandra, non-blocking I/O to communicate between system processes, and so on.

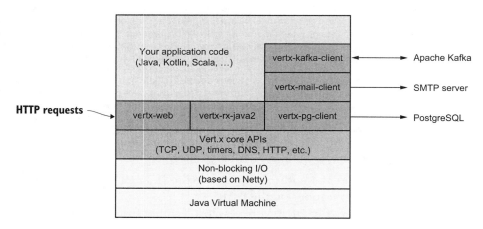

Figure 1.5   Overview of the structure of a Vert.x application

Vert.x is *polyglot* as it supports most of the popular JVM languages: JavaScript, Ruby, Kotlin, Scala, Groovy, and more. Interestingly, these languages are not just supported through their interoperability with Java. Idiomatic bindings are being generated, so you can write Vert.x code that still feels natural in these languages. For example, the Scala bindings use the Scala future APIs, and the Kotlin bindings leverage custom DSLs and functions with named parameters to simplify some code constructs. And, of course, you can mix and match different supported languages within the same Vert.x application.

1.11 Your first Vert.x application

It's finally time for us to write a Vert.x application!

Let's continue with the echo TCP protocol that we have used in various forms in this chapter. It will still expose a TCP server on port 3000, where any data is sent back to the client. We will add two other features:

- The number of open connections will be displayed every five seconds.
- An HTTP server on port 8080 will respond with a string giving the current number of open connections.

1.11.1 Preparing the project

While not strictly necessary for this example, it is easier to use a build tool. In this book, I will show examples with Gradle, but you can find the equivalent Maven build descriptors in the book's source code Git repository.

For this project, the only third-party dependency that we need is the `vertx-core` artifact plus its dependencies. This artifact is on Maven Central under the `io.vertx` group identifier.

An integrated development environment (IDE) like IntelliJ IDEA Community Edition is great, and it knows how to create Maven and Gradle projects. You can equally use Eclipse, NetBeans, or even Visual Studio Code.

> **TIP** You can also use the Vert.x starter web application at https://start.vertx .io and generate a project skeleton to download.

For this chapter let's use Gradle. A suitable build.gradle.kts file would look like the next listing.

Listing 1.12 Gradle configuration to build and run `VertxEcho`

```
plugins {
  java
  application
}

repositories {
  mavenCentral()
}

dependencies {
  implementation("io.vertx:vertx-core:VERSION")      ⟵  Replace VERSION with a
}                                                        release version of Vert.x
                                                         like 3.9.1 or 4.0.0.
java {
  sourceCompatibility = JavaVersion.VERSION_1_8
}
                                                       This is the fully qualified
application {                                          name of the class containing
  mainClassName = "chapter1.firstapp.VertxEcho"   ⟵   a main method so that we
}                                                      can use the run Gradle task.
```

TIP You may be more familiar with Apache Maven than Gradle. This book uses Gradle because it is a modern, efficient, and flexible build tool. It also uses a concise domain-specific language for writing build files, which works better than Maven XML files in the context of a book. You will find Maven build descriptors equivalent to those of Gradle in the source code Git repository.

1.11.2 The VertxEcho class

The `VertxEcho` class implementation is shown in listing 1.15. You can run the application with Gradle using the `run` task (`gradle run` or `./gradlew run`), as follows.

Listing 1.13   Running `VertxEcho`

```
$ ./gradlew run

> Task :run
We now have 0 connections
We now have 0 connections
We now have 0 connections
We now have 1 connections
We now have 1 connections
Jul 07, 2018 11:44:14 PM io.vertx.core.net.impl.ConnectionBase
SEVERE: Connection reset by peer
We now have 0 connections
<=============----> 75% EXECUTING [34s]
> :run
```

TIP If you prefer Maven, run `mvn compile exec:java` instead of `./gradlew run` from the chapter1 folder in the book's source code Git repository.

You can, of course, interact with the service with the `netcat` command to echo text, and you can make an HTTP request to see the number of open connections, as shown in the following listing.

Listing 1.14   Interacting with `VertxEcho` over TCP and HTTP

```
$ netcat localhost 3000
Hello from Tassin-La-Demi-Lune, France
Hello from Tassin-La-Demi-Lune, France

$ http :8080
HTTP/1.1 200 OK
content-length: 25

We now have 0 connections
```

TIP The `http` command comes from the HTTPie project at https://httpie.org. This tool is a developer-friendly alternative to `curl`, and you can easily install it on your operating system.

Let's now see the code of `VertxEcho`.

> **Listing 1.15 Implementation of the `VertxEcho` class**

```java
package chapter1.firstapp;

import io.vertx.core.Vertx;
import io.vertx.core.net.NetSocket;

public class VertxEcho {

  private static int numberOfConnections = 0;

  public static void main(String[] args) {
    Vertx vertx = Vertx.vertx();

    vertx.createNetServer()
      .connectHandler(VertxEcho::handleNewClient)
      .listen(3000);

    vertx.setPeriodic(5000, id -> System.out.println(howMany()));

    vertx.createHttpServer()
      .requestHandler(request -> request.response().end(howMany()))
      .listen(8080);
  }
  private static void handleNewClient(NetSocket socket) {
    numberOfConnections++;
    socket.handler(buffer -> {
      socket.write(buffer);
      if (buffer.toString().endsWith("/quit\n")) {
        socket.close();
      }
    });
    socket.closeHandler(v -> numberOfConnections--);
  }

  private static String howMany() {
    return "We now have " + numberOfConnections + " connections";
  }
}
```

As you will see in the next chapter, event handlers are always executed on the same thread, so there is no need for JVM locks or using AtomicInteger.

Creating a TCP server requires passing a callback for each new connection.

This defines a periodic task with a callback being executed every five seconds.

Similar to a TCP server, an HTTP server is configured by giving the callback to be executed for each HTTP request.

The buffer handler is invoked every time a buffer is ready for consumption. Here we just write it back, and we use a convenient string conversion helper to look for a terminal command.

Another event is when the connection closes. We decrement a connections counter that was incremented upon connection.

This example is interesting in that it has few lines of code. It is centered around a plain old Java `main` method, because there is no framework to bootstrap. All we need to create is a `Vertx` context, which in turns offers methods to create tasks, servers, clients, and more, as you will discover in the next chapters.

While it's not apparent here, an event loop is managing the processing of events, be it a new TCP connection, the arrival of a buffer, a new HTTP request, or a periodic task that is being fired. Also, every event handler is being executed on the same (event-loop) thread.

1.11.3   *The role of callbacks*

As you just saw in listing 1.15, *callbacks* are the primary method Vert.x uses to notify the application code of asynchronous events and pass them to some handlers. Combined with lambda expressions in Java, callbacks make for a concise way to define event handling.

You may have heard or experienced the infamous *callback hell* where callbacks get nested into callbacks, leading to code that is difficult to read and reason about.

```
Listing 1.16   Callback hell illustrated
```

```
dothis(a -> {
  dothat(b -> {
    andthis(c -> {
      andthat(d -> {
        alsothis(e -> {
          alsothat(f -> {
            // ...
          });
        });
      });
    });
  });
});
```

Be reassured: although the Vert.x core APIs indeed use callbacks, Vert.x provides support for more programming models. Callbacks are the canonical means for notification in event-driven APIs, but as you will see in upcoming chapters, it is possible to build other abstractions on top of callbacks, such as futures and promises, reactive extensions, and coroutines.

While callbacks have their issues, there are many cases with minimal levels of nesting where they remain a very good programming model with minimal dispatch overhead.

1.11.4   *So is this a reactive application?*

This is a very good question to ask. It is important to remember that while Vert.x is a toolkit for building reactive applications, using the Vert.x API and modules does not "auto-magically" make an application a reactive one. Yet the event-driven, non-blocking APIs that Vert.x provides tick the first box.

The short answer is that no, this application is not reactive. Resiliency is not the issue, as the only errors that can arise are I/O related—and they simply result in discarding the connections. The application is also responsive, as it does not perform any complicated processing. If we benchmarked the TCP and HTTP servers, we would get very good latencies with low deviation and very few outliers. The following listing shows an imperfect, yet telling, quick benchmark with `wrk` (https://github.com/wg/wrk) running from a terminal.

Listing 1.17 Output of a benchmark session with `wrk`

```
$ wrk --latency http://localhost:8080/
Running 10s test @ http://localhost:8080/
  2 threads and 10 connections
  Thread Stats   Avg      Stdev     Max   +/- Stdev
    Latency   136.98us  106.91us   7.26ms   97.37%
    Req/Sec    36.62k     4.09k   45.31k    85.64%
  Latency Distribution
     50%  125.00us
     75%  149.00us
     90%  199.00us
     99%  340.00us
  735547 requests in 10.10s, 44.89MB read
Requests/sec:  72830.90
Transfer/sec:     4.45MB
```

The culprit for not being reactive clearly is elasticity. Indeed, if we create new instances, each instance maintains its own connection counter. The counter scope is the application, so it should be a shared global counter between all instances.

As this example shows, designing reactive applications is more subtle than just implementing responsive and resource-efficient systems. Ensuring that an application can run as many replaceable instances is surprisingly more engaging, especially as we need to think about *instance state* versus *application state* to make sure that instances are interchangeable.

> **What if I am a Windows user?**
>
> `wrk` is a command-line tool that works on Unix systems like Linux and macOS.
>
> In this book we prefer Unix-style tooling and command-line interfaces over graphical user interfaces. We will use Unix tools that are powerful, intuitive, and maintained by active open source communities.
>
> Fortunately, you don't have to leave Windows to benefit from these tools! While some of these tools work natively on Windows, starting from Windows 10 you can install the Windows Subsystem for Linux (WSL) and benefit from a genuine Linux environment alongside your more traditional Windows desktop environment. Microsoft markets WSL as a major feature for developers on Windows, and I can only recommend that you invest some time and get familiar with it. You can see Microsoft's WSL FAQ for more details: https://docs.microsoft.com/en-us/windows/wsl/faq.

1.12 *What are the alternatives to Vert.x?*

As you will see in this book, Vert.x is a compelling technology for building end-to-end reactive applications. Reactive application development is a trendy topic, and it is more important to understand the principles than to blindly become an expert in one specific technology. What you will learn in this book easily transfers to other technologies, and I highly encourage you to check them out.

Here are the most popular alternatives to Vert.x for asynchronous and reactive programming:

- *Node.js*—Node.js is an event-driven runtime for writing asynchronous JavaScript applications. It is based on the V8 JavaScript engine that is used by Google Chrome. At first sight, Vert.x and Node.js have lots of similarities. Still, they differ greatly. Vert.x runs multiple event loops by default, unlike Node.js. Also, the JVM has a better JIT compiler and garbage collector, so the JVM is better suited for long-running processes. Last, but not least, Vert.x supports JavaScript.

- *Akka*—Akka is a faithful implementation of the *actor* model. It runs on the JVM and primarily offers Scala APIs, although Java bindings are also being promoted. Akka is particularly interesting, as actors are message driven and location transparent, and actors offer supervision features that are interesting for error recovery. Akka clearly targets the design of reactive applications. As you will see in this book, Vert.x is no less capable for the task. Vert.x has a concept of *verticles*, a loose form of actors, that are used for processing asynchronous events. Interestingly, Vert.x is significantly faster than Akka and most alternatives in established benchmarks, such as TechEmpower benchmarks (www .techempower.com/benchmarks/).

- *Spring Framework*—The older and widespread Spring Framework now integrates a reactive stack. It is based on Project Reactor, an API for reactive programming that is very similar to RxJava. The focus of the Spring reactive stack is essentially on reactive programming APIs, but it does not necessarily lead to end-to-end reactive applications. Many parts of the Spring Framework employ blocking APIs, so extra care must be taken to limit the exposure to blocking operations. Project Reactor is a compelling alternative to RxJava, but the Spring reactive stack is tied to this API, and it may not always be the best way to express certain asynchronous constructions. Vert.x provides more flexibility as it supports callbacks, futures, Java `CompletionStage`, Kotlin coroutines, RxJava, and fibers. This means that with Vert.x it is easier to select the right asynchronous programming model for a certain task. Also like with Akka, Vert.x remains significantly faster in TechEmpower benchmarks, and applications boot faster than Spring-based ones.

- *Quarkus*—Quarkus is a new framework for developing Java applications that run exceptionally well in container environments like Kubernetes (https:// quarkus.io). Indeed, in such environments, boot time and memory consumption are critical cost-saving factors. Quarkus employs techniques at compilation time to make sensible gains when running using traditional Java virtual machines and as native executables. It is based on popular libraries like Hibernate, Eclipse MicroProfile, RESTEasy, and Vert.x. Quarkus unifies imperative and reactive programming models, and Vert.x is a cornerstone of the framework. Vert.x is not just used to power some pieces of the networking stack; some client modules are directly based on those from Vert.x, such as the Quarkus mail service and reactive routes. You can also use Vert.x APIs in a Quarkus application, with the unification between reactive and imperative helping you to bridge both worlds. Vert.x and Quarkus have different programming paradigms: Vert.x will appeal to developers who prefer a toolkit approach, or developers who have affinities with Node.js. In contrast, Quarkus will appeal to developers who prefer an opinionated stack approach with dependency injection and convention over configuration. In the end, both projects work together, and anything you develop with Vert.x can be reused in Quarkus.

- *Netty*—The Netty framework provides non-blocking I/O APIs for the JVM. It provides abstractions and platform-specific bug fixes compared to using raw NIO APIs. It also provides threading models. The target of Netty is low-latency and high-performance network applications. While you can certainly build reactive applications with Netty, the APIs remain somewhat low-level. Vert.x is one of the many technologies built on top of Netty (Spring Reactive and Akka have Netty integration), and you can get all the performance benefits of Netty with the simpler APIs of Vert.x.

- *Scripting languages*—Scripting languages such as Python and Ruby also provide non-blocking I/O libraries, such as Async (Ruby) and Twisted (Python). You can certainly build reactive systems with them. Again, the JVM performance is an advantage for Vert.x, along with the ability to use alternative JVM languages (Ruby is officially supported by Vert.x).

- *Native languages*—Native languages are becoming trendy again. Instead of using the venerable C/C++ languages, Go, Rust, and Swift are gaining mindshare. They all tick the boxes for building highly scalable applications, and they certainly can be used for creating reactive applications. That being said, most efficient libraries in these languages are fairly low-level, and ultimately the JVM-based Vert.x/Netty combination still ranks favorably in benchmarks.

The following books are good resources for many of the preceding topics:

- *Node.js in Action* by Mike Cantelon, Marc Harter, T.J. Holowaychuk, and Nathan Rajlich (Manning, 2013)
- *Akka in Action* by Raymond Roestenburg, Rob Bakker, and Rob Williams (Manning, 2016)
- *Reactive Application Development* by Duncan K. DeVore, Sean Walsh, and Brian Hanafee (Manning, 2018)
- *Spring in Action*, fifth edition, by Craig Walls (Manning, 2018)
- *Netty in Action* by Norman Maurer and Marvin Allen Wolfthal (Manning, 2015)
- *Go in Action* by William Kennedy with Brian Ketelsen and Erik St. Martin (Manning, 2015)
- *Rust in Action* by Tim McNamara (Manning, 2019)
- *Swift in Depth* by Tjeerd in 't Veen (Manning, 2018)

In the next chapter, we will dissect the fundamentals of asynchronous programming with Vert.x.

Summary

- Asynchronous programming allows you to multiplex multiple networked connections on a single thread.
- Managing non-blocking I/O is more complex than the equivalent imperative code based on blocking I/O, even for simple protocols.
- The event loop and the reactor pattern simplify asynchronous event processing.
- A reactive system is both scalable and resilient, producing responses with consistent latencies despite demanding workloads and failures.
- Vert.x is an approachable, efficient toolkit for writing asynchronous and reactive applications on the JVM.

Verticles: The basic processing units of Vert.x

This chapter covers

- What verticles are
- How to write, configure, and deploy verticles
- The Vert.x threading model
- How to mix Vert.x and non-Vert.x threads

Put simply, a *verticle* is the fundamental processing unit in Vert.x. The role of a verticle is to encapsulate a *technical functional unit* for processing events, such as exposing an HTTP API and responding to requests, providing a repository interface on top of a database, or issuing requests to a third-party system. Much like components in technologies like Enterprise JavaBeans, verticles can be deployed, and they have a life cycle.

Asynchronous programming is key to building reactive applications, since they have to scale, and verticles are fundamental in Vert.x for structuring (asynchronous) event-processing code and business logic.

2.1   *Writing a verticle*

If you're familiar with the *actor concurrency model*, you will find similarities between Vert.x verticles and actors.[1] Put simply, in the actor model, autonomous entities (the actors) exclusively communicate with other entities by sending and responding to messages. The similarities between Vert.x verticles and actors is no fortuitous coincidence: verticles have private state that may be updated when receiving events, they can deploy other verticles, and they can communicate via message-passing (more on that in the next chapter). Verticles do not necessarily follow the orthodox definition of actors, but it is fair to consider Vert.x as being at least inspired by actors.

Since verticles are a key concept in Vert.x, we will look into how they work. Before that, though, we'll write a small verticle that processes two types of events: periodic timers and HTTP requests.

2.1.1   *Preparing the project*

We will use a common project for all of the examples in this chapter, making use of the Gradle project descriptor in the following listing.

> Listing 2.1   Gradle `build.gradle.kts` for the examples in chapter 2

```
plugins {
  java
}

repositories {
  mavenCentral()
}

dependencies {
  implementation("io.vertx:vertx-core:VERSION")
  implementation("ch.qos.logback:logback-classic:1.2.3")
}

tasks.create<JavaExec>("run") {
  main = project.properties.getOrDefault("mainClass",
    "chapter2.hello.HelloVerticle") as String
  classpath = sourceSets["main"].runtimeClasspath
  systemProperties["vertx.logger-delegate-factory-class-name"] =
    "io.vertx.core.logging.SLF4JLogDelegateFactory"
}

java {
  sourceCompatibility = JavaVersion.VERSION_1_8
}
```

This is the Vert.x core library dependency. Replace "VERSION" with a recent release number like 3.9.0.

The logback-classic dependency provides the SLF4J logger API and the logback implementation.

This will allow you to run samples with Gradle from the command line.

This ensures that Vert.x itself also uses SLF4J logging.

---

[1]For more on the actor concurrency model, see the 1973 article by Carl Hewitt, Peter Bishop, and Richard Steiger that introduced the model: "A universal modular ACTOR formalism for artificial intelligence," in *Proceedings of the 3rd international joint conference on Artificial intelligence* (IJCAI'73), p. 235–245 (Morgan Kaufmann, 1973).

The Gradle build is a very simple one for a Java project. Since we will have several examples to run, we won't rely on the Gradle `application` plugin, but will define our own custom `run` task, where we can pass the name of the class to execute. We'll also use it to ensure that logging is properly configured and unified to SLF4J.

Listing 2.2 Logback configuration to reduce Netty verbosity

This defines an appender to send events to the console.

The pattern defines what the log events look like.

```
<configuration>
  <appender name="STDOUT" class="ch.qos.logback.core.ConsoleAppender">
    <encoder>
      <pattern>%level [%thread] %logger{0} - %msg%n</pattern>
    </encoder>
  </appender>

  <logger name="io.netty" level="warn"/>

  <root level="debug">
    <appender-ref ref="STDOUT"/>
  </root>
</configuration>
```

We drop Netty log events that are more verbose than warnings.

> **TIP** Vert.x uses Netty, and logging in Netty is quite verbose with the default Logback configuration. We can reduce the number of log entries by creating an src/main/resources/logback.xml file and adding the configuration as in listing 2.2. To make the log samples shorter in this book, I've also removed event dates and shortened logger class names ($logger{0}). Please refer to the Logback documentation to learn how to configure it (https://logback .qos.ch/manual/index.html).

2.1.2 The verticle class

The whole verticle and application fits in the following Java class.

Listing 2.3 A sample verticle

```
package chapter2.hello;

import io.vertx.core.AbstractVerticle;
import io.vertx.core.Vertx;
import org.slf4j.Logger;
import org.slf4j.LoggerFactory;

public class HelloVerticle extends AbstractVerticle {
  private final Logger logger = LoggerFactory.getLogger(HelloVerticle.class);
  private long counter = 1;

  @Override
  public void start() {
    vertx.setPeriodic(5000, id -> {
```

This defines a periodic task every five seconds.

```
      logger.info("tick");
    });

    vertx.createHttpServer()                        The HTTP server calls this
      .requestHandler(req -> {                      handler on every request.
        logger.info("Request #{} from {}", counter++,
          req.remoteAddress().host());
        req.response().end("Hello!");
      })
      .listen(8080);
    logger.info("Open http://localhost:8080/");
  }
                                                    We need a global Vert.x instance.
  public static void main(String[] args) {
    Vertx vertx = Vertx.vertx();                    This is the simplest way
    vertx.deployVerticle(new HelloVerticle());      to deploy a verticle.
  }
}
```

This verticle defines two event handlers: one for periodic tasks every five seconds, and one for processing HTTP requests in an HTTP server. The `main` method instantiates a global Vert.x instance and deploys an instance of the verticle.

Defining a verticle in Java is typically done by specializing the `AbstractVerticle` class. There is a `Verticle` interface that you could in theory implement, but `AbstractVerticle` provides all the event processing, configuration, and execution plumbing that Vert.x users need.

> **NOTE** Since Vert.x is a library and not a framework, you can create a Vert.x instance from a main method, or from any other class, and then deploy verticles.

The life cycle of a verticle consists of start and stop events. The `AbstractVerticle` class provides `start` and `stop` methods that can be overridden:

- The `start` method typically contains setup and initialization for handlers, like setting a periodic task handler and starting an HTTP server in listing 2.3.
- The `stop` method is implemented when housekeeping tasks are required, such as closing open database connections.

By default these methods do nothing.

2.1.3   *Running and first observations*

The application can be launched as a regular Java application by running the `main` method either from an IDE or from the command line. To run it on the command line using Gradle, you can use the following command:

```
$ ./gradlew run -PmainClass=chapter2.hello.HelloVerticle
```

I am again assuming that you will run this from a Unix shell, be it under Linux, macOS, or Windows through WSL. If you run the command from a traditional

Windows terminal, there is a .bat file for Gradle, so you will need to replace `./gradlew` with `gradlew.bat`.

Once the application runs, you can perform a few HTTP requests at http://localhost:8080/ with a web browser, or by using command-line tools such as curl and HTTPie. The logs will be similar to the one shown in the following listing.

Listing 2.4 Sample log output when running `HelloVerticle`

The HTTP server is now ready.   **A periodic task event log**

```
INFO [vert.x-eventloop-thread-0] HelloVerticle - Open http://localhost:8080/
INFO [vert.x-eventloop-thread-0] HelloVerticle - tick
INFO [vert.x-eventloop-thread-0] HelloVerticle -
   Request #1 from 0:0:0:0:0:0:0:1
INFO [vert.x-eventloop-thread-0] HelloVerticle -
   Request #2 from 0:0:0:0:0:0:0:1
INFO [vert.x-eventloop-thread-0] HelloVerticle -
   Request #3 from 0:0:0:0:0:0:0:1
INFO [vert.x-eventloop-thread-0] HelloVerticle -
   Request #4 from 0:0:0:0:0:0:0:1
INFO [vert.x-eventloop-thread-0] HelloVerticle - tick
```

An HTTP request event log

> **TIP** In some of the remaining examples, I have shortened the class definitions. I have especially removed package definitions, imports, and `main` methods that are similar to the one in listing 2.3. To see the full source code, please consult the book's code repository.

The Logback configuration that we are using shows the name of the thread associated with an event. We can already check an important property of Vert.x verticles in log entries: event processing happens on a single event-loop thread. Both the periodic tasks and HTTP request processing happen on a thread that appears as `vert.x -eventloop-thread-0` in the logs.

An obvious benefit of this design is that a verticle instance always executes event processing on the same thread, so there is no need for using thread synchronization primitives. In a multithreaded design, updating the `counter` field would require either a `synchronized` block or the use of `java.util.concurrent.AtomicLong`. There is no such issue here, so a plain `long` field can be safely used.

Preparation methods, such as `createHttpServer` or `setTimer`, may be called from a non-Vert.x thread. This may happen when you're directly using a `Vertx` object without a verticle, or when you're writing unit tests. This is, however, not a problem, because the use of the `Vertx` class methods is thread-safe.

Figure 2.1 shows the (simplified) interactions between the verticle, the handlers, Vert.x, and the event sources. Each arrow represents a method call between the participants. For instance, `HelloVerticle` creates a periodic task handler by calling `setPeriodic` on the `Vertx` object, which in turns creates a periodic task using an internal Vert.x timer. In turn, the timer periodically calls back the `timerHandler` handler in `HelloVerticle`.

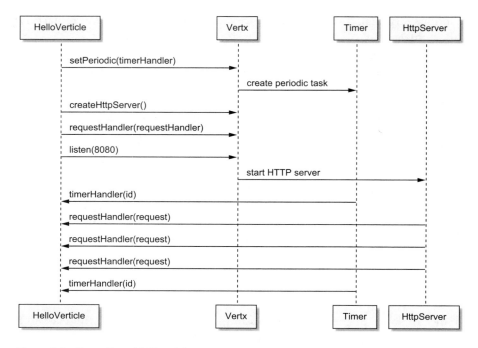

Figure 2.1   Execution of listing 2.3

Note that I represented the calls to `requestHandler` and `listen` as being to the `Vertx` object as a shortcut; in reality, they are on an object that implements the `HttpServer` interface. The actual class is internal to Vert.x, and since it doesn't serve the diagram to add another participant, I merged it into `Vertx`.

2.2   *More on verticles*

There are more things to know about writing and deploying verticles:

- What happens when the event loop is being blocked?
- How can you defer notification of life-cycle completion in the presence of asynchronous initialization work?
- How can you deploy and undeploy verticles?
- How can you pass configuration data?

We'll cover each of these topics using very simple yet focused examples.

2.2.1   *Blocking and the event loop*

Handler callbacks are run from event-loop threads. It is important that code running on an event loop takes as little time as possible, so that the event-loop thread can have a higher throughput in the number of processed events. This is why no long-running or blocking I/O operations should happen on the event loop.

That being said, it may not always be easy to spot blocking code, especially when using third-party libraries. Vert.x provides a checker that detects when an event loop is being blocked for too long.

To illustrate that, let's see what happens when we introduce an infinite loop in an event-handler callback.

Listing 2.5 An example where the event loop is being blocked

```
public class BlockEventLoop extends AbstractVerticle {

  @Override
  public void start() {
    vertx.setTimer(1000, id -> {
      while (true);              ⟵──── Infinite loop!
    });
  }

  public static void main(String[] args) {
    Vertx vertx = Vertx.vertx();
    vertx.deployVerticle(new BlockEventLoop());
  }
}
```

The code in listing 2.5 defines a one-second timer, and the handler callback enters into an infinite loop.

Listing 2.6 Log output when running listing 2.5

```
WARN [vertx-blocked-thread-checker] BlockedThreadChecker - Thread
➡ Thread[vert.x-eventloop-thread-0,5,main] has been blocked for 2871
➡ ms, time limit is 2000
WARN [vertx-blocked-thread-checker] BlockedThreadChecker - Thread
➡ Thread[vert.x-eventloop-thread-0,5,main] has been blocked for 3871 ms,
➡ time limit is 2000              ⟵──┐
(...)                                 │  The thread checker is not happy.
WARN [vertx-blocked-thread-checker] BlockedThreadChecker - Thread
➡ Thread[vert.x-eventloop-thread-0,5,main] has been blocked for 5879
➡ ms, time limit is 2000
io.vertx.core.VertxException: Thread blocked
  at chapter2.blocker.BlockEventLoop.lambda$start$0(BlockEventLoop.java:11)
  at chapter2.blocker.BlockEventLoop$$Lambda$10/152379791.handle(Unknown
  ➡ Source)
(...)
```

Listing 2.6 shows a typical log output when running the code from listing 2.5. As you can see, warnings start to appear while the event-loop thread is running the infinite loop and hence is not available for processing other events. After some iterations (five seconds by default), the warning is enriched with stack trace dumps, so you can clearly identify the culprit in your code. Note that this is only a warning. The event-loop thread checker cannot kill the handler that is taking too long to complete its task.

Of course, you sometimes will need to use blocking or long-running code, and Vert.x offers solutions to run such code without blocking the event loop. This is the subject of section 2.3.

Configuring the Vert.x blocked thread checker

The time limit before the blocked thread checker complains is two seconds by default, but it can be configured to a different value. There are environments, such as embedded devices, where processing power is slower, and it is normal to increase the thread-checker threshold for them.

You can use system properties to change the settings:

- `-Dvertx.options.blockedThreadCheckInterval=5000` changes the interval to five seconds.
- `-Dvertx.threadChecks=false` disables the thread checker.

Note that this configuration is global and cannot be fine-tuned on a per-verticle basis.

2.2.2   *Asynchronous notification of life-cycle events*

So far we have looked at examples with `start()` life-cycle methods. The contract in these methods is that a verticle has successfully completed its `start` life-cycle event processing unless the method throws an exception. The same applies for `stop()` methods.

There is, however, a problem: some of the operations in a `start` or a `stop` method may be asynchronous, so they may complete after a call to `start()` or `stop()` has returned.

Let's see how to properly notify the caller of deferred success or failure. A good example is starting a HTTP server, which is a non-blocking operation.

Listing 2.7   Example of an asynchronous start life-cycle method

```
public class SomeVerticle extends AbstractVerticle {

    @Override
    public void start(Promise<Void> promise) {
        vertx.createHttpServer()
          .requestHandler(req -> req.response().end("Ok"))
          .listen(8080, ar -> {
            if (ar.succeeded()) {
              promise.complete();
            } else {
              promise.fail(ar.cause());
            }
        });
    }
}
```

The Promise is of type void because Vert.x is only interested in the deployment completion, and there is no value to carry along.

The listen variant that supports an asynchronous result indicates whether the operation failed or not.

complete() is used to mark the Promise as completed (when the Promise is not of type void, a value can be passed).

If the listen operation fails, we mark the Promise as failed and propagate the error.

Listing 2.7 shows an example where the verticle reports an asynchronous notification when it starts. This is important because starting a HTTP server *can* fail. Indeed, the TCP port may be used by another process, in which case the HTTP server cannot start, and hence the verticle has not successfully deployed. To report the asynchronous notification, we use a variant of the `listen` method with callback called when the operation completes.

The `start` and `stop` methods in `AbstractVerticle` support variants with an argument of type `io.vertx.core.Promise`. As the name suggests, a Vert.x `Promise` is an adaptation of the *futures and promises* model for processing asynchronous results.[2] A *promise* is used to *write* an asynchronous result, whereas a *future* is used to *view* an asynchronous result. Given a `Promise` object, you can call the `future()` method to obtain a future of type `io.vertx.core.Future`.

In listing 2.7, the `Promise` object is set to be completed when the verticle has successfully completed its `start` or `stop` life cycle. If an error arises, the `Promise` object is failed with an exception describing the error, and the verticle deployment is failed.

To better understand what happens here, figure 2.2 illustrates the interactions between the verticle, the Vert.x object, and the internal Vert.x deployer object responsible for calling the `start` method. We can check that the deployer waits for the

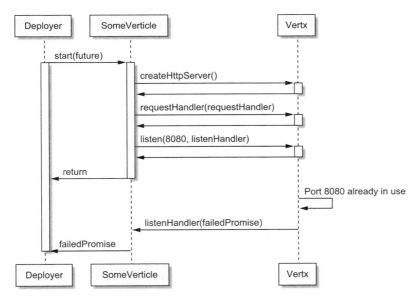

Figure 2.2 Sequence diagram of starting an HTTP server with a promise and a `listen` handler

---

[2]The paper that introduced the concept of promises and futures was B. Liskov and L. Shrira, "Promises: linguistic support for efficient asynchronous procedure calls in distributed systems," in R.L. Wexelblat, ed., *Proceedings of the ACM SIGPLAN 1988 conference on Programming language design and implementation (PLDI'88)*, p. 260–267 (ACM, 1988).

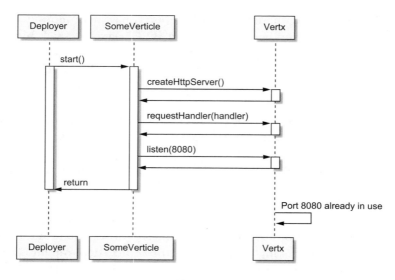

Figure 2.3   Sequence diagram of starting an HTTP server without a promise and a `listen` handler

promise completion to know if the deployment was a success or not, even after the call to the start method has returned. In contrast, figure 2.3 shows the interactions when not using the variant of start that accepts a Promise object. There is no way the deployer can be notified of an error.

> **TIP** It is a good robustness practice to use the asynchronous method variants that accept a callback to notify of errors, like the listen method in listing 2.7. I will not always do this in the remainder of this book if it allows me to reduce the verbosity of code samples.

2.2.3   *Deploying verticles*

So far we have been deploying verticles from a main method embedded in a single verticle class.

Verticles are always deployed (and undeployed) through the Vertx object. You can do so from any method, but the typical way to deploy an application composed of verticles is as follows:

1   Deploy a main verticle.
2   The main verticle deploys other verticles.
3   The deployed verticles may in turn deploy further verticles.

Note that while this sounds hierarchical, Vert.x has no formal notion of parent/child verticles.

To illustrate that, let's define some verticles.

Listing 2.8 A sample verticle to deploy

```java
public class EmptyVerticle extends AbstractVerticle {
  private final Logger logger = LoggerFactory.getLogger(EmptyVerticle.class);

  @Override
  public void start() {
    logger.info("Start");        // ◁—— We log when the verticle starts.
  }

  @Override
  public void stop() {
    logger.info("Stop");
  }
}
```

Listing 2.8 defines a simple verticle. It does not do anything interesting except logging when it starts and stops.

Listing 2.9 A verticle that deploys and undeploys other verticles

```java
public class Deployer extends AbstractVerticle {
  private final Logger logger = LoggerFactory.getLogger(Deployer.class);

  @Override
  public void start() {                         // We deploy a new instance of
    long delay = 1000;                          // EmptyVerticle every second.
    for (int i = 0; i < 50; i++) {
      vertx.setTimer(delay, id -> deploy());  // ◁—┘
      delay = delay + 1000;
    }                                           // Deploying a verticle
  }                                             // is an asynchronous
                                                // operation, and there is
  private void deploy() {                       // a variant of the deploy
    vertx.deployVerticle(new EmptyVerticle(), ar -> {  // ◁— method that supports
      if (ar.succeeded()) {                     // an asynchronous result.
        String id = ar.result();
        logger.info("Successfully deployed {}", id);
        vertx.setTimer(5000, tid -> undeployLater(id));  // ◁—┐ We will undeploy
      } else {                                            //    a verticle after
        logger.error("Error while deploying", ar.cause()); //  five seconds.
      }
    });
  }

  private void undeployLater(String id) {      // Undeploying is very
    vertx.undeploy(id, ar -> {                 // similar to deploying.
      if (ar.succeeded()) {                    // ◁—┘
        logger.info("{} was undeployed", id);
      } else {
        logger.error("{} could not be undeployed", id);
```

```
      }
    });
  }
}
```

Listing 2.9 defines a verticle that deploys 50 instances of the `EmptyVerticle` class from 2.8. The use of a timer allows us to separate each deployment by one second. The `deploy` method uses another timer for undeploying a verticle five seconds after it has been deployed. Deployment assigns a unique identifier string to a verticle, which can later be used for undeploying.

Listing 2.10   Main class to deploy the `Deployer` verticle

```
public static void main(String[] args) {
  Vertx vertx = Vertx.vertx();
  vertx.deployVerticle(new Deployer());
}
```

Last but not least, the `Deployer` verticle itself can be deployed from a `main` method and class, as shown in listing 2.10. Running this example yields log entries like those in the following listing.

Listing 2.11   Log excerpts of running the code in listing 2.10

A verticle has been deployed.
```
INFO [vert.x-eventloop-thread-1] EmptyVerticle - Start
INFO [vert.x-eventloop-thread-0] Deployer - Successfully deployed
➥ 05553394-b6ce-4f47-9076-2c6648d65329
INFO [vert.x-eventloop-thread-2] EmptyVerticle - Start
INFO [vert.x-eventloop-thread-0] Deployer - Successfully deployed
➥ 6d920f33-f317-4964-992f-e712185fe514
(...)
INFO [vert.x-eventloop-thread-0] Deployer -
➥ 8153abb7-fc64-496e-8155-75c27a93b56d was undeployed
INFO [vert.x-eventloop-thread-13] EmptyVerticle - Start
INFO [vert.x-eventloop-thread-0] Deployer - Successfully deployed
➥ 0f69ccd8-1344-4b70-8245-020a4815cc96
(...)
```

A verticle has been undeployed.

You can see the log entries from the `vert.x-eventloop-thread-0` thread; they correspond to the `Deployer` verticle. You can then see life-cycle log events from `EmptyVerticle` instances; they use other event-loop threads.

Interestingly, we are deploying 50 verticles from `Deployer`, yet there are likely fewer threads than verticles appearing in the logs. By default, Vert.x creates twice the number of event-loop threads as CPU cores. If you have 8 cores, then a Vert.x application has 16 event loops. The assignment of verticles to event loops is done in a round-robin fashion.

This teaches us an interesting lesson: while a verticle always uses the same event-loop thread, the event-loop threads are being shared by multiple verticles. This design results in a predictable number of threads for running an application.

> **TIP**   It is possible to tweak how many event loops should be available, but it is not possible to manually allocate a given verticle to a specific event loop. This should never be a problem in practice, but in the worst case you can always plan the deployment order of verticles.

2.2.4   Passing configuration data

Application code often needs configuration data. A good example is code that connects to a database server: it typically needs a host name, a TCP port, a login, and a password. Since the values change from one deployment configuration to another, such configuration needs to be accessed from a configuration API.

Vert.x verticles can be passed such configuration data when they are deployed. You will see later in this book that some more advanced forms of configuration can be used, but the Vert.x core API already provides a generic API that is very useful.

Configuration needs to be passed as JSON data, using the Vert.x JSON API materialized by the `JsonObject` and `JsonArray` classes in the `io.vertx.core.json` package.

Listing 2.12   Passing configuration data to a verticle

config() returns the JsonObject configuration instance, and the accessor method supports optional default values. Here, if there is no "n" key in the JSON object, -l is returned.

```
public class SampleVerticle extends AbstractVerticle {
    private final Logger logger = LoggerFactory.getLogger(SampleVerticle.class);

    @Override
    public void start() {
        logger.info("n = {}", config().getInteger("n", -1));
    }

    public static void main(String[] args) {
        Vertx vertx = Vertx.vertx();
        for (int n = 0; n < 4; n++) {
            JsonObject conf = new JsonObject().put("n", n);
            DeploymentOptions opts = new DeploymentOptions()
                .setConfig(conf)
                .setInstances(n);
            vertx.deployVerticle("chapter2.opts.SampleVerticle", opts);
        }
    }
}
```

We can deploy multiple instances at once.

We create a JSON object and put an integer value for key "n."

The DeploymentOption allows more control on a verticle, including passing configuration data.

Since we deploy multiple instances, we need to point to the verticle using its *fully qualified class name* (FQCN) rather than using the new operator. For deploying just one instance, you can elect either an instance created with new or using a FQCN.

Listing 2.12 shows an example of deploying many verticles and passing configuration data. Running the example gives the output in listing 2.13, and you can check the different values of the configuration data.

Listing 2.13   Sample execution output when running the code in listing 2.12

```
INFO [vert.x-eventloop-thread-2] SampleVerticle - n = 2
INFO [vert.x-eventloop-thread-5] SampleVerticle - n = 3
INFO [vert.x-eventloop-thread-4] SampleVerticle - n = 3
INFO [vert.x-eventloop-thread-1] SampleVerticle - n = 2
INFO [vert.x-eventloop-thread-3] SampleVerticle - n = 3
INFO [vert.x-eventloop-thread-0] SampleVerticle - n = 1
```

2.3   When code needs to block

The basic rule when running code on an event loop is that it should not block, and it should run "fast enough." You saw earlier that, by default, Vert.x detects and warns when an event loop is being blocked for too long.

There are inevitably cases where you will have a hard time avoiding blocking code. It may happen because you are using a third-party library with another threading model, such as drivers for some networked services. Vert.x provides two options for dealing with such cases: worker verticles and the `executeBlocking` operation.

2.3.1   Worker verticles

Worker verticles are a special form of verticles that do not execute on an event loop. Instead, they execute on *worker threads*, that is, threads taken from special worker pools. You can define your own worker thread pools and deploy worker verticles to them, but in most cases you will be just fine using the default Vert.x worker pool.

A worker verticle processes events just like an event-loop verticle, except that it can take an arbitrarily long time to do so. It is important to understand two things:

- A worker verticle is not tied to a single worker thread, so unlike an event-loop verticle, successive events may not execute on the same thread.
- Worker verticles may only be accessed by a single worker thread at a given time.

To put it simply, like event-loop verticles, worker verticles are single-threaded, but unlike event-loop verticles, the thread may not always be the same.

Listing 2.14   A sample worker verticle

```
public class WorkerVerticle extends AbstractVerticle {
  private final Logger logger = LoggerFactory.getLogger(WorkerVerticle.class);

  @Override
  public void start() {
    vertx.setPeriodic(10_000, id -> {
      try {
        logger.info("Zzz...");
        Thread.sleep(8000);          ◁──────  We can block and
        logger.info("Up!");                   get no warning!
      } catch (InterruptedException e) {
        logger.error("Woops", e);
      }
    });
```

```
    }

    public static void main(String[] args) {
        Vertx vertx = Vertx.vertx();
        DeploymentOptions opts = new DeploymentOptions()
            .setInstances(2)
            .setWorker(true);
        vertx.deployVerticle("chapter2.worker.WorkerVerticle", opts);
    }
}
```

Making a worker verticle is a deployment options flag.

Listing 2.14 shows an example where a worker verticle is being deployed with two instances. Every 10 seconds, the code blocks for 8 seconds. Running this example produces output similar to that of listing 2.15. As you can see, different worker threads are being used for successive events.

> #### Listing 2.15 Sample output of running listing 2.14

```
INFO [vert.x-worker-thread-2] WorkerVerticle - Zzz...
INFO [vert.x-worker-thread-3] WorkerVerticle - Zzz...
INFO [vert.x-worker-thread-3] WorkerVerticle - Up!
INFO [vert.x-worker-thread-2] WorkerVerticle - Up!
INFO [vert.x-worker-thread-5] WorkerVerticle - Zzz...
INFO [vert.x-worker-thread-4] WorkerVerticle - Zzz...
INFO [vert.x-worker-thread-4] WorkerVerticle - Up!
INFO [vert.x-worker-thread-5] WorkerVerticle - Up!
(...)
```

> **WARNING** When deploying a verticle, there is an option for enabling multi-threading for worker verticles, which allows multiple events to be processed concurrently by a verticle, breaking the single-threaded processing assumption. This was always considered fairly advanced usage, and many users ended up using it the wrong way and catching concurrency bugs. The feature is no longer publicly documented and may even disappear in future Vert.x releases. Users are encouraged to simply adjust worker pool sizes to match the workload, rather than enabling worker multi-threading.

2.3.2 The executeBlocking operation

Worker verticles are a sensible option for running blocking tasks, but it may not always make sense to extract blocking code into worker verticles. Doing so can lead to an explosion in the number of worker verticle classes performing small duties, and each class may not form a sensible standalone functional unit.

The other option for running blocking code is to use the executeBlocking method from the Vertx class. This method takes some blocking code to execute, offloads it to a worker thread, and sends the result back to the event loop as a new event, as illustrated in figure 2.4.

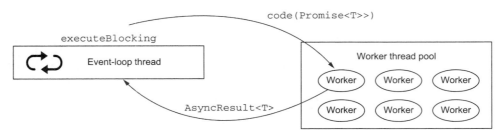

Figure 2.4   Interactions in an `executeBlocking` call

The following listing shows a sample usage.

Listing 2.16   Using `executeBlocking`

```
public class Offload extends AbstractVerticle {
  private final Logger logger = LoggerFactory.getLogger(Offload.class);

  @Override
  public void start() {
    vertx.setPeriodic(5000, id -> {
      logger.info("Tick");
      vertx.executeBlocking(this::blockingCode, this::resultHandler);
    });
  }

  private void blockingCode(Promise<String> promise) {
    logger.info("Blocking code running");
    try {
      Thread.sleep(4000);
      logger.info("Done!");
      promise.complete("Ok!");
    } catch (InterruptedException e) {
      promise.fail(e);
    }
  }

  private void resultHandler(AsyncResult<String> ar) {
    if (ar.succeeded()) {
      logger.info("Blocking code result: {}", ar.result());
    } else {
      logger.error("Woops", ar.cause());
    }
  }
}
```

executeBlocking takes two parameters: the code to run and a callback for when it has run.

The blocking code takes a Promise object of any type. It is used to eventually pass the result.

The Promise object needs to either complete or fail, marking the end of the blocking code execution.

Processing the result on the event loop is just another asynchronous result.

The following listing shows some sample output from running the code in listing 2.16. As you can see, the execution is offloaded to worker threads, but the result processing still happens on the event loop.

```
Listing 2.17  Sample output when running listing 2.16
```

```
INFO [vert.x-eventloop-thread-0] Offload - Tick
INFO [vert.x-worker-thread-0] Offload - Blocking code running
INFO [vert.x-worker-thread-0] Offload - Done!
INFO [vert.x-eventloop-thread-0] Offload - Blocking code result: Ok!
INFO [vert.x-eventloop-thread-0] Offload - Tick
INFO [vert.x-worker-thread-1] Offload - Blocking code running
INFO [vert.x-worker-thread-1] Offload - Done!
INFO [vert.x-eventloop-thread-0] Offload - Blocking code result: Ok!
INFO [vert.x-eventloop-thread-0] Offload - Tick
INFO [vert.x-worker-thread-2] Offload - Blocking code running
(...)
```

TIP By default, successive executeBlocking operations have their results processed in the same order as the calls to executeBlocking. There is a variant of executeBlocking with an additional boolean parameter, and when it's set to false, results are made available as event-loop events as soon as they are available, regardless of the order of the executeBlocking calls.

2.4 So what is really in a verticle?

So far you've seen how to write verticles, how to deploy and configure them, and how to deal with blocking code. By using informative logs in the examples, you have seen the elements of the Vert.x threading model.

Now is a good time to step back and dissect what is inside a verticle, and make sure you leave this chapter with a comprehensive understanding of how verticles work and how you can properly use them.

2.4.1 Verticles and their environment

Figure 2.5 gives an overview of the relationships between a verticle and its environment.

A verticle object is essentially the combination of two objects:

- The Vert.x instance the verticle belongs to
- A dedicated context instance that allows events to be dispatched to handlers

The Vert.x instance exposes the core APIs for declaring event handlers. We have used it already in the previous code samples with methods such as setTimer, setPeriodic, createHttpServer, deployVerticle, and so on. The Vert.x instance is being shared by multiple verticles, and there is generally only one instance of Vertx per JVM process.

The context instance holds the access to the thread for executing handlers. Events may originate from various sources such as timers, database drivers, HTTP servers, and more. As such, they are more often than not being triggered from other threads, such as Netty accepting threads or timer threads.

Event handling in user-defined callbacks happens through the context. The context instance allows us to call the handler back on the verticle event-loop thread, hence respecting the Vert.x threading model.

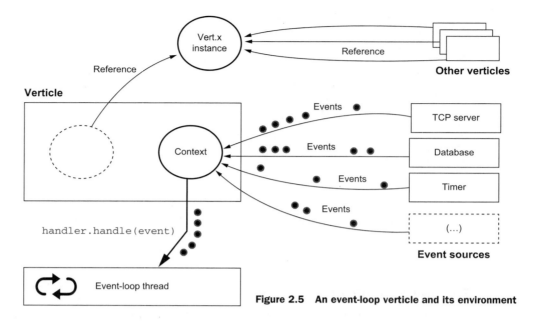

Figure 2.5 An event-loop verticle and its environment

The case of worker verticles is not much different, except that handlers are executed using one worker thread in a worker thread pool, as illustrated in figure 2.6. They are still verticles, just like their event-loop counterparts, and the code can assume single-threaded access. There is just no stability in which a worker thread is going to be used for processing a worker verticle's events.

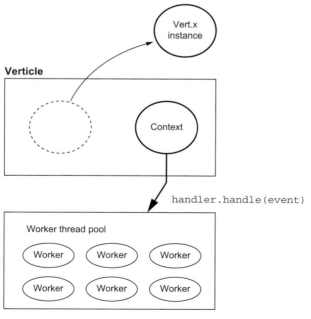

Figure 2.6 A worker verticle and its environment

2.4.2 More on contexts

Context objects can be accessed using the `getOrCreateContext()` method from the `Vertx` class. While a context is almost always associated with a verticle, it is possible to create event-loop contexts outside of a verticle. As the name of the method suggests

- Calling `getOrCreateContext()` from a context thread like that of a verticle returns the context.
- Calling `getOrCreateContext()` from a non-context thread creates a new context.

Listing 2.18 shows an example where a global `Vertx` instance is being created, and two calls to `getOrCreateContext` are being made on the JVM process main thread. Each call is followed by a call to `runOnContext`, which allows us to run a block of code on the context thread.

Listing 2.18 Creating contexts without a verticle

```
Vertx vertx = Vertx.vertx();

vertx.getOrCreateContext()
  .runOnContext(v -> logger.info("ABC"));

vertx.getOrCreateContext()
  .runOnContext(v -> logger.info("123"));
```

> The lambda is executed on a Vert.x context thread.

As you can see in the next listing, each context gets assigned to an event loop.

Listing 2.19 Sample output of running listing 2.18

```
INFO [vert.x-eventloop-thread-1] ThreadsAndContexts - 123
INFO [vert.x-eventloop-thread-0] ThreadsAndContexts - ABC
```

Context objects support more operations, such as holding context-wide arbitrary key/value data and declaring exception handlers. The following listing shows an example where a `foo` key holds string `bar`, and an exception handler is declared to catch and process exceptions while a handler is executed on the event-loop thread.

Listing 2.20 Using context data and exception handling

```
Vertx vertx = Vertx.vertx();
Context ctx = vertx.getOrCreateContext();
ctx.put("foo", "bar");

ctx.exceptionHandler(t -> {
  if ("Tada".equals(t.getMessage())) {
    logger.info("Got a _Tada_ exception");
  } else {
    logger.error("Woops", t);
  }
});
```

```
ctx.runOnContext(v -> {
  throw new RuntimeException("Tada");
});

ctx.runOnContext(v -> {
  logger.info("foo = {}", (String) ctx.get("foo"));
});
```

Context data may be useful when event processing is spread across multiple classes. It is otherwise much simpler (and faster!) to use class fields.

Exception handlers are important when event processing may throw exceptions. By default, exceptions are simply logged by Vert.x, but overriding a context exception handler is useful when performing custom actions to deal with errors.

Listing 2.21   Sample output of running listing 2.20

```
INFO [vert.x-eventloop-thread-0] ThreadsAndContexts - Got a _Tada_ exception
INFO [vert.x-eventloop-thread-0] ThreadsAndContexts - foo = bar
```

Running the code in listing 2.20 produces output similar to that of listing 2.21.

2.4.3   *Bridging Vert.x and non-Vert.x threading models*

You will probably not have to deal with Vert.x contexts when writing Vert.x applications. Still, there is one case where it makes the most sense: when you have to use third-party code that has its own threading model, and you want to make it work properly with Vert.x.

The code in the next listing shows an example where a non-Vert.x thread is being created. By passing a context obtained from a verticle, we are able to execute some code back on the event loop from some code running on a non-Vert.x thread.

Listing 2.22   Mixing different threading models

```
public class MixedThreading extends AbstractVerticle {
  private final Logger logger = LoggerFactory.getLogger(MixedThreading.class);

  @Override
  public void start() {
    Context context = vertx.getOrCreateContext();    <───┐  We get the context of the
    new Thread(() -> {                                    │  verticle because start is
      try {                                               │  running on an event-loop
        run(context);                                     │  thread.
      } catch (InterruptedException e) {
        logger.error("Woops", e);
      }
    }).start();    <─── We start a plain Java thread.
  }

  private void run(Context context) throws InterruptedException {
```

```
    CountDownLatch latch = new CountDownLatch(1);
    logger.info("I am in a non-Vert.x thread");
    context.runOnContext(v -> {                    <—————
      logger.info("I am on the event-loop");
      vertx.setTimer(1000, id -> {
        logger.info("This is the final countdown");
        latch.countDown();
      });
    });
    logger.info("Waiting on the countdown latch...");
    latch.await();
    logger.info("Bye!");
  }
}
```

runOnContext ensures we run some code back on the verticle event-loop thread.

The logs in the following listing show that.

Listing 2.23 Sample output when running listing 2.22

```
INFO [Thread-3] MixedThreading - I am in a non-Vert.x thread
INFO [Thread-3] MixedThreading - Waiting on the countdown latch...
INFO [vert.x-eventloop-thread-0] MixedThreading - I am on the event-loop
INFO [vert.x-eventloop-thread-0] MixedThreading - This is the final countdown
INFO [Thread-3] MixedThreading - Bye!
```

You can use the technique of having a verticle context and issuing calls to runOnContext whenever you need to integrate non-Vert.x threading models into your applications.

> **TIP** This example shows another important property of contexts: they are propagated when defining handlers. Indeed, the block of code run with runOnContext sets a timer handler after one second. You can see that the handler is executed with the same context as the one that was used to define it.

The next chapter discusses the event bus, the privileged way verticles can communicate with each other and articulate event processing in a Vert.x application.

Summary

- Verticles are the core component for asynchronous event processing in Vert.x applications.
- Event-loop verticles process asynchronous I/O events and should be free of blocking and long-running operations.
- Worker verticles can be used to process blocking I/O and long-running operations.
- It is possible to mix code with both Vert.x and non-Vert.x threads by using event-loop contexts.

Event bus: The backbone of a Vert.x application

This chapter covers

- What the event bus is
- How to have point-to-point, request-reply, and publish/subscribe communications over the event bus
- The distributed event bus for verticle-to-verticle communication across the network

The previous chapter introduced *verticles*. A Vert.x application is made up of one or more verticles, and each verticle forms a unit for processing asynchronous events. It is common to specialize verticles by functional and technical concerns, such as having one verticle for exposing an HTTP API and another for dealing with a data store. This design also encourages the deployment of several instances of a given verticle for scalability purposes.

What we have *not* covered yet is how verticles can communicate with each other. For example, an HTTP API verticle needs to *talk* to the data store verticle if the larger Vert.x application is to do anything useful.

Connecting verticles and making sure they can cooperate is the role of the *event bus*. This is important when building reactive applications—the event bus offers a way to transparently distribute event-processing work both inside a process and across several nodes over the network.

3.1 *What is the event bus?*

The event bus is a means for sending and receiving messages in an asynchronous fashion. Messages are sent to and retrieved from *destinations*. A destination is simply a free-form string, such as `incoming.purchase.orders` or `incoming-purchase-orders`, although the former format with dots is preferred.

Messages have a body, optional headers for storing metadata, and an expiration timestamp after which they will be discarded if they haven't been processed yet.

Message bodies are commonly encoded using the Vert.x JSON representation. The advantage of using JSON is that it is a serialization format that can be easily transported over the network, and all programming languages understand it. It is also possible to use Java primitive and string types, especially as JVM languages that may be used for writing verticles have direct bindings for them. Last but not least, it is possible to register custom encoder/decoders (codecs) to support more specialized forms of message body serialization. For instance, you could write a codec for converting Java objects to a binary encoding of your own. It is rarely useful to do so, however, and JSON and string data cover most Vert.x applications' needs.

The event bus allows for decoupling between verticles. There is no need for one verticle to access another verticle class—all that is needed is to agree on destination names and data representation. Another benefit is that since Vert.x is polyglot, the event bus allows verticles written in different languages to communicate with each other without requiring any complex language interoperability layer, whether for communications inside the same JVM process or across the network.

An interesting property of the event bus is that it can be extended outside of the application process. You will see in this chapter that the event bus also works across distributed members of a cluster. Later in this book you will see how to extend the event bus to embedded or external message brokers, to remote clients, and also to JavaScript applications running in a web browser.

Communications over the event bus follow three patterns:

- Point-to-point messaging
- Request-reply messaging
- Publish/subscribe messaging

3.1.1 *Is the event bus just another message broker?*

Readers familiar with message-oriented middleware will have spotted the obvious resemblance between the event bus and a message broker. After all, the event bus exhibits familiar messaging patterns, such as the publish/subscribe pattern, which is popular for integrating distributed and heterogeneous applications.

The short answer is that no, the Vert.x event bus is not an alternative to Apache ActiveMQ, RabbitMQ, ZeroMQ, or Apache Kafka. The longer explanation is that it is an *event* bus for verticle-to-verticle communications inside an application, not a *message* bus for application-to-application communications. As you will see later in this book, Vert.x integrates with message brokers, but the event bus is no replacement for this type of middleware. Specifically, the event bus does not do the following:

- Support message acknowledgments
- Support message priorities
- Support message durability to recover from crashes
- Provide routing rules
- Provide transformation rules (schema adaptation, scatter/gather, etc.)

The event bus simply carries *volatile* events that are being processed asynchronously by verticles.

Not all events are created equal, and while some may be lost, some may not. In our quest for writing *reactive applications*, you will see where to use data replication or message brokers such as Apache Kafka in combination with the event bus.[1]

The event bus is a simple and fast event conveyor, and we can take advantage of it for most verticle-to-verticle interactions, while turning to more costly middleware for events that cannot be lost.

TIP Readers familiar with messaging patterns may want to skim the next three subsections, or even skip them.

3.1.2 *Point-to-point messaging*

Messages are sent by producers to destinations, such as a.b.c in figure 3.1. Destination names are free-form strings, but the convention in the Vert.x community is to use separating dots. For example, we could use datastore.new-purchase-orders to send new purchase orders to be stored in a database.

With point-to-point messaging, one of the possibly multiple consumers picks a message and processes it. Figure 3.1 shows this with messages M1, M2, and M3.

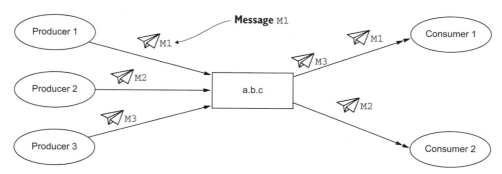

Figure 3.1 Point-to-point messaging over the event bus

---

[1]For a thorough discussion of using Kafka, see Dylan Scott's *Kafka in Action* (Manning, 2019).

Messages are distributed in a round-robin fashion among the consumers, so they split message processing in equal proportions. This is why in figure 3.1 the first consumer processes M1 and M3, while the second consumer processes M2. Note that there is no fairness mechanism to distribute fewer messages to an overloaded consumer.

3.1.3 Request-reply messaging

In Vert.x, the request-reply messaging communication pattern is a variation on point-to-point messaging. When a message is sent in point-to-point messaging, it is possible to register a *reply* handler. When you do, the event bus generates a temporary destination name dedicated solely to communications between the request message producer that is expecting a reply, and the consumer that will eventually receive and process the message.

This messaging pattern works well for mimicking remote procedure calls, but with the response being sent in an asynchronous fashion, so there is no need to keep waiting until it comes back. For example, an HTTP API verticle can send a request to a data store verticle to fetch some data, and the data store verticle eventually returns a reply message.

This pattern is illustrated in figure 3.2. When a message expects a reply, a reply destination is generated by the event bus and attached to the message before it reaches a consumer. You can inspect the reply destination name through the event-bus message API if you want, but you will rarely need to know the destination, since you will simply call a `reply` method on the message object. Of course, a message consumer needs to be programmed to provide a reply when this pattern is being used.

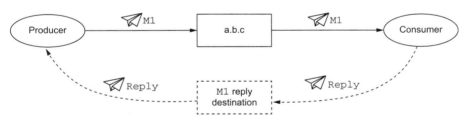

Figure 3.2 Request-reply messaging over the event bus

3.1.4 Publish/subscribe messaging

In publish/subscribe communications, there is even more decoupling between producers and consumers. When a message is sent to a destination, all subscribers receive it, as illustrated by figure 3.3. Messages M1, M2, and M3 are each sent by a different producer, and all subscribers receive the messages, unlike in the case of point-to-point messaging (see figure 3.1). It is not possible to specify reply handlers for publish/subscribe communications on the event bus.

Publish/subscribe is useful when you are not sure how many verticles and handlers will be interested in a particular event. If you need message consumers to get back to

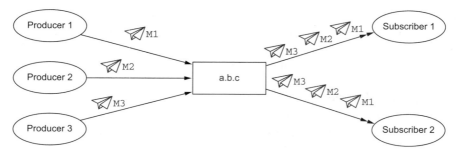

Figure 3.3   Publish/subscribe messaging over the event bus

the entity that sent the event, go for request-reply. Otherwise, opting for point-to-point versus publish/subscribe is a matter of functional requirements, mostly whether all consumers should process an event or just one consumer should.

3.2   *The event bus in an example*

Let's put the event bus to use and see how we can communicate between independent verticles. The example that we'll use involves several temperature sensors. Of course, we won't use any hardware. Instead we'll let temperatures evolve using pseudo-random numbers. We will also expose a simple web interface where temperatures and their average will be updated live.

A screenshot of the web interface is shown in figure 3.4. It displays the temperatures from four sensors and keeps their average up to date. The communication between the web interface and the server will happen using *server-sent events*, a simple yet effective protocol supported by most web browsers.[2]

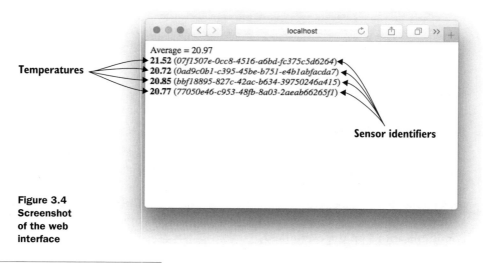

**Figure 3.4
Screenshot
of the web
interface**

---

[2]The W3C specification for server-sent events is available at www.w3.org/TR/eventsource.

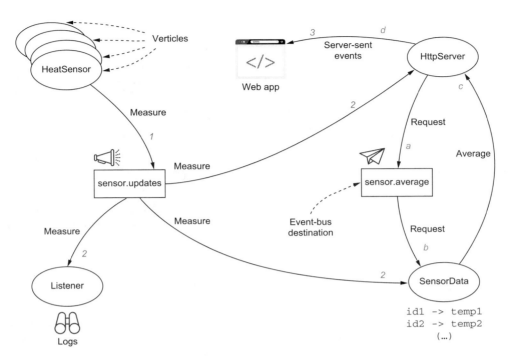

Figure 3.5 Overview of the example architecture

Figure 3.5 gives an overview of the application architecture. The figure shows two concurrent event communications annotated with ordering sequences [1, 2, 3] (a temperature update is being sent) and [a, b, c, d] (a temperature average computation is being requested).

The application is structured around four verticles:

- HeatSensor generates temperature measures at non-fixed rates and publishes them to subscribers to the sensor.updates destination. Each verticle has a unique sensor identifier.
- Listener monitors new temperature measures and logs them using SLF4J.
- SensorData keeps a record of the latest observed values for each sensor. It also supports request-response communications: sending a message to sensor.average triggers a computation of the average based on the latest data, and the result is sent back as a response.
- HttpServer exposes the HTTP server and serves the web interface. It pushes new values to its clients whenever a new temperature measurement has been observed, and it periodically asks for the current average and updates all the connected clients.

3.2.1 Heat sensor verticle

The following listing shows the implementation of the `HeatSensor` verticle class.

Listing 3.1 Heatsensor verticle implementation

```
public class HeatSensor extends AbstractVerticle {
  private final Random random = new Random();
  private final String sensorId = UUID.randomUUID().toString();   ⟵
  private double temperature = 21.0;
```
The sensor identifier is generated using a UUID.

```
  @Override
  public void start() {
    scheduleNextUpdate();
  }
```
Updates are scheduled with a random delay between one and six seconds.

```
  private void scheduleNextUpdate() {
    vertx.setTimer(random.nextInt(5000) + 1000, this::update);   ⟵
  }

  private void update(long timerId) {
    temperature = temperature + (delta() / 10);
    JsonObject payload = new JsonObject()
      .put("id", sensorId)
      .put("temp", temperature);
    vertx.eventBus().publish("sensor.updates", payload);   ⟵
    scheduleNextUpdate();
  }
```
We schedule the next update.

publish sends a message to subscribers.

```
  private double delta() {   ⟵
    if (random.nextInt() > 0) {
      return random.nextGaussian();
    } else {
      return -random.nextGaussian();
    }
  }
}
```
This computes a random positive or negative value to slightly modify the current temperature.

The `HeatSensor` verticle class does not use any realistic temperature model but instead uses random increments or decrements. Hence, if you run it long enough, it may report absurd values, but this is not very important in our journey through reactive applications.

The event bus is accessed through the `Vertx` context and the `eventBus()` method. Since this verticle does not know what the published values will be used for, we use the `publish` method to send them to subscribers on the `sensor.updates` destination. We also use JSON to encode data, which is idiomatic with Vert.x.

Let's now look at a verticle that consumes temperature updates.

3.2.2   *Listener verticle*

The following listing shows the implementation of the `Listener` verticle class.

**We don't need the full double value, so we format all
temperatures to two-decimal string representations.**

```
public class Listener extends AbstractVerticle {
    private final Logger logger = LoggerFactory.getLogger(Listener.class);
    private final DecimalFormat format = new DecimalFormat("#.##");

    @Override
    public void start() {
        EventBus bus = vertx.eventBus();
        bus.<JsonObject>consumer("sensor.updates", msg -> {
            JsonObject body = msg.body();
            String id = body.getString("id");
            String temperature = format.format(body.getDouble("temp"));
            logger.info("{} reports a temperature ~{}C", id, temp);
        });
    }
}
```

**The consumer method
allows subscribing to
messages, and a
callback handles all
event-bus messages.**

**The message
payload is in
the body.**

**We simply
log.**

The purpose of the `Listener` verticle class is to log all temperature measures, so all it does is listen to messages received on the `sensor.updates` destination. Since the emitter in the `HeatSensor` class uses a publish/subscribe pattern, `Listener` is not the only verticle that can receive the messages.

We did not take advantage of message headers in this example, but it is possible to use them for any metadata that does not belong to the message body. A common header is that of an "action," to help receivers know what the message is about. For instance, given a `database.operations` destination, we could use an action header to specify whether we intend to query the database, update an entry, store a new entry, or delete a previously stored one.

Let's now look at another verticle that consumes temperature updates.

3.2.3   *Sensor data verticle*

The following listing shows the implementation of the `SensorData` verticle class.

**We store the latest measurement of
each sensor by its unique identifier.**

```
public class SensorData extends AbstractVerticle {
    private final HashMap<String, Double> lastValues = new HashMap<>();

    @Override
    public void start() {
        EventBus bus = vertx.eventBus();
```

**The start method only declares two
event-bus destination handlers.**

```
    bus.consumer("sensor.updates", this::update);
    bus.consumer("sensor.average", this::average);
  }

  private void update(Message<JsonObject> message) {     ◁─┐
    JsonObject json = message.body();
    lastValues.put(json.getString("id"), json.getDouble("temp"));
  }

  private void average(Message<JsonObject> message) {     ◁─┐
    double avg = lastValues.values().stream()
      .collect(Collectors.averagingDouble(Double::doubleValue));
    JsonObject json = new JsonObject().put("average", avg);
 ┌▷ message.reply(json);
 │  }
 │ }
```

When a new measurement is being received, we extract the data from the JSON body.

The incoming message for average requests is not used, so it can just contain an empty JSON document.

The reply method is used to reply to a message.

The `SensorData` class has two event-bus handlers: one for sensor updates and one for average temperature computation requests. In one case, it updates entries in a `Hash-Map`, and in the other case, it computes the average and responds to the message sender.

The next verticle is the HTTP server.

3.2.4   HTTP server verticle

The HTTP server is interesting as it requests temperature averages from the `Sensor-Data` verticle via the event bus, and it implements the server-sent events protocol to consume temperature updates.

Let's start with the backbone of this verticle implementation.

SERVER IMPLEMENTATION

The following listing shows a classical example of starting an HTTP server and declaring a request handler.

Listing 3.4   Prologue of the HTTP server verticle implementation

The HTTP server port is configured with 8080 as the default value.

```
  public class HttpServer extends AbstractVerticle {
    @Override
    public void start() {
      vertx.createHttpServer()
        .requestHandler(this::handler)
 ┌───▷ .listen(config().getInteger("port", 8080));
 │    }
 │
 │    private void handler(HttpServerRequest request) {
 │      if ("/".equals(request.path())) {
 │        request.response().sendFile("index.html");     ◁─┐
```

The sendFile method allows the content of any local file to be streamed to the client. This closes the connection automatically.

```
    } else if ("/sse".equals(request.path())) {
        sse(request);                                ◁────────── Server-sent events will use the
    } else {                                                    /sse resource, and we provide
        request.response().setStatusCode(404);  ◁──────         a method for handling these
    }                                                           requests.
}                           Anything else triggers an HTTP
// (...)                    404 (not found) response.
}
```

The handler deals with three cases:

- Serving the web application to browsers
- Providing a resource for server-sent events
- Responding with 404 errors for any other resource path

TIP Manually dispatching custom actions depending on the requested resource path and HTTP method is tedious. As you will see later, the vertx-web module provides a nicer *router* API for conveniently declaring handlers.

THE WEB APPLICATION

Let's now see the client-side application, which is served by the HTTP server. The web application fits in a single HTML document shown in the following listing (I removed the irrelevant HTML portions, such as headers and footers).

Listing 3.5   Web application code

```
<div id="avg"></div>              EventSource objects
<div id="main"></div>             deal with server-sent         This callback listens for server-sent
<script language="JavaScript">    events.                     events of type update.
  const sse = new EventSource("/sse")    ◁──
  const main = document.getElementById("main")
  const avg = document.getElementById("avg")          The response data is plain
                                                      text, and since the server will
  sse.addEventListener("update", (evt) => {  ◁───     be sending JSON, we need to
    const data = JSON.parse(evt.data)        ◁──────  parse it.
    let div = document.getElementById(data.id);
    if (div === null) {                         If the sensor doesn't have a div for
      div = document.createElement("div")   ◁── displaying its data, we create it.
      div.setAttribute("id", data.id)
      main.appendChild(div)
    }
    div.innerHTML = `<strong>${data.temp.toFixed(2)}</strong>
    ➥ (<em>${data.id}</em>)`            ◁──
  })                                       This updates a temperature div.

  sse.addEventListener("average", (evt) => {   ◁──────  This callback listens
    const data = JSON.parse(evt.data)                   to server-sent events
    avg.innerText = `Average = ${data.average.toFixed(2)}`   of type average.
  })
</script>
```

The JavaScript code in the preceding listing deals with server-sent events and reacts to update the displayed content. We could have used one of the many popular JavaScript frameworks, but sometimes it's good to get back to basics.

> **NOTE** You may have noticed that listing 3.5 uses a modern version of Java-Script, with arrow functions, no semicolons, and string templates. This code should work as is on any recent web browser. I tested it with Mozilla Firefox 63, Safari 12, and Google Chrome 70.

SUPPORTING SERVER-SENT EVENTS

Let's now focus on how server-sent events work, and how they can be easily implemented with Vert.x.

Server-sent events are a very simple yet effective protocol for a server to push events to its clients. The protocol is text-based, and each event is a block with an event type and some data:

```
event: foo
data: bar
```

Each block event is separated by an empty line, so two successive events look like this:

```
event: foo
data: abc

event: bar
data: 123
```

Implementing server-sent events with Vert.x is very easy.

Listing 3.6   Supporting server-sent events

The text/event-stream MIME type is specified for server-sent events.

Since this is a live stream, we need to prevent browsers and proxies from caching it.

```
private void sse(HttpServerRequest request) {
  HttpServerResponse response = request.response();
  response
    .putHeader("Content-Type", "text/event-stream")
    .putHeader("Cache-Control", "no-cache")
    .setChunked(true);

  MessageConsumer<JsonObject> consumer =
    vertx.eventBus().consumer("sensor.updates");
  consumer.handler(msg -> {
    response.write("event: update\n");
    response.write("data: " + msg.body().encode() + "\n\n");
  });

  TimeoutStream ticks = vertx.periodicStream(1000);
  ticks.handler(id -> {
```

We call consumer without a handler, as we need an object to cancel the subscription when the client disconnects.

Sending event blocks is just sending text.

We update the average every second, so we need a periodic timer. Since it needs to be cancelled, we also use a form without a handler to get an object.

```
      vertx.eventBus().<JsonObject>request("sensor.average", "",
➡️   reply -> {                                                    ◁─────────────────┐
        if (reply.succeeded()) {
          response.write("event: average\n");
          response.write("data: " + reply.result().body().encode() + "\n\n");
        }
      });                            request sends a message that expects a
    });                              response. The reply is an asynchronous
                                     object, as it may have failed.

    response.endHandler(v -> {    ◁──┐
      consumer.unregister();         │  When the client disconnects (or refreshes the page) we
      ticks.cancel();                │  need to unregister the event-bus message consumer
    });                              │  and cancel the periodic task that computes averages.
}
```

Listing 3.6 provides the implementation of the `sse` method that deals with HTTP requests to the `/sse` resource. It declares one consumer for each HTTP request for temperature updates, and it pushes new events. It also declares a periodic task to query the `SensorData` verticle and maintain the average in a request-reply manner.

Since these two handlers are for an HTTP request, we need to be able to stop them when the connection is lost. This may happen because a web browser tab is closed, or simply on page reloads. To do that, we obtain *stream* objects, and we declare a handler for each, just like we would with forms that accept callbacks. You will see in the next chapter how to deal with stream objects, and when they are useful.

We can also use a command-line tool, such as HTTPie or curl, against the running application to see the event stream, as in the following listing.

Listing 3.7 Stream of SSE events using HTTPie

```
$ http http://localhost:8080/sse --stream  ◁──┐  The --stream flag allows streaming the
HTTP/1.1 200 OK                                │  response to the console rather than waiting
Cache-Control: no-cache                        │  for the server to end the connection.
Content-Type: text/event-stream
Transfer-Encoding: chunked

event: average                          ◁──────── Each event has a type.
data: {"average":21.132465880152044}    ◁──┐
                                            │  Since JSON is just text, it
event: update                               │  transports well as event data.
data: {"id":"3fa8321d-7600-42d3-b114-9fb6cdab7ecd","temp":21.043921061475107}

event: update
data: {"id":"8626e13f-9114-4f7d-acc3-bd60b00f3028","temp":21.47111113365458}

event: average
data: {"average":21.123126848463464}
```

WARNING At the time of writing, server-sent events are supported by all major web browsers except those from Microsoft. There are some JavaScript polyfills that provide the missing functionality to Microsoft's browsers, albeit with some limitations.

3.2.5 *Bootstrapping the application*

Now that we have all the verticles ready, we can assemble them as a Vert.x application. The following listing shows a main class for bootstrapping the application. It deploys four sensor verticles and one instance of each other verticle.

Listing 3.8   Main class to bootstrap the application

```
public class Main {
  public static void main(String[] args) {
    Vertx vertx = Vertx.vertx();
    vertx.deployVerticle("chapter3.HeatSensor", new        We start four
    ➥ DeploymentOptions().setInstances(4));        ◄      sensors.
    vertx.deployVerticle("chapter3.Listener");       ◄
    vertx.deployVerticle("chapter3.SensorData");           We are using the variants
    vertx.deployVerticle("chapter3.HttpServer");           of deployVerticle that use
  }                                                        reflection to instantiate
}                                                          the verticle classes.
```

Running the `main` method of this class allows us to connect with a web browser to http://localhost:8080/. When you do, you should see a graphical interface similar to that in figure 3.4, with continuous live updates. The console logs will also display temperature updates.

3.3 *Clustering and the distributed event bus*

Our use of the event bus so far has been *local*: all communications happened within the same JVM process. What is even more interesting is to use Vert.x *clustering* and benefit from a *distributed* event bus.

3.3.1 *Clustering in Vert.x*

Vert.x applications can run in clustering mode where a set of Vert.x application nodes can work together over the network. They may be node instances of the same application and have the same set of deployed verticles, but this is not a requirement. Some nodes can have one set of verticles, while others have a different set.

Figure 3.6 shows an overview of Vert.x clustering. A *cluster manager* ensures nodes can exchange messages over the event bus, enabling the following set of functionalities:

- Group membership and discovery allow discovering new nodes, maintaining the list of current nodes, and detecting when nodes disappear.
- Shared data allows maps and counters to be maintained cluster-wide, so that all nodes share the same values. Distributed locks are useful for some forms of coordination between nodes.
- Subscriber topology allows knowing what event-bus destinations each node has interest in. This is useful for efficiently dispatching messages over the distributed event bus. If one node has no consumer on destination `a.b.c`, there is no point in sending events from that destination to that node.

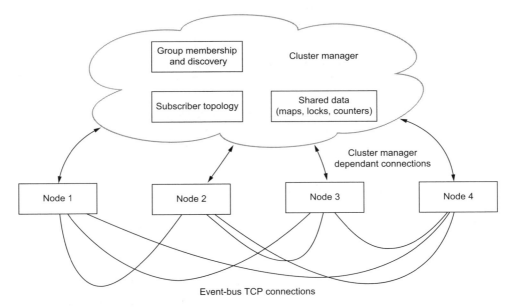

Figure 3.6 **Overview of Vert.x clustering**

There are several cluster manager implementations for Vert.x based on Hazelcast, Infinispan, Apache Ignite, and Apache ZooKeeper. Historically Hazelcast was the cluster manager for Vert.x, and then other engines were added. They all support the same Vert.x clustering abstractions for membership, shared data, and event-bus message passing. They are all functionally equivalent, so you will have to choose one depending on your needs and constraints. If you have no idea which one to pick, I recommend going with Hazelcast, which is a good default.

Finally, as shown in figure 3.6, the event-bus communications between nodes happen through direct TCP connections, using a custom protocol. When a node sends a message to a destination, it checks the subscriber topology with the cluster manager and dispatches the message to the nodes that have subscribers for that destination.

What cluster manager should you use?

There is no good answer to the question of which cluster manager you should use. It depends on whether you need special integration with one library, and also on what type of environment you need to deploy. If, say, you need to use the Infinispan APIs in your code, and not just Infinispan as the cluster manager engine for Vert.x, you should go with Infinispan to cover both needs.

You should also consider your deployment environment. If you deploy to some environment where Apache ZooKeeper is being used, perhaps it would be a good choice to also rely on it for the Vert.x cluster manager.

(continued)

By default, some cluster managers use multicast communications for node discovery, which may be disabled on some networks, especially those found in containerized environments like Kubernetes. In this case, you will need to configure the cluster manager to work in these environments.

As mentioned earlier, in case of doubt, choose Hazelcast, and check the project documentation for specific network configuration, like when deploying to Kubernetes. You can always change to another cluster manager implementation later.

3.3.2   *From event bus to distributed event bus*

Let's get back to the heat sensor application that we developed earlier in this chapter. Moving to a distributed event bus is transparent for the verticles.

We will prepare two main classes with different verticle deployments, as illustrated in figure 3.7:

- Four instances of `HeatSensor`, and one instance of `HttpServer` on port 8080
- Four instances of `HeatSensor`, one instance of `Listener`, one instance of `Sensor-Data`, and one instance of `HttpServer` on port 8081 (so you can run and test it on the same host)

The goal is to show that by launching one instance of each deployment in clustering mode, verticles communicate just as if they were running within the same JVM process. Connecting with a web browser to either of the instances will give the same view of the eight sensors' data. Similarly, the `Listener` verticle on the second instance will get temperature updates from the first instance.

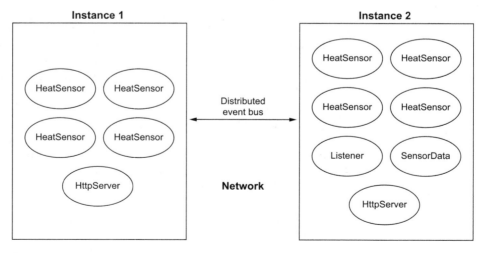

Figure 3.7   Clustered application overview

We will use Infinispan as the cluster manager, but you can equally use another one. Supposing your project is built with Gradle, you'll need to add `vertx-infinispan` as a dependency:

```
implementation("io.vertx:vertx-infinispan:version")
```

The following listing shows the implementation of the main class `FirstInstance` that we can use to start one node that doesn't deploy all of the application verticles.

Listing 3.9   Code of the main class for the first instance

```
public class FirstInstance {
  private static final Logger logger =
➥   LoggerFactory.getLogger(FirstInstance.class);

  public static void main(String[] args) {
    Vertx.clusteredVertx(new VertxOptions(), ar -> {        ⬅   Starting a clustered
      if (ar.succeeded()) {                                     Vert.x application is
        logger.info("First instance has been started");        an asynchronous
        Vertx vertx = ar.result();                       ⬅    operation.
        vertx.deployVerticle("chapter3.HeatSensor",
➥         new DeploymentOptions().setInstances(4));            Upon success,
        vertx.deployVerticle("chapter3.HttpServer");           we retrieve the
      } else {                                                 Vertx instance.
        logger.error("Could not start", ar.cause());   ⬅
      }                                                        A potential cause of failure
    });                                                        could be the absence of a
  }                                                            cluster manager library.
}
```

As you can see, starting an application in clustered mode requires calling the `clustered-Vertx` method. The remainder is just classic verticle deployment.

The code of the second instance's main method is very similar and is shown in the following listing.

Listing 3.10   Code of the main class for the second instance

```
public class SecondInstance {
  private static final Logger logger =
➥   LoggerFactory.getLogger(SecondInstance.class);

  public static void main(String[] args) {
    Vertx.clusteredVertx(new VertxOptions(), ar -> {
      if (ar.succeeded()) {
        logger.info("Second instance has been started");
        Vertx vertx = ar.result();
        vertx.deployVerticle("chapter3.HeatSensor",
➥         new DeploymentOptions().setInstances(4));
        vertx.deployVerticle("chapter3.Listener");
        vertx.deployVerticle("chapter3.SensorData");
```

```
        JsonObject conf = new JsonObject().put("port", 8081);
        vertx.deployVerticle("chapter3.HttpServer",
          new DeploymentOptions().setConfig(conf));
      } else {
        logger.error("Could not start", ar.cause());
      }
    });
  }
}
```

We use a different port so you can start both instances on the same host.

Both main classes can be run on the same host, and the two instances will discover each other. As before, you can start them from your IDE, or by running `gradle run -PmainClass=chapter3.cluster.FirstInstance` and `gradle run -PmainClass=chapter3.cluster.SecondInstance` in two different terminals.

> **TIP** If you are using IPv6 and encountering issues, you can add the `-Djava.net.preferIPv4Stack=true` flag to the JVM parameters.

By default, the Vert.x Infinispan cluster manager is configured to perform discovery using network broadcast, so the two instances discover each other when they're run on the same machine. You can also use two machines on the same network.

> **WARNING** Network broadcast rarely works in cloud environments and many data centers. In these cases, the cluster manager needs to be configured to use other discovery and group membership protocols. In the case of Infinispan, the documentation has specific details at https://infinispan.org/documentation/.

Figure 3.8 shows the application running with one browser connected to the instance with port 8080 and another browser connected to the second instance with port 8081, and we see logs from the `Listener` verticle in the background. As you can see, both instances display events from the eight sensors, and the first instance has its average temperature updated so it can interact with the `SensorData` verticle on the second instance.

The distributed event bus is an interesting tool, as it is transparent to the verticles.

> **TIP** The event-bus API has `localConsumer` methods for declaring message handlers that only work locally when running with clustering. For instance, a consumer for destination `a.b.c` will not receive messages sent to that destination from another instance in the cluster.

The next chapter discusses asynchronous data and event streams.

Console outputs of the
application instances

Web browsers connected
to different instances

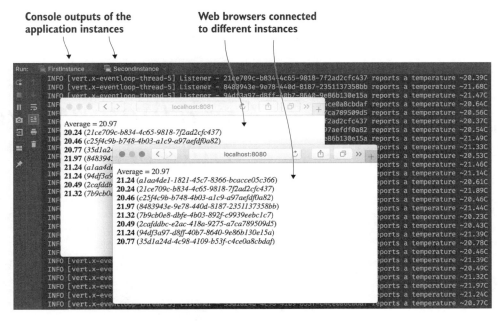

Figure 3.8   Screenshot of the application running in clustered mode

Summary

- The event bus is the preferred way for verticles to communicate, and it uses asynchronous message passing.
- The event bus implements both publish/subscribe (one-to-many) and point-to-point (many-to-one) communications.
- While it looks like a traditional message broker, the event bus does not provide durability guarantees, so it must only be used for transient data.
- Clustering allows networked instances to communicate over the distributed event bus in a transparent fashion, and to scale the workload across several application instances.

Asynchronous data and event streams

So far we have been processing events using *callbacks*, and from various sources such as HTTP or TCP servers. Callbacks allow us to reason about events one at a time.

Processing an incoming data buffer from a TCP connection, from a file, or from an HTTP request is not very different: you need to declare a callback handler that reacts to each event and allows custom processing.

That being said, most events need to be processed as a series rather than as isolated events. Processing the body of an HTTP request is a good example, as several buffers of different sizes need to be assembled to reconstitute the full body payload.

Since reactive applications deal with non-blocking I/O, efficient and correct stream processing is key. In this chapter we'll look at why streams pose challenges and how Vert.x offers a comprehensive unified stream model.

4.1 Unified stream model

Vert.x offers a unified abstraction of streams across several types of resources, such as files, network sockets, and more. A *read stream* is a source of events that can be read, whereas a *write stream* is a destination for events to be sent to. For example, an HTTP request is a read stream, and an HTTP response is a write stream.

Streams in Vert.x span a wide range of sources and sinks, including those listed in table 4.1.

Table 4.1 Vert.x common read and write streams

Stream resource	Read support	Write support
TCP sockets	Yes	Yes
UDP datagrams	Yes	Yes
HTTP requests and responses	Yes	Yes
WebSockets	Yes	Yes
Files	Yes	Yes
SQL results	Yes	No
Kafka events	Yes	Yes
Periodic timers	Yes	No

Read and write stream are defined through the `ReadStream` and `WriteStream` interfaces of the `io.vertx.core.streams` package. You will mostly deal with APIs that implement these two interfaces rather than implement them yourself, although you may have to do so if you want to connect to some third-party asynchronous event API.

These interfaces can be seen as each having two parts:

- Essential methods for reading or writing data
- Back-pressure management methods that we will cover in the next section

Table 4.2 lists the essential methods of read streams. They define callbacks for being notified of three types of events: some data has been read, an exception has arisen, and the stream has ended.

Table 4.2 `ReadStream` essential methods

Method	Description
`handler(Handler<T>)`	Handles a new read value of type `T` (e.g., `Buffer`, `byte[]`, `JsonObject`, etc.)
`exceptionHandler(Handler<Throwable>)`	Handles a read exception
`endHandler(Handler<Void>)`	Called when the stream has ended, either because all data has been read or because an exception has been raised

Similarly, the essential methods of write streams listed in table 4.3 allow us to write data, end a stream, and be notified when an exception arises.

Table 4.3 `WriteStream` essential methods

Method	Description
`write(T)`	Writes some data of type, `T` (e.g., `Buffer`, `byte[]`, `JsonObject`, etc.)
`exceptionHandler(Handler<Throwable>)`	Handles a write exception
`end()`	Ends the stream
`end(T)`	Writes some data of type, `T`, and then ends the stream

We already manipulated streams in the previous chapters without knowing it, such as with TCP and HTTP servers.

The `java.io` APIs form a classic stream I/O abstraction for reading and writing data from various sources in Java, albeit using blocking APIs. It is interesting to compare the JDK streams with the Vert.x non-blocking stream APIs.

Suppose we want to read the content of a file and output its content to the standard console output.

Listing 4.1 Reading a file using JDK I/O APIs

```
public static void main(String[] args) {
  File file = new File("build.gradle.kts");
  byte[] buffer = new byte[1024];
  try (FileInputStream in = new FileInputStream(file)) {
    int count = in.read(buffer);
    while (count != -1) {
      System.out.println(new String(buffer, 0, count));
      count = in.read(buffer);
    }
  } catch (IOException e) {
    e.printStackTrace();
  } finally {
    System.out.println("\n--- DONE");
  }
}
```

Using try-with-resources we ensure that reader.close() is always going to be called, whether the execution completes normally or exceptionally.

We insert two lines to the console once reading has finished.

Listing 4.1 shows a classic example of using JDK I/O streams to read a file and then output its content to the console, while taking care of possible errors. We read data to a buffer and then immediately write the buffer content to the standard console before recycling the buffer for the next read.

The following listing shows the same code as in listing 4.1, but using the Vert.x asynchronous file APIs.

Listing 4.2 Reading a file using Vert.x streams

Opening a file with Vert.x requires options, such as
whether the file is in read, write, append mode, and more.

```
public static void main(String[] args) {
   Vertx vertx = Vertx.vertx();
   OpenOptions opts = new OpenOptions().setRead(true);
   vertx.fileSystem().open("build.gradle.kts", opts, ar -> {
     if (ar.succeeded()) {
       AsyncFile file = ar.result();
       file.handler(System.out::println)
         .exceptionHandler(Throwable::printStackTrace)
         .endHandler(done -> {
           System.out.println("\n--- DONE");
           vertx.close();
         });
     } else {
       ar.cause().printStackTrace();
     }
   });
}
```

- Opening a file is an asynchronous operation.
- AsyncFile is the interface for Vert.x asynchronous files.
- The callback for new buffer data
- The callback when an exception arises
- The callback when the stream ends

The approach is declarative here, as we define handlers for the different types of events when reading the stream. We are being *pushed* data, whereas in listing 4.1 we were *pulling* data from the stream.

This difference may seem cosmetic at first sight, with data being pulled in one example, while being pushed in the other. However, the difference is major, and we need to understand it to master asynchronous streams, whether with Vert.x or with other solutions.

This brings us to the notion of *back-pressure*.

4.2   What is back-pressure?

Back-pressure is a mechanism for a consumer of events to signal an event's producer that it is emitting events at a faster rate than the consumer can handle them. In reactive systems, back-pressure is used to pause or slow down a producer so that consumers avoid accumulating unprocessed events in unbounded memory buffers, possibly exhausting resources.

To understand why back-pressure matters with asynchronous streams, let's take the example of an HTTP server used for downloading Linux distribution images, and consider the implementation without any back-pressure management strategy in place.

Linux distribution images are often distributed as .iso files and can easily weigh several gigabytes. Implementing a server that could distribute such files would involve doing the following:

1 Open an HTTP server.
2 For each incoming HTTP request, find the corresponding file.
3 For each buffer read from the file, write it to the HTTP response body.

Figure 4.1 provides an illustration of how this would work with Vert.x, although this also applies to any non-blocking I/O API. Data buffers are read from the file stream, and then passed to a handler. The handler is unlikely to do anything but directly write each buffer to the HTTP response stream. Each buffer is eventually written to the underlying TCP buffer, either directly or as smaller chunks. Since the TCP buffer may be full (either because of the network or because the client is busy), it is necessary to maintain a buffer of pending buffers to be written (the write queue in figure 4.1). Remember, a write operation is non-blocking, so buffering is needed. This sounds like a very simple processing pipeline, so what could possibly go wrong?

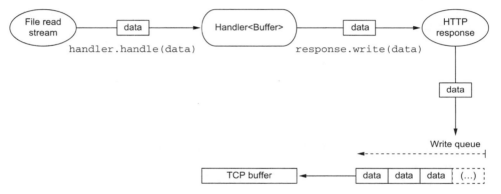

Figure 4.1   Reading and then writing data between streams without any back-pressure signaling

Reading from a filesystem is generally fast and low-latency, and given several read requests, an operating system is likely to cache some pages into RAM. By contrast, writing to the network is much slower, and bandwidth depends on the weakest network link. Delays also occur.

As the reads are much faster than writes, a write buffer, as shown in figure 4.1, may quickly grow very large. If we have several thousand concurrent connections to download ISO images, we may have lots of buffers accumulated in write buffer queues. We may actually have several gigabytes worth of ISO images in a JVM process memory, waiting to be written over the network! The more buffers there are in write queues, the more memory the process consumes.

The risk here is clearly that of exhaustion, either because the process eats all available physical memory, or because it runs in a memory-capped environment such as a container. This raises the risk of consuming too much memory and even crashing.

As you can probably guess, one solution is *back-pressure signaling*, which enables the read stream to adapt to the throughput of the write stream. In the previous example, when the HTTP response write queue grows too big, it should be able to notify the file read stream that it is going too fast. In practice, pausing the source stream is a good way to manage back-pressure, because it gives time to write the items in the write buffer while not accumulating new ones.

> **TIP** Blocking I/O APIs have an implicit form of back-pressure by blocking execution threads until I/O operations complete. Write operations block when buffers are full, which prevents blocked threads from pulling more data until write operations have completed.

Table 4.4 lists the back-pressure management methods of ReadStream. By default, a read stream reads data as fast as it can, unless it is being paused. A processor can pause and then resume a read stream to control the data flow.

Table 4.4 `ReadStream` back-pressure management methods

Method	Description
pause()	Pauses the stream, preventing further data from being sent to the handler.
resume()	Starts reading data again and sending it to the handler.
fetch(n)	Demands a number, n, of elements to be read (at most). The stream must be paused before calling fetch(n).

When a read stream has been paused, it is possible to ask for a certain number of elements to be fetched, which is a form of asynchronous pulling. This means that a processor can ask for elements using fetch, setting its own pace. You will see concrete examples of that in the last section of this chapter.

In any case, calling resume() causes the stream to start pushing data again as fast as it can.

Table 4.5 shows the corresponding back-pressure management methods for Write-Stream.

Table 4.5 `WriteStream` back-pressure management methods

Method	Description
setWriteQueueMaxSize(int)	Defines what the maximum write buffer queue size should be before being considered full. This is a size in terms of queued Vert.x buffers to be written, not a size in terms of actual bytes, because the queued buffers may be of different sizes.
boolean writeQueueFull()	Indicates when the write buffer queue size is full.
drainHandler(Handler<Void>)	Defines a callback indicating when the write buffer queue has been drained (typically when it is back to half of its maximum size).

The write buffer queue has a maximum size after which it is considered to be full. Write queues have default sizes that you will rarely want to tweak, but you can do so if you want to. Note that writes can still be made, and data will accumulate in the queue. A writer is supposed to check when the queue is full, but there is no enforcement on writes. When the writer knows that the write queue is full, it can be notified through a *drain handler* when data can be written again. In general this happens when half the write queue has been drained.

Now that you have seen the back-pressure operations provided in `ReadStream` and `WriteStream`, here is the recipe for controlling the flow in our example of providing ISO images via HTTP:

1 For each read buffer, write it to the HTTP response stream.
2 Check if the write buffer queue is full.
3 If it is full

   a Pause the file read stream.
   b Install a drain handler that resumes the file read stream when it is called.

Note that this back-pressure management strategy is not always what you need:

- There may be cases where dropping data when a write queue is full is functionally correct and even desirable.
- Sometimes the source of events does not support pausing like a Vert.x `ReadStream` does, and you will need to choose between dropping data or buffering even if it may cause memory exhaustion.

The appropriate strategy for dealing with back-pressure depends on the functional requirements of the code you are writing. In general, you will prefer flow control like Vert.x streams offer, but when that's not possible, you will need to adopt another strategy.

Let's now assemble all that we've seen into an application.

4.3   *Making a music-streaming jukebox*

We are going to illustrate Vert.x streams and back-pressure management through the example of a music-streaming jukebox (see figure 4.2).

The idea is that the jukebox has a few MP3 files stored locally, and clients can connect over HTTP to listen to the stream. Individual files can also be downloaded over HTTP. In turn, controlling when to play, pause, and schedule a song happens over a simple, text-based TCP protocol. All connected players will be listening to the same audio at the same time, apart from minor delays due to the buffering put in place by the players.

This example will allow us to see how we can deal with custom flow pacing and different back-pressure management strategies, and also how to parse streams.

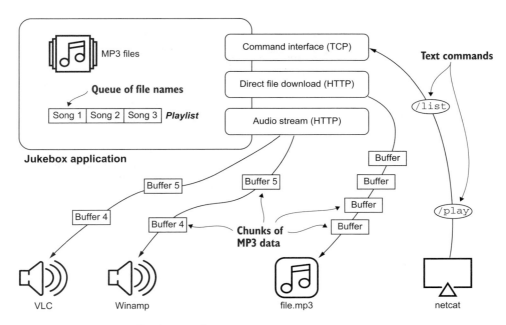

Figure 4.2   **Jukebox application overview**

4.3.1   *Features and usage*

The application that we will build can be run from the code in the book's GitHub repository using a Gradle task, as shown in the console output of listing 4.3.

> **NOTE**   You will need to copy some of your MP3 files to a folder named tracks/ in the project directory if you want the jukebox to have music to play.

Listing 4.3   Running the jukebox application

The main class is chapter4.jukebox.Jukebox.

We are deploying two verticles.

```
$ ./gradlew run -PmainClass=chapter4.jukebox.Main

> Task :run
[vert.x-eventloop-thread-0] chapter4.jukebox.Jukebox - Start
[vert.x-eventloop-thread-1] chapter4.jukebox.NetControl - Start
```

There are two verticles being deployed in this application:

- `Jukebox` provides the main music-streaming logic and HTTP server interface for music players to connect to.
- `NetControl` provides a text-based TCP protocol for remotely controlling the jukebox application.

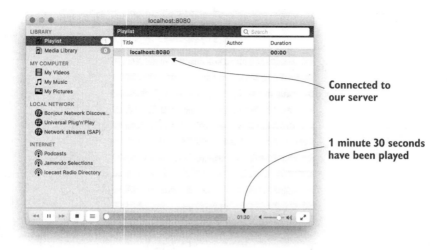

Figure 4.3   VLC connected to the jukebox

To listen to music, the user can connect a player such as VLC (see figure 4.3) or even open a web browser directly at http://localhost:8080/.

   On the other hand, the player can be controlled via a tool like `netcat`, with plain text commands to list all files, schedule a track to be played, and pause or restart the stream. Listing 4.4 shows an interactive session using `netcat`.

Listing 4.4   Controlling the jukebox with `netcat`

The control TCP server listens on port 3000.

```
$ netcat localhost 3000
/list                                        ← This command lists all files.
Daniela-La-Luz-Did-you-Ever-(Original-Mix).mp3
The-Revenge-Let-Love-Take-The-Blame-(Original-Mix).mp3
intro.mp3
SQL-Surrender-(Original-Mix).mp3
/schedule SQL-Surrender-(Original-Mix).mp3   ← Scheduling adds the file to a playlist.
/pause
/play                      This pauses the stream for all connected players.
/schedule Daniela-La-Luz-Did-you-Ever-(Original-Mix).mp3   ← We schedule another track when the first has finished.
^C
```

This resumes the stream.   **We can exit the netcat session with Ctrl+C with no harm.**

TIP   `netcat` may be available as `nc` on your Unix environment. I am not aware of a friendly and equivalent tool for Windows, outside of a WSL environment.

Finally, we want to be able to download any MP3 for which we know the filename over HTTP:

```
curl -o out.mp3 http://localhost:8080/download/intro.mp3
```

Let's now dissect the various parts of the implementation.

4.3.2   HTTP processing: The big picture

There will be many code snippets referring to HTTP server processing, so it is good to look at figure 4.4 to understand how the next pieces of code will fit together.

There are two types of incoming HTTP requests: either a client wants to directly download a file by name, or it wants to join the audio stream. The processing strategies are very different.

In the case of downloading a file, the goal is to perform a direct copy from the file read stream to the HTTP response write stream. This will be done with back-pressure management to avoid excessive buffering.

Streaming is a bit more involved, as we need to keep track of all the streamers' HTTP response write streams. A timer periodically reads data from the current MP3 file, and the data is duplicated and written for each streamer.

Let's look at how these parts are implemented.

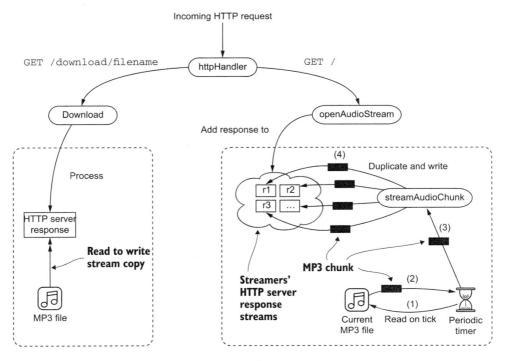

Figure 4.4   Big picture of the HTTP server processing

4.3.3   *Jukebox verticle basics*

The next listing shows that the state of the Jukebox verticle class is defined by a play status and a playlist.

Listing 4.5   State of the Jukebox class

```
private enum State {PLAYING, PAUSED}

private State currentMode = State.PAUSED;

private final Queue<String> playlist = new ArrayDeque<>();
```

An enumerated type, State, defines two states, while a Queue holds all scheduled tracks to be played next. Again, the Vert.x threading model ensures single-threaded access, so there is no need for concurrent collections and critical sections.

The start method of the Jukebox verticle (listing 4.6) needs to configure a few event-bus handlers that correspond to the commands and actions that can be used from the TCP text protocol. The NetControl verticle, which we will dissect later, deals with the inners of the TCP server and sends messages to the event bus.

Listing 4.6   Setting up the event-bus handlers in the Jukebox verticle

```
@Override
public void start() {
  EventBus eventBus = vertx.eventBus();
  eventBus.consumer("jukebox.list", this::list);
  eventBus.consumer("jukebox.schedule", this::schedule);
  eventBus.consumer("jukebox.play", this::play);
  eventBus.consumer("jukebox.pause", this::pause);

  // (...more later!)
}
```

Note that because we've abstracted the transfer of commands over the event-bus, we can easily plug in new ways to command the jukebox, such as using mobile applications, web applications, and so on.

The following listing provides the play/pause and schedule handlers. These methods directly manipulate the play and playlist state.

Listing 4.7   Play/pause and schedule operations in the Jukebox verticle

```
private void play(Message<?> request) {
  currentMode = State.PLAYING;
}

private void pause(Message<?> request) {
  currentMode = State.PAUSED;
}
```

```
private void schedule(Message<JsonObject> request) {
  String file = request.body().getString("file");
  if (playlist.isEmpty() && currentMode == State.PAUSED) {
    currentMode = State.PLAYING;
  }
  playlist.offer(file);
}
```

This allows us to automatically resume playing when no track is playing and we schedule a new one.

Listing the available files is a bit more involved, as the next listing shows.

Listing 4.8 Listing all available files in the `Jukebox` verticle

```
private void list(Message<?> request) {
  vertx.fileSystem().readDir("tracks", ".*mp3$", ar -> {
    if (ar.succeeded()) {
      List<String> files = ar.result()
        .stream()
        .map(File::new)
        .map(File::getName)
        .collect(Collectors.toList());
      JsonObject json = new JsonObject().put("files", new JsonArray(files));
      request.reply(json);
    } else {
      logger.error("readDir failed", ar.cause());
      request.fail(500, ar.cause().getMessage());
    }
  });
}
```

We asynchronously get all files ending with .mp3 in the tracks/ folder.

We build a JSON response.

This is an example of sending a failure code and error message in a request/reply communication over the event bus.

4.3.4   Incoming HTTP connections

There are two types of incoming HTTP clients: either they want the audio stream or they want to download a file.

The HTTP server is started in the `start` method of the verticle (see the next listing).

Listing 4.9 Setting up the HTTP server in the `Jukebox` verticle

```
@Override
public void start() {
  EventBus eventBus = vertx.eventBus();
  eventBus.consumer("jukebox.list", this::list);
  eventBus.consumer("jukebox.schedule", this::schedule);
  eventBus.consumer("jukebox.play", this::play);
  eventBus.consumer("jukebox.pause", this::pause);

  vertx.createHttpServer()
    .requestHandler(this::httpHandler)
    .listen(8080);

  // (...more later!)
}
```

We will expand on this later with MP3 streaming.

The request handler used by the Vert.x HTTP server is shown in the following listing. It forwards HTTP requests to the `openAudioStream` and `download` utility methods, which complete the requests and proceed.

Listing 4.10   HTTP request handler and dispatcher

```
private void httpHandler(HttpServerRequest request) {
  if ("/".equals(request.path())) {
    openAudioStream(request);
    return;
  }
  if (request.path().startsWith("/download/")) {
    String sanitizedPath = request.path().substring(10).replaceAll("/", "");
    download(sanitizedPath, request);
    return;
  }
  request.response().setStatusCode(404).end();
}
```

> **This string substitution prevents malicious attempts to read files from other directories (think of someone willing to read /etc/passwd).**

> **When nothing matches, we give a 404 (not found) response.**

The implementation of the `openAudioStream` method is shown in the following listing. It prepares the stream to be in chunking mode, sets the proper content type, and sets the response object aside for later.

Listing 4.11   Dealing with new stream players

```
private final Set<HttpServerResponse> streamers = new HashSet<>();

private void openAudioStream(HttpServerRequest request) {
  HttpServerResponse response = request.response()
    .putHeader("Content-Type", "audio/mpeg")
    .setChunked(true);
  streamers.add(response);
  response.endHandler(v -> {
    streamers.remove(response);
    logger.info("A streamer left");
  });
}
```

> **We track all current streamers in a set of HTTP responses.**

> **It is a stream, so the length is unknown.**

> **When a stream exits, it is no longer tracked.**

4.3.5   *Downloading as efficiently as possible*

Downloading a file is a perfect example where back-pressure management can be used to coordinate a source stream (the file) and a sink stream (the HTTP response).

The following listing shows how we look for the file, and when it exists, we forward the final download duty to the `downloadFile` method.

Listing 4.12   Download method

```
private void download(String path, HttpServerRequest request) {
  String file = "tracks/" + path;
```

```
if (!vertx.fileSystem().existsBlocking(file)) {
  request.response().setStatusCode(404).end();
  return;
}
OpenOptions opts = new OpenOptions().setRead(true);
vertx.fileSystem().open(file, opts, ar -> {
  if (ar.succeeded()) {
    downloadFile(ar.result(), request);
  } else {
    logger.error("Read failed", ar.cause());
    request.response().setStatusCode(500).end();
  }
});
}
```

⟵ **Unless you are on a networked filesystem, the possible blocking time is marginal, so we avoid a nested callback level.**

The implementation of the downloadFile method is shown in the following listing.

Listing 4.13 Downloading a file

```
private void downloadFile(AsyncFile file, HttpServerRequest request) {
  HttpServerResponse response = request.response();
  response.setStatusCode(200)
    .putHeader("Content-Type", "audio/mpeg")
    .setChunked(true);

  file.handler(buffer -> {
    response.write(buffer);
    if (response.writeQueueFull()) {
      file.pause();
      response.drainHandler(v -> file.resume());
    }
  });

  file.endHandler(v -> response.end());
}
```

Writing too fast!

Back-pressure application by pausing the read stream ⟵

Resuming when drained ⟵

Back-pressure is taken care of while copying data between the two streams. This is so commonly done when the strategy is to pause the source and not lose any data that the same code can be rewritten as in the following listing.

Listing 4.14 Pipe helper

```
HttpServerResponse response = request.response();
response.setStatusCode(200)
  .putHeader("Content-Type", "audio/mpeg")
  .setChunked(true);

file.pipeTo(response);
```

Pipes data from file to response ⟵

A pipe deals with back-pressure when copying between a pausable ReadStream and a WriteStream. It also manages the end of the source stream and errors on both streams. The code of listing 4.14 does exactly what's shown in listing 4.13, but without the boilerplate. There are other variants of `pipeTo` for specifying custom handlers.

4.3.6 *Reading MP3 files, but not too fast*

MP3 files have a header containing metadata such as the artist name, genre, bit rate, and so on. Several frames containing compressed audio data follow, which decoders can turn into *pulse-code modulation* data, which can eventually be turned into sound.

MP3 decoders are very resilient to errors, so if they start decoding in the middle of a file, they will still manage to figure out the bit rate, and they will align with the next frame to start decoding the audio. You can even concatenate multiple MP3 files and send them to a player. The audio will be decoded as long as all files are using the same bit rate and stereo mode.

This is interesting for us as we design a music-streaming jukebox: if our files have been encoded in the same way, we can simply push each file of a playlist one after the other, and the decoders will handle the audio just fine.

WHY BACK-PRESSURE ALONE IS NOT ENOUGH

Feeding MP3 data to many connected players is not as simple as it may seem. The main issue is ensuring that all current and future players are listening to the same music at roughly the same time. All players have different local buffering strategies to ensure smooth playback, even when the network suffers delays, but if the server simply pushes files as fast as it can, not all clients will be synchronized. Worse, when a new player connects, it may receive nothing to play while the current players have several minutes of music remaining in their buffers. To provide a sensible playback experience, we need to control the pace at which files are read, and for that we will use a timer.

This is illustrated in figure 4.5, which shows what happens *without* and *with* rate control on the streams. In both cases, suppose that Player A joined the stream at the beginning, while Player B joined, say, 10 seconds later. Without read-rate control, we find ourselves in a similar case to that of downloading an MP3 file. We may have back-pressure in place to ensure efficient resource usage while copying MP3 data chunks to the connected clients, but the streaming experience will be very bad.

Since we are basically streaming data as fast as we can, Player A finds its internal buffers filled with almost all the current file data. While it may be playing at position 0 minutes 15 seconds, it has already received data beyond the 3-minute mark. When Player B joins, it starts receiving MP3 data chunks from much farther on in the file, so it starts playing at position 3 minutes and 30 seconds. If we extend our reasoning to multiple files, a new player can join and receive no data at all, while the previously connected players may have multiple songs to play in their internal buffers.

By contrast, if we control the read rate of the MP3 file, and hence the rate at which MP3 chunks are being copied and written to the connected players, we can ensure that they are all, more or less, at the same position.

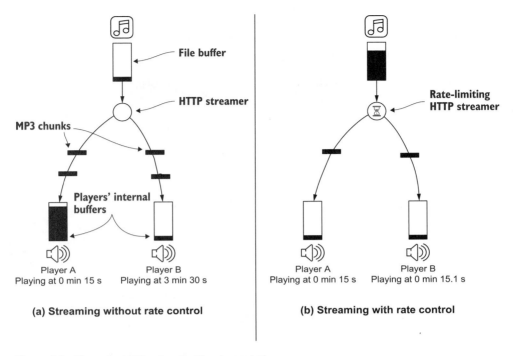

Figure 4.5   Streaming without and with rate control

Rate control here is all about ensuring that all players receive data fast enough so that they can play without interruption, but not too quickly so they do not buffer too much data.

RATE-LIMITED STREAMING IMPLEMENTATION

Let's look at the complete `Jukebox` verticle `start` method, as it shows that much needed timer.

Listing 4.15   Jukebox verticle class `start` method

```
@Override
public void start() {
  EventBus eventBus = vertx.eventBus();
  eventBus.consumer("jukebox.list", this::list);
  eventBus.consumer("jukebox.schedule", this::schedule);
  eventBus.consumer("jukebox.play", this::play);
  eventBus.consumer("jukebox.pause", this::pause);

  vertx.createHttpServer()
    .requestHandler(this::httpHandler)
    .listen(8080);

  vertx.setPeriodic(100, this::streamAudioChunk);
}
```

streamAudioChunk periodically pushes new MP3 data (100 ms is purely empirical, so feel free to adjust it).

Beyond connecting the event-bus handlers and starting an HTTP server, the `start` method also defines a timer so that data is streamed every 100 milliseconds.

Next, we can look at the implementation of the `streamAudioChunk` method.

Listing 4.16   Streaming file chunks

```
private AsyncFile currentFile;
private long positionInFile;

private void streamAudioChunk(long id) {
  if (currentMode == State.PAUSED) {
    return;
  }
  if (currentFile == null && playlist.isEmpty()) {
    currentMode = State.PAUSED;
    return;
  }
  if (currentFile == null) {
    openNextFile();
  }
  currentFile.read(Buffer.buffer(4096), 0, positionInFile, 4096, ar -> {
    if (ar.succeeded()) {
      processReadBuffer(ar.result());
    } else {
      logger.error("Read failed", ar.cause());
      closeCurrentFile();
    }
  });
}
```

> **Buffers cannot be reused across I/O operations, so we need a new one.**

> **This is where data is being copied to all players.**

Why these values?

Why do we read data every 100 milliseconds? And why read buffers of 4096 bytes?

I have empirically found these values work well for 320 KBps constant bit rate MP3 files on my laptop. They ensured no drops in tests while preventing players from buffering too much data, and thus ending several seconds apart in the audio stream.

Feel free to tinker with these values as you run the examples.

The code of `streamAudioChunk` reads blocks of, at most, 4096 bytes. Since the method will always be called 10 times per second, it also needs to check whether anything is being played at all. The `processReadBuffer` method streams data, as shown in the following listing.

Listing 4.17   Streaming data chunks to players

```
private void processReadBuffer(Buffer buffer) {
  positionInFile += buffer.length();
  if (buffer.length() == 0) {
```

> **This happens when the end of the file has been reached.**

```
        closeCurrentFile();
        return;
    }
    for (HttpServerResponse streamer : streamers) {
        if (!streamer.writeQueueFull()) {
            streamer.write(buffer.copy());
        }
    }
}
```

Back-pressure again → (pointing to `if (!streamer.writeQueueFull()) {`)

← **Remember, buffers cannot be reused.** (pointing to `streamer.write(buffer.copy());`)

For every HTTP response stream to a player, the method copies the read data. Note that we have another case of back-pressure management here: when the write queue of a client is full, we simply discard data. On the player's end, this will result in audio drops, but since the queue is full on the server, it means that the player will have delays or drops anyway. Discarding data is fine, as MP3 decoders know how to recover, and it ensures that playback will remain closely on time with the other players.

> **WARNING** Vert.x buffers cannot be reused once they have been written, as they are placed in a write queue. Reusing buffers will always result in bugs, so don't look for unnecessary optimizations here.

Finally, the helper methods in the following listing enable the opening and closing of files.

Listing 4.18 Opening and closing files

```
private void openNextFile() {
    OpenOptions opts = new OpenOptions().setRead(true);
    currentFile = vertx.fileSystem()
        .openBlocking("tracks/" + playlist.poll(), opts);
    positionInFile = 0;
}

private void closeCurrentFile() {
    positionInFile = 0;
    currentFile.close();
    currentFile = null;
}
```

← **Again, we use the blocking variant, but it will rarely be an issue for opening a file.** (pointing to `.openBlocking("tracks/" + playlist.poll(), opts);`)

4.4 Parsing simple streams

So far our dissection of the jukebox example has focused on the `Jukebox` verticle used to download and stream MP3 data. Now it's time to dissect the `NetControl` verticle, which exposes a TCP server on port 3000 for receiving text commands to control what the jukebox plays. Extracting data from asynchronous data streams is a common requirement, and Vert.x provides effective tools for doing that.

The commands in our text protocol are of the following form:

```
/action [argument]
```

These are the actions:

- /list—Lists the files available for playback
- /play—Ensures the stream plays
- /pause—Pauses the stream
- /schedule file—Appends file at the end of the playlist

Each text line can have exactly one command, so the protocol is said to be *newline-separated*.

We need a parser for this, as buffers arrive in chunks that rarely correspond to one line each. For example, a first read buffer could contain the following:

```
ettes.mp3
/play
/pa
```

The next one may look like this:

```
use
/schedule right-here-righ
```

And it may be followed by this:

```
t-now.mp3
```

What we actually want is reasoning about *lines*, so the solution is to concatenate buffers as they arrive, and split them again on newlines so we have one line per buffer. Instead of manually assembling intermediary buffers, Vert.x offers a handy parsing helper with the RecordParser class. The parser ingests buffers and emits new buffers with parsed data, either by looking for delimiters or by working with chunks of fixed size.

In our case, we need to look for newline delimiters in the stream. The following listing shows how to use RecordParser in the NetControl verticle.

Listing 4.19 A recordparser based on newlines over a TCP server stream

```
@Override
public void start() {
  vertx.createNetServer()
    .connectHandler(this::handleClient)
    .listen(3000);
}

private void handleClient(NetSocket socket) {
  RecordParser.newDelimited("\n", socket)          ⟵  Parse by looking
    .handler(buffer -> handleBuffer(socket, buffer))    for new lines.
    .endHandler(v -> logger.info("Connection ended"));  ⟵  Now buffers
}                                                            are lines.
```

The parser is both a read and a write stream, as it functions as an adapter between two streams. It ingests intermediate buffers coming from the TCP socket, and it emits parsed data as new buffers. This is fairly transparent and simplifies the rest of the verticle implementation.

In the next listing, each buffer is known to be a line, so we can go directly to processing commands.

Listing 4.20 Handling parsed buffers

```
private void handleBuffer(NetSocket socket, Buffer buffer) {
  String command = buffer.toString();        ◁──── Buffer-to-string
  switch (command) {                                decoding with the
    case "/list":                                   default charset
      listCommand(socket);
      break;
    case "/play":
      vertx.eventBus().send("jukebox.play", "");
      break;
    case "/pause":
      vertx.eventBus().send("jukebox.pause", "");
      break;
    default:
      if (command.startsWith("/schedule ")) {
        schedule(command);
      } else {
        socket.write("Unknown command\n");
      }
  }
}
```

The simple commands are in the case clauses, and the other commands are in separate methods shown in the following listing.

Listing 4.21 Other commands

```
private void schedule(String command) {
  String track = command.substring(10);          ◁──── The first 10 characters
  JsonObject json = new JsonObject().put("file", track);    are for /schedule and
  vertx.eventBus().send("jukebox.schedule", json);          a space.
}

private void listCommand(NetSocket socket) {
  vertx.eventBus().request("jukebox.list", "", reply -> {
    if (reply.succeeded()) {
      JsonObject data = (JsonObject) reply.result().body();
      data.getJsonArray("files")
        .stream().forEach(name -> socket.write(name + "\n"));    ◁────
    } else {
      logger.error("/list error", reply.cause());
    }                                                    We write each filename
  });                                                    to the standard console
}                                                                       output.
```

4.5   *Parsing complex streams*

Streams can be more complex than just lines of text, and `RecordParser` can also simplify our work with these. Let's take the example of key/value database storage, where each key and value is a string.

In such a database, we could have entries such as 1 -> {foo} and 2 -> {bar, baz}, with 1 and 2 being keys. There are countless ways to define a serialization scheme for this type of data structure, so imagine that we must use the stream format in table 4.6.

Table 4.6   Database stream format

Data	Description
Magic header	A sequence of bytes 1, 2, 3, and 4 to identify the file type
Version	An integer with the database stream format version
Name	Name of the database as a string, ending with a newline character
Key length	Integer with the number of characters for the next key
Key name	A sequence of characters for the key name
Value length	Integer with the number of characters for the next value
Value	A sequence of characters for the value
(…)	Remaining {key, value} sequences

The format mixes binary and text records, as the stream starts with a magic number, a version number, a name, and then a sequence of key and value entries. While the format in itself is questionable on some points, it is a good example to illustrate more complex parsing.

First of all, let's have a program that writes a database to a file with two key/value entries. The following listing shows how to use the Vert.x filesystem APIs to open a file, append data to a buffer, and then write it.

Listing 4.22   Writing a sample database to a file

```
AsyncFile file = vertx.fileSystem().openBlocking("sample.db",
  new OpenOptions().setWrite(true).setCreate(true));
Buffer buffer = Buffer.buffer();

buffer.appendBytes(new byte[] { 1, 2, 3, 4});        Magic number
buffer.appendInt(2);                                 Version
buffer.appendString("Sample database\n");            Database name

String key = "abc";                                  First entry
String value = "123456-abcdef";
buffer
  .appendInt(key.length())
```

```
    .appendString(key)
    .appendInt(value.length())
    .appendString(value);

key = "foo@bar";        ◁──── Second entry
value = "Foo Bar Baz";
buffer
    .appendInt(key.length())
    .appendString(key)
    .appendInt(value.length())
    .appendString(value);

file.end(buffer, ar -> vertx.close());
```

In this example we had little data, so we used a single buffer that we prepared wholly before writing it to the file, but we could equally use a buffer for the header and new buffers for each key/value entry.

Writing is easy, but what about reading it back? The interesting property of `RecordParser` is that its parsing mode can be switched on the fly. We can start parsing buffers of fixed size 5, then switch to parsing based on tab characters, then chunks of 12 bytes, and so on.

The parsing logic is better expressed by splitting it into methods where each method corresponds to a parsing state: a method for parsing the database name, a method for parsing a value entry, and so on.

The following listing opens the file that we previously wrote and puts the `Record-Parser` object into fixed mode, as we are looking for a sequence of four bytes that represents the magic header. The handler that we install is called when a magic number is read.

Listing 4.23 Reading a database stream, step 1

```
AsyncFile file = vertx.fileSystem().openBlocking("sample.db",
    new OpenOptions().setRead(true));                        We first want to
                                                             read the magic
RecordParser parser = RecordParser.newFixed(4, file);   ◁──┐ number.
parser.handler(header -> readMagicNumber(header, parser));
```

The next listing provides the implementation of further methods.

Listing 4.24 Reading a database stream, step 2

```
private static void readMagicNumber(Buffer header, RecordParser parser) {
    logger.info("Magic number: {}:{}:{}:{}", header.getByte(0),
  ➥ header.getByte(1), header.getByte(2), header.getByte(3));
    parser.handler(version -> readVersion(version, parser));
}

private static void readVersion(Buffer header, RecordParser parser) {
    logger.info("Version: {}", header.getInt(0));
```

```
    parser.delimitedMode("\n");                        ←──┐  The parser mode can
    parser.handler(name -> readName(name, parser));       │  be switched on the fly.
}

private static void readName(Buffer name, RecordParser parser) {
    logger.info("Name: {}", name.toString());
    parser.fixedSizeMode(4);
    parser.handler(keyLength -> readKey(keyLength, parser));
}
```

The `readMagicNumber` method extracts the four bytes of the magic number from a buffer. We know that the buffer is exactly four bytes since the parser was in fixed-sized mode.

The next entry is the database version, and it is an integer, so we don't have to change the parser mode because an integer is four bytes. Once the version has been read, the `readVersion` method switches to delimited mode to extract the database name. We then start looking for a key length, so we need a fixed-sized mode in `readName`.

The following listing reads the key name, the value length, and the proper value, and `finishEntry` sets the parser to look for an integer and delegates to `readKey`.

Listing 4.25   Reading a database stream, step 3

```
private static void readKey(Buffer keyLength, RecordParser parser) {
    parser.fixedSizeMode(keyLength.getInt(0));
    parser.handler(key -> readValue(key.toString(), parser));
}

private static void readValue(String key, RecordParser parser) {
    parser.fixedSizeMode(4);
    parser.handler(valueLength -> finishEntry(key, valueLength, parser));
}

private static void finishEntry(String key, Buffer valueLength,
➥ RecordParser parser) {
    parser.fixedSizeMode(valueLength.getInt(0));
    parser.handler(value -> {
        logger.info("Key: {} / Value: {}", key, value);
        parser.fixedSizeMode(4);
        parser.handler(keyLength -> readKey(keyLength, parser));
    });
}
```

The next listing shows some sample output when reading the database file with the parsing methods of listings 4.23 through 4.25.

Listing 4.26   Logs of reading the database stream

```
DatabaseReader - Magic number: 1:2:3:4
DatabaseReader - Version: 2
DatabaseReader - Name: Sample database
DatabaseReader - Key: abc / Value: 123456-abcdef
DatabaseReader - Key: foo@bar / Value: Foo Bar Baz
```

These on-the-fly parser mode and handler changes form a very simple yet effective way to parse complex streams.

> **TIP** You may wonder how the parsing mode can be changed on the fly, while some further data is already available to the parser from the read stream. Remember that we are on an event loop, so parser handlers are processing parser records one at a time. When we switch from, say, delimiter mode to fixed-size mode, the next record is emitted by processing the remaining stream data based on a number of bytes rather than looking for a string. The same reasoning applies when switching from fixed-sized mode to delimiter mode.

4.6 *A quick note on the stream fetch mode*

Before we wrap up this chapter, let's go back to a detail of the `ReadStream` interface that I deliberately left aside.

Introduced in Vert.x 3.6, the fetch mode that I mentioned earlier in this chapter allows a stream consumer to request a number of data items, rather than the stream pushing data items to the consumer. This works by pausing the stream and then asking for a varying number of items to be fetched later on, as data is needed.

We could rewrite the jukebox file-streaming code with the fetch mode, but we would still need a timer to dictate the pace. In this case, manually reading a buffer of 4096 bytes or requesting 4096 to be fetched is not that different.

Instead, let's go back to the database reading example. The read stream pushed events in listings 4.23 through 4.25. Switching to fetch mode and pulling data does not require many changes. The following listing shows the stream initialization code.

> **Listing 4.27 Putting a read stream in fetch mode**

The stream won't push events.

```
RecordParser parser = RecordParser.newFixed(4, file);
parser.pause();
parser.fetch(1);
parser.handler(header -> readMagicNumber(header, parser));
```

We ask for one element (here, a buffer).

Remember that the `RecordParser` decorates the file stream. It is paused, and then the `fetch` method asks for one element. Since the parser emits buffers of parsed data, asking for one element in this example means asking for a buffer of four bytes (the magic number). Eventually, the parser handler will be called to process the requested buffer, and nothing else will happen until another call to the `fetch` method is made.

The following listing shows two of the parsing handler methods and their adaptation to the fetch mode.

Listing 4.28 Fetching stream data as needed

```
private static void readMagicNumber(Buffer header, RecordParser parser) {
  logger.info("Magic number: {}:{}:{}:{}", header.getByte(0),
  ➡ header.getByte(1), header.getByte(2), header.getByte(3));
  parser.handler(version -> readVersion(version, parser));
  parser.fetch(1);          ←——┐
}                               |   Here one item is a parser record.
// (...)

private static void finishEntry(String key, Buffer valueLength,
➡ RecordParser parser) {
  parser.fixedSizeMode(valueLength.getInt(0));
  parser.handler(value -> {
    logger.info("Key: {} / Value: {}", key, value);
    parser.fixedSizeMode(4);
    parser.handler(keyLength -> readKey(keyLength, parser));
    parser.fetch(1);
  });
  parser.fetch(1);
}
```

The only difference between the two modes is that we need to request elements by calling `fetch`. You will not likely need to play with fetch mode while writing Vert.x applications, but if you ever need to manually control a read stream, it is a useful tool to have.

In many circumstances, having data being pushed is all you need, and the requester can manage the back-pressure by signaling when pausing is needed. If you have a case where it is easier for the requester to let the source know how many items it can handle, then pulling data is a better option for managing the back-pressure. Vert.x streams are quite flexible here.

The next chapter focuses on other models besides callbacks for asynchronous programming with Vert.x.

Summary

- Vert.x streams model asynchronous event and data flows, and they can be used in both push and pull/fetch modes.
- Back-pressure management is essential for ensuring the coordinated exchange of events between asynchronous systems, and we illustrated this through MP3 audio streaming across multiple devices and direct downloads.
- Streams can be parsed for simple and complex data, illustrated here by a networked control interface for an audio streaming service.

Beyond callbacks

5

This chapter covers

- Callbacks and their limitations, as shown with a gateway/edge service example
- Futures and promises—a simple model to chain asynchronous operations
- Reactive extensions—a more powerful model that is especially well suited to composing streams of asynchronous events
- Kotlin coroutines—language-level support for asynchronous code execution flows

You will need to write all sorts of business logic while developing a reactive application, and not all logic is easy to express in an asynchronous form. While callbacks are a simple form of asynchronous event notification, they can easily render asynchronous code complicated.

Let's look at a real example of why callbacks are not always the best asynchronous programming model. Then we'll explore the multiple options supported in Vert.x.

5.1   *Composing asynchronous operations: The edge service example*

We'll take the example of an *edge service* to illustrate composing asynchronous operations with different asynchronous programming models.

An edge service is also frequently called an *API gateway*. It is a service that serves as a facade for other services, so that a requester just has to deal with one service interface rather than having to talk to each service. An edge service may also perform other tasks, such as data transformation and interacting with other services, so it does not just conveniently aggregate data from multiple services.

5.1.1   *Scenario*

Let's go back to the heat sensor verticles we used in chapter 3. Suppose that we have several heat sensors, and we want to expose an API to fetch and aggregate all of the sensors' heat data. This is a very simple yet effective example of an edge service, as it abstracts the need for a requester to know about and contact all the sensors. To make things even more interesting, we'll also have a *snapshot* service that captures and logs the sensor values before they are returned to the requester. The whole scenario is illustrated in figure 5.1.

The requester issues a request to the edge service, which in turn fetches temperature data from the sensor services. Each sensor exposes an HTTP/JSON API, and the edge service aggregates all responses in a larger JSON document. This document is

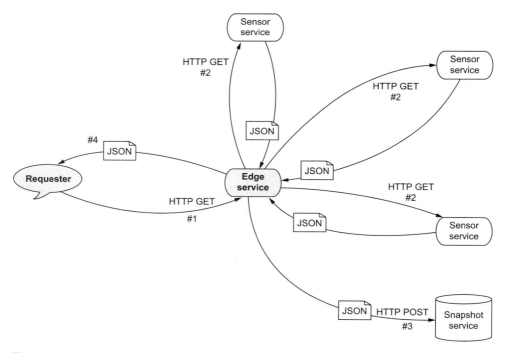

Figure 5.1   Edge service scenario

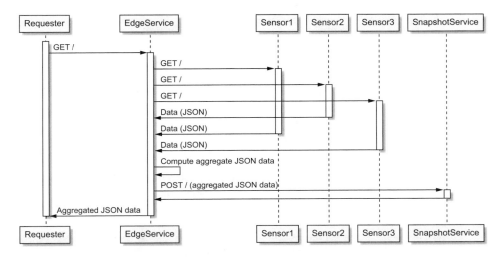

Figure 5.2 Interactions between the edge, sensor, and snapshot services

then sent to the snapshot service, before it's sent back to the requester. The interactions are summarized in figure 5.2.

This example allows us to reason about parallel and sequential operations:

- Parallel asynchronous operations: fetching heat sensor data
- Sequential asynchronous operations: aggregating heat sensor data, sending it to the snapshot service, and then returning it to the requester

5.1.2 Heat sensor verticles

We could deploy our heat sensors as multiple independent processes, each exposing an HTTP API. To simplify our example, we will deploy them within the same process, albeit with HTTP servers listening on different TCP ports.

The following `HeatSensor` class is a simple adaptation of the one we used earlier. Listing 5.1 shows the preamble of the class, directly ported from the code in chapter 3.

Listing 5.1 Heat sensor verticle

```
public class HeatSensor extends AbstractVerticle {            Each sensor has a
                                                             generated unique
  private final Random random = new Random();                   identifier.
  private final String sensorId = UUID.randomUUID().toString();  ◄
  private double temperature = 21.0;

  private void scheduleNextUpdate() {
    vertx.setTimer(random.nextInt(5000) + 1000, this::update);
  }

  private void update(long timerId) {
    temperature = temperature + (delta() / 10);
```

```
    scheduleNextUpdate();
  }

  private double delta() {
    if (random.nextInt() > 0) {
      return random.nextGaussian();
    } else {
      return -random.nextGaussian();
    }
  }
}
// (...)
```

The code keeps the same logic of updating the temperature by a random amount, with a random delay of between one and six seconds.

The following listing shows the code added to expose an HTTP API.

Listing 5.2 Heat sensor verticle HTTP API code

```
@Override
public void start() {
  vertx.createHttpServer()
    .requestHandler(this::handleRequest)
    .listen(config().getInteger("http.port", 3000));   ⟵ The server TCP port
  scheduleNextUpdate();                                    is configurable.
}

private void handleRequest(HttpServerRequest req) {
  JsonObject data = new JsonObject()
    .put("id", id)
    .put("temp", temp);
  req.response()
    .putHeader("Content-Type", "application/json")
    .end(data.encode());
}
```

This is a very straightforward use of the Vert.x HTTP server, with the HTTP port being passed by configuration. The response is encoded in JSON.

5.1.3 *Snapshot service verticle*

The snapshot service exposes an HTTP server as well, as you can see in the following listing.

Listing 5.3 Snapshot service verticle

```
public class SnapshotService extends AbstractVerticle {
  private final Logger logger = LoggerFactory.getLogger(SnapshotService.class);

  @Override
  public void start() {
    vertx.createHttpServer()
```

```
        .requestHandler(req -> {
          if (badRequest(req)) {
            req.response().setStatusCode(400).end();
          }
          req.bodyHandler(buffer -> {            ◁─────
            logger.info("Latest temperatures: {}",
              buffer.toJsonObject().encodePrettily());
            req.response().end();
          });
        })
        .listen(config().getInteger("http.port", 4000));
    }

    private boolean badRequest(HttpServerRequest req) {
      return !req.method().equals(HttpMethod.POST) ||
        !"application/json".equals(req.getHeader("Content-Type"));
    }
  }
```

> This waits for the whole body to be received rather than assembling intermediate buffers.

The HTTP request handler expects an HTTP POST request, extracts the body using a body handler, and logs the received data.

With these two verticles defined, the fun can now begin, and we can look into making our edge service.

5.2 Callbacks

We are first going to implement the edge service using callbacks, as we have been doing since the beginning of this book.

The dependencies we need for our project are *Vert.x Core*, *Vert.x Web Client* (to simplify making HTTP requests), and *Logback*. The following listing shows the dependencies for a Gradle build. The artifacts are exactly the same when using Maven or any other compatible build tool.

Listing 5.4 Edge service dependencies (callbacks version)

```
dependencies {
    implementation("io.vertx:vertx-core:${vertxVersion}")        ◁─────
    implementation("io.vertx:vertx-web-client:${vertxVersion}")
    implementation("ch.qos.logback:logback-classic:1.2.3")
}
```

> Replace ${vertxVersion} with the current Vert.x version of your choice.

NOTE All classes other than chapter5.future.CollectorService compile on Vert.x 3.9. This class requires the newer Vert.x 4 future-based APIs, as mentioned in section 5.3.2 on Vert.x futures and promises.

5.2.1   *Implementation*

We'll start with the preamble of the `CollectorService` verticle class implementation.

Listing 5.5   Callbacks implementation preamble

```
public class CollectorService extends AbstractVerticle {

  private final Logger logger =
  ➥ LoggerFactory.getLogger(CollectorService.class);
  private WebClient webClient;

  @Override
  public void start() {
    webClient = WebClient.create(vertx);
    vertx.createHttpServer()
      .requestHandler(this::handleRequest)
      .listen(8080);
  }
  // (...)
}
```

A Vert.x web client needs a vertx context.

The `start` method first creates a `WebClient` instance and then starts an HTTP server on port 8080. The web client class comes from the `vertx-web-client` module and greatly simplifies making HTTP requests compared to the HTTP client in the Vert.x core APIs. It especially simplifies HTTP body handling and conversions: you can convert a body to plain text, to JSON, or to general-purpose Vert.x buffers.

The HTTP request handler is the `handleRequest` method shown in the following listing.

Listing 5.6   Request-handling with callbacks

We need a list to collect the JSON responses.

We also need a counter for tracking responses, since the number of responses may be less than the number of requests when there are errors.

```
private void handleRequest(HttpServerRequest request) {
  List<JsonObject> responses = new ArrayList<>();
  AtomicInteger counter = new AtomicInteger(0);
  for (int i = 0; i < 3; i++) {
    webClient
      .get(3000 + i, "localhost", "/")
      .expect(ResponsePredicate.SC_SUCCESS)
      .as(BodyCodec.jsonObject())
      .send(ar -> {
        if (ar.succeeded()) {
          responses.add(ar.result().body());
        } else {
          logger.error("Sensor down?", ar.cause());
        }
        if (counter.incrementAndGet() == 3) {
```

This issues an HTTP GET request on resource / on localhost and port 3000 + i.

This predicate triggers an error when the HTTP status code is not in the 2xx range.

This treats the body as a JSON object and performs automatic conversion.

When all requests (or errors) have been received, we can move to the next operation.

```
        JsonObject data = new JsonObject()
          .put("data", new JsonArray(responses));
        sendToSnapshot(request, data);
      }
    });
  }
}
```

This method shows how easy it is to use the web client API to perform HTTP requests. The main difficulty lies in coordinating the parallel HTTP requests. We need a loop to issue the requests, and since they are asynchronous, we also need to keep track of the number of received responses and the response values. This is done by having a list of responses, and using a counter for responses. Note that we use an `AtomicInteger` here not because of concurrency, but rather because we need an object to increment an integer from the callbacks.

Once all responses have been received, we can move to the next operation, which is sending the data to the snapshot service.

Listing 5.7 Sending data to the snapshot service

```
private void sendToSnapshot(HttpServerRequest request, JsonObject data) {
  webClient
    .post(4000, "localhost", "/")
    .expect(ResponsePredicate.SC_SUCCESS)
    .sendJsonObject(data, ar -> {
      if (ar.succeeded()) {
        sendResponse(request, data);
      } else {
        logger.error("Snapshot down?", ar.cause());
        request.response().setStatusCode(500).end();   <-- In case of error, we end the HTTP request here with a 500 status code.
      }
    });
}
```

This method implementation simply uses the web client to issue an HTTP POST request.

Upon success, the code moves to the `sendResponse` method to end the HTTP request, shown next.

Listing 5.8 Sending the response

```
private void sendResponse(HttpServerRequest request, JsonObject data) {
  request.response()
    .putHeader("Content-Type", "application/json")
    .end(data.encode());   <-- Gives a compact JSON text representation
}
```

5.2.2   *Running*

To run the edge service, we first need to deploy verticles, as in the following listing.

Listing 5.9   Main method

```
Vertx vertx = Vertx.vertx();

vertx.deployVerticle("chapter5.sensor.HeatSensor",
   new DeploymentOptions().setConfig(new JsonObject()
     .put("http.port", 3000)));

vertx.deployVerticle("chapter5.sensor.HeatSensor",
   new DeploymentOptions().setConfig(new JsonObject()
     .put("http.port", 3001)));

vertx.deployVerticle("chapter5.sensor.HeatSensor",
   new DeploymentOptions().setConfig(new JsonObject()
     .put("http.port", 3002)));

vertx.deployVerticle("chapter5.snapshot.SnapshotService");
vertx.deployVerticle("chapter5.callbacks.CollectorService");
```

Each instance can use a different port number.

We can issue HTTP requests to test the service with HTTPie, as shown next.

Listing 5.10   Calling the edge service

```
$ http :8080
HTTP/1.1 200 OK
Content-Type: application/json
content-length: 224

{
    "data": [
        {
            "id": "66e310a6-9068-4552-b4aa-6130b3e17cb6",
            "temp": 21.118902894421108
        },
        {
            "id": "3709b24b-cef2-4341-b64a-af68b11e2c0d",
            "temp": 20.96576368750857
        },
        {
            "id": "79f9fa27-b341-4ce5-a335-03caef6e8935",
            "temp": 21.01792006568459
        }
    ]
}
```

Using HTTPie, :8080 is a shortcut for http://localhost:8080.

On the server side, we can check that the snapshot service outputs some logs, as in the following listing.

Listing 5.11 Logs of the edge service

```
15:10:25.576 SnapshotService - Lastest temperatures: {      Each entry has the
  "data" : [ {                                               aggregated JSON data.
    "id" : "66e310a6-9068-4552-b4aa-6130b3e17cb6",
    "temp" : 21.118902894421108
  }, {
    "id" : "3709b24b-cef2-4341-b64a-af68b11e2c0d",
    "temp" : 20.96576368750857
  }, {
    "id" : "79f9fa27-b341-4ce5-a335-03caef6e8935",
    "temp" : 21.01792006568459
  } ]
}
```

5.2.3 The "callback hell" is not the problem

Many people will scream "Callback hell!" when discussing callbacks. Callback hell is when nested callbacks are being used to chain asynchronous operations, resulting in code that is harder to understand, due to the deep nesting. Error handling is especially more difficult with nested callbacks.

While this is true, callback hell can easily be mitigated using one method for each asynchronous operation callback, as we did with the `handleRequest`, `sendToSnapshot`, and `sendResponse` methods. Each method does exactly one thing, and we avoid nesting the callbacks.

The following listing shows equivalent code to the preceding, but compacted as a single piece with nested callbacks.

Listing 5.12 Variant with nested callbacks

```
List<JsonObject> responses = new ArrayList<>();
AtomicInteger counter = new AtomicInteger(0);
for (int i = 0; i < 3; i++) {
  webClient
    .get(3000 + i, "localhost", "/")
    .expect(ResponsePredicate.SC_SUCCESS)
    .as(BodyCodec.jsonObject())            Send a sensor request in
    .send(ar -> {                          parallel with the others.
      if (ar.succeeded()) {
        responses.add(ar.result().body());
      } else {
        logger.error("Sensor down?", ar.cause());
      }                                       All HTTP responses
      if (counter.incrementAndGet() == 3) {   have been received.
        JsonObject data = new JsonObject()
          .put("data", new JsonArray(responses));
        webClient
          .post(4000, "localhost", "/")
          .expect(ResponsePredicate.SC_SUCCESS)    Post to the
          .sendJsonObject(data, ar1 -> {           snapshot service.
            if (ar1.succeeded()) {
              request.response()
```

Respond to
the requester.

```
              .putHeader("Content-Type", "application/json")
              .end(data.encode());
          } else {
            logger.error("Snapshot down?", ar1.cause());
            request.response().setStatusCode(500).end();
          }
        });
      }
    });
  }
```

Nested callbacks certainly do not render the code more readable, but I argue that the real issue lies in the fact that the functional code is entangled with asynchronous coordination code. You need to decipher from the loop, callbacks, and branching that three HTTP requests are being made in parallel and that their results are being assembled, sent to a third-party service, and then given back as a response.

Callbacks aren't perfect, but a bit of discipline keeps the code readable, especially when all you have is sequential composition of asynchronous operations, like send-ToSnapshot passing the work to sendResponse.

Let's now look at other asynchronous programming models that can be more interesting than callbacks.

5.3   *Futures and promises*

You have already been exposed to Vert.x *futures* and *promises* due to the signature of the verticle start methods. You may also have been exposed to them in other languages, like JavaScript. We'll explore this model further and see how they are interesting primitives for composing asynchronous operations with Vert.x.

Vert.x implements a model of futures and promises that is in line with the original research results from Barbara Liskov and Liuba Shrira.[1] They introduced promises as a language abstraction for composing asynchronous remote procedure calls.

A promise holds the value of some computation for which there is no value right now. A promise is eventually completed with a result value or an error. In the context of asynchronous I/O, a promise is a natural fit for holding the result of an asynchronous operation. In turn, a future allows you to read a value that will eventually be available from a promise.

To summarize: a promise is used to write an eventual value, and a future is used to read it when it is available. Let's now see how it works in Vert.x.

5.3.1   *Futures and promises in Vert.x*

A promise is created by a piece of code that is about to perform an asynchronous operation. As an example, imagine that you want to report that an asynchronous operation

---

[1] B. Liskov and L. Shrira, "Promises: linguistic support for efficient asynchronous procedure calls in distributed systems," in R.L. Wexelblat, ed., *Proceedings of the ACM SIGPLAN 1988 conference on Programming language design and implementation (PLDI'88)*, p. 260–267 (ACM, 1988).

has completed, not now but in five seconds. In Vert.x you would use a timer for that, and a promise would be used to hold the result, as shown in the following listing.

Listing 5.13 Creating a promise

Create a promise.

```
Promise<String> promise = Promise.promise();
vertx.setTimer(5000, id -> {                          Asynchronous operation
   if (System.currentTimeMillis() % 2L == 0L) {
      promise.complete("Ok!");                         Complete the promise
   } else {                                            with a value.
      promise.fail(new RuntimeException("Bad luck..."));   Fail the promise
   }                                                       with an exception.
});
// (...)        See listing 5.14.
```

Here the asynchronous operation is a timer of five seconds, after which the promise is completed. Depending on whether the current time is odd or even, the promise completes with a value or fails with an exception. This is great, but how do we actually *get* the value from the promise?

The code that wants to react when the result is available needs a future object. A Vert.x future is created from a promise, then passed to the code that wants to read the value, as shown in the next listing, which is the rest of listing 5.13.

Listing 5.14 Creating a future from a promise

```
Future<String> future = promise.future();       Derive a future from a
return future;                                   promise, and then return it.
// (...)                      Callback for when the
                              promise is completed
future
   .onSuccess(System.out::println)
   .onFailure(err -> System.out.println(err.getMessage()));   Callback for when
                                                              the future is failed
```

The `Future` interface defines two methods, `onSuccess` and `onFailure`, for handling values and errors. When we run the corresponding code, we see that either "Ok!" or "Bad luck…" is printed after five seconds.

We can perform more advanced asynchronous operations with futures, as shown in the following listing.

Listing 5.15 Advanced future composition operations

Recover from an error
with another value.

```
promise.future()
   .recover(err -> Future.succeededFuture("Let's say it's ok!"))
   .map(String::toUpperCase)            Map a value to
                                        another value.
```

```
.flatMap(str -> {
  Promise<String> next = Promise.promise();
  vertx.setTimer(3000, id -> next.complete(">>> " + str));
  return next.future();
})
.onSuccess(System.out::println);
```
> Compose with another asynchronous operation.

The recover operation is called when the promise is failed, and it is used to replace the error with another value. You can see recover as the equivalent of a catch block in Java, where you can handle an error. Here we simply provide a recovery value using a succeeded future, but you can also report a failed future in more advanced cases when there is nothing you can do to recover.

The map operation transforms a value using a function, whereas flatMap composes with another asynchronous operation. You can think of flatMap as "and then." Here the operation takes the string value and prepends it with ">>>" after three seconds. We also see the typical promise/future pattern where we first create a promise, then perform an asynchronous operation that eventually completes the promise, and finally return a future so the value can be consumed by another piece of code.

5.3.2 *Future-based APIs in Vert.x 4*

Vert.x 4 brings Vert.x futures to the core APIs alongside callbacks. While callbacks remain the canonical model, most APIs are available with variants that return a Future.

This means that given a method, void doThis(Handler<AsyncResult<T>>), there is a variant of the form Future<T> doThis(). A good example is shown in the following listing where we start an HTTP server.

Listing 5.16 Starting an HTTP server with future methods

Returns a Future<HttpServer>
```
@Override
public void start(Promise<Void> promise) {
  vertx.createHttpServer()
    .requestHandler(this::handleRequest)
    .listen(8080)
    .onFailure(promise::fail)              Called when the server
    .onSuccess(ok -> {                     could not be started
      System.out.println("http://localhost:8080/");
      promise.complete();
    });
}
```
Called on success

The listen method that we saw in earlier examples took a callback, and here it returns a Future<HttpServer>. We can then chain calls to onFailure and onSuccess to define what to do when the server starts, or when an error occurs.

NOTE You can use the new promise/future interfaces starting from Vert.x 3.8, but the future-based APIs are only available in Vert.x 4.

5.3.3 Interoperability with CompletionStage APIs

Vert.x futures are also interoperable with the `CompletionStage` interface of the `java.util.concurrent` package in the JDK. The `CompletionStage` interface represents a step in an asynchronous operation, so you can think of it as being a future, especially as there is a class called `CompletableFuture` that implements `CompletionStage`. For instance, the HTTP client API in Java 11 offers `sendAsync` methods that return `CompletableFuture` to make asynchronous HTTP requests.

The interoperability between Vert.x futures and `CompletionStage` is useful when you need to interact with libraries that use `CompletionStage` in their APIs.

NOTE The Vert.x `Future` interface is not a subtype of `CompletionStage`. The Vert.x team thought about it while preparing the roadmap for Vert.x 4, but we ultimately opted for our own interface definition, since `CompletionStage` is more agnostic regarding the threading model. Indeed, the "async"-suffixed methods provide variants where you can pass an executor like `CompletionStage<Void> thenRunAsync(Runnable,Executor)`, while the variants without an executor parameter dispatch by default to a `ForkJoinPool` instance. These methods allow stepping out of Vert.x event loops or worker thread pools too easily, so we chose to offer interoperability and not use `CompletionStage` directly in the Vert.x APIs.

The following listing shows how we can move from a Vert.x `Future` to a `CompletionStage`.

Listing 5.17 From a Vert.x `Future` to a `CompletionStage`

Converts a Future to a CompletionStage

```
CompletionStage<String> cs = promise.future().toCompletionStage();
cs
  .thenApply(String::toUpperCase)          ◁──┐  thenApply is similar to
  .thenApply(str -> "~~~ " + str)             │  map in Vert.x Future.
  .whenComplete((str, err) -> {         ◁──────┐
    if (err == null) {                         │  Takes a value or an error
      System.out.println(str);
    } else {
      System.out.println("Oh... " + err.getMessage());
    }
  });
```

Here we convert the string result to uppercase, prefix it with a string, and eventually call `whenComplete`. Note that this is a `BiConsumer`, and you need to test which of the values or exception parameters is `null` to know whether the promise completed successfully. It is also important to note that unless you call an asynchronous `CompletionStage` method, the calls are performed on a Vert.x thread.

Last but not least, you can convert a `CompletionStage` to a Vert.x `Future`, as follows.

Listing 5.18   From a `CompletionStage` to a Vert.x `Future`

```
CompletableFuture<String> cf = CompletableFuture.supplyAsync(() -> {
  try {
    Thread.sleep(5000);
  } catch (InterruptedException e) {
    e.printStackTrace();
  }
  return "5 seconds have elapsed";
});

Future
  .fromCompletionStage(cf, vertx.getOrCreateContext())
  .onSuccess(System.out::println)
  .onFailure(Throwable::printStackTrace);
```

> Create a CompletableFuture from an asynchronous operation.

> Convert to a Vert.x future, and dispatch on a Vert.x context.

`CompletableFuture` implements `CompletionStage`, and `supplyAsync` dispatches a call to the default `ForkJoinPool`. A thread from that pool will be used, sleeping for five seconds before returning a string, which will be the `CompletableFuture` result. The `fromCompletionStage` method converts to a Vert.x `Future`. The method has two variants: one with a Vert.x context to call `Future` methods like `onSuccess` on the context, and one where the calls will happen on whatever thread completed the provided `CompletionStage` instance.

5.3.4   *Collector service with Vert.x futures*

Going back to the edge service example, we can make use of the Vert.x APIs that use `Future`. We'll use the earlier verticle `start` method from listing 5.16.

First of all, we can define the `fetchTemperature` method in the following listing to get the temperature from a service.

Listing 5.19   Fetching temperature with future-based APIs

```
private Future<JsonObject> fetchTemperature(int port) {
  return webClient
    .get(port, "localhost", "/")
    .expect(ResponsePredicate.SC_SUCCESS)
    .as(BodyCodec.jsonObject())
    .send()
    .map(HttpResponse::body);
}
```

> A Future<HttpResponse>

> Extract and return just the body.

This method returns a future of a `JsonObject`, and to achieve that we use the future-returning variant of the `WebClientsend` method, and then map the result to extract just the JSON data.

Temperatures are collected in the `handleRequest` method shown next.

Listing 5.20 Collecting temperatures with future-based APIs

Compose several futures.

```
private void handleRequest(HttpServerRequest request) {
  CompositeFuture.all(
      fetchTemperature(3000),      ⟵——— Fetch temperatures.
      fetchTemperature(3001),
      fetchTemperature(3002))      ⟶ Chain with another asynchronous operation.
      .flatMap(this::sendToSnapshot)  ⟵——┘
      .onSuccess(data -> request.response()      ⟵——— Handle success.
        .putHeader("Content-Type", "application/json")
        .end(data.encode())))
      .onFailure(err -> {                  ⟵——— Handle failure.
        logger.error("Something went wrong", err);
        request.response().setStatusCode(500).end();
      });
}
```

You can use `CompositeFuture` to make one future out of several. The `all` static method results in a future that is completed when all futures are completed, and that fails when any future has failed. There are also `any` and `join` methods that have different semantics.

Once all temperatures have been successfully received, the call to `flatMap` sends data to the snapshot service, which is an asynchronous operation. The code for the `sendToSnapshot` method is shown in the following listing.

Listing 5.21 Sending data to the snapshot service with future-based APIs

```
private Future<JsonObject> sendToSnapshot(CompositeFuture temps) {
  List<JsonObject> tempData = temps.list();
  JsonObject data = new JsonObject()
    .put("data", new JsonArray()
      .add(tempData.get(0))
      .add(tempData.get(1))
      .add(tempData.get(2)));
  return webClient
    .post(4000, "localhost", "/")
    .expect(ResponsePredicate.SC_SUCCESS)
    .sendJson(data)                  ⟵——— Future-based variant
    .map(response -> data);
}
```

This code is similar to that of `fetchTemperature` because we use a method of `WebClient` that returns a `Future`. The code of the main method that deploys verticles is the same as in the callbacks variant, except that we deploy a different `CollectorService` verticle:

```
// (...)
vertx.deployVerticle("chapter5.future.CollectorService");
```

Let's now move on to reactive extension, another asynchronous programming model.

5.4   *Reactive extensions*

Reactive extensions are an elaborated form of the *observable* design pattern.[2] They were first popularized by Erik Meijer in the *Microsoft .NET* ecosystem. Modern applications are increasingly composed of asynchronous event streams, not just on the server, but also in web, desktop, and mobile clients.[3] Indeed, we can think of graphical user interface events as a stream of events that an application has to respond to.

Reactive extensions are defined by three things:

- Observing event or data streams (e.g., an incoming HTTP request can be observed)
- Composing operators to transform streams (e.g., merge multiple HTTP request streams as one)
- Subscribing to streams and reacting to events and errors

The *ReactiveX* initiative offers a common API and implementations in many languages, both for backend and frontend projects (http://reactivex.io/). The RxJS project offers reactive extensions for JavaScript applications in the browser, whereas a project like RxJava offers a general-purpose reactive extensions implementation for the Java ecosystem.

Vert.x offers bindings for RxJava versions 1 and 2. Using version 2 is recommended because it supports back-pressure, while version 1 does not.

5.4.1   *RxJava in a nutshell*

Let's explore the basics of what RxJava is and see what it does and how it nicely it integrates with Vert.x

> **TIP** Timo Tuominen's *RxJava for Android Developers* (Manning, 2019) is a solid resource for learning RxJava.

OBSERVABLE TYPES

First of all, RxJava 2 offers five different types of observable sources, listed in table 5.1.

Table 5.1   Observable types in RxJava

Type	Description	Example
Observable<T>	A stream of events of type T. Does not support back-pressure.	Timer events, observable source where we cannot apply back-pressure like GUI events
Flowable<T>	A stream of events of type T where back-pressure can be applied	Network data, filesystem inputs

---

[2]Erich Gamma, Richard Helm, Ralph Johnson, and John Vlissides, *Design Patterns: Elements of Reusable Object-Oriented Software* (Addison-Wesley Professional, 1995).
[3]Erik Meijer, "Your Mouse is a Database," *Queue* 10, 3 (March 2012), http://mng.bz/v96M.

Table 5.1 Observable types in RxJava *(continued)*

Type	Description	Example
Single<T>	A source that emits exactly one event of type T	Fetching an entry from a data store by key
Maybe<T>	A source that may emit one event of type T, or none	Fetching an entry from a data store by key, but the key may not exist
Completable	A source that notifies of some action having completed, but no value is being given	Deleting files

You may sometimes read about *hot* and *cold* sources. A hot source is a source where events are being emitted whether there are subscribers or not. A cold source is a source where events only start being emitted after the first subscription. A periodic timer is a hot source, whereas a file to read is a cold source. With a cold source, you can get all events, but with a hot source, you will only get those emitted after you have subscribed.

BASIC EXAMPLES

We'll start with the simple example in listing 5.22, illustrated in figure 5.3.

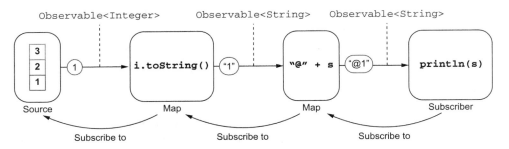

Figure 5.3 RxJava pipeline of listing 5.22

Listing 5.22 A first RxJava example

This is an observable of a predefined sequence.

```
Observable.just(1, 2, 3)
    .map(Object::toString)
    .map(s -> "@" + s)
    .subscribe(System.out::println);
```

We map to a string.

We transform the string.

For each item, we print to the standard output.

Running the code in listing 5.22 yields the following console output:

```
@1
@2
@3
```

This example creates an observable of three integers. The `just` factory method creates an `Observable<Integer>` source. We then use two `map` operators to transform the stream. The first one converts from an `Observable<Integer>` to an `Observable<String>`. The second one prepends the @ character to each item. Finally, `subscribe` performs a subscription where `System.out.println` is called for each item.

Sources may emit errors, in which case the subscriber can be notified. Consider the observable in the following listing.

Listing 5.23   Error handling with RxJava

The observable emits one error.

```
Observable.<String>error(() -> new RuntimeException("Woops"))     This is never
    .map(String::toUpperCase)                                      called.
    .subscribe(System.out::println, Throwable::printStackTrace);
```

The stacktrace will be printed.

The observable of string values will emit one error. The `map` operator will never be called, since it operates only on values, not errors. We can see that `subscribe` now has two parameters; the second one is the callback to process errors. In this example, we just print the stack trace, but in networked applications, for example, we would do error recovery.

> **NOTE**   Using the `just` factory method is great in examples and tests, but in real-world scenarios you'll want to adapt a more complex source to produce events to an RxJava observable type. To do that, there is a general-purpose `Publisher` interface that you can implement to emit items to subscribers using the `fromPublisher` method (instead of `just`). There are also adapter methods for JDK futures, for iterable objects, and for generating items from a JDK callable object.

LIFE CYCLE

The previous example didn't show the full life cycle of an observable. Once a subscription has been made, zero or many items are emitted. Then the stream terminates with either an error or a notification that it has completed.

Let's look at a more elaborated example.

Listing 5.24   Dealing with all life-cycle events in RxJava

```
Observable                         Actions can be inserted, such as when a subscription happens.
    .just("--", "this", "is", "--", "a", "sequence", "of", "items", "!")
    .doOnSubscribe(d -> System.out.println("Subscribed!"))
```

```
.delay(5, TimeUnit.SECONDS)          ◁───┐   This delays emitting
.filter(s -> !s.startsWith("--"))        │   events by five seconds.
.doOnNext(System.out::println)    ◁──┐
.map(String::toUpperCase)            │       Another action, here called for
.buffer(2)                   ◁──┐    │       each item flowing in the stream
.subscribe(
  System.out::println,           This groups events 2 by 2.
  Throwable::printStackTrace,
  () -> System.out.println(">>> Done"));   ◁─── Called when the stream has completed
```

Running the preceding code gives the following output.

Listing 5.25   Output of running listing 5.24

```
Subscribed!               ◁───┐   This is the sole output for
doOnNext: this                │   five seconds. Then the
doOnNext: is                  │   next lines appear.
next: [THIS, IS]
doOnNext: a
doOnNext: sequence
next: [A, SEQUENCE]
doOnNext: of
doOnNext: items
next: [OF, ITEMS]
doOnNext: !
next: [!]
~Done~
```

This example shows us the form of subscribe where all events can be handled: an event, an error, and the completion of the stream. The example also shows further operators:

- doOnSubscribe and doOnNext are actions (with potential side effects) that can be triggered as items pass along the stream.
- delay allows delaying when events start to be emitted further down the stream.
- buffer groups events (into lists), so here we get events in pairs.

There is, of course, more to RxJava than we've discussed in this section, but we've covered enough to dive into the Vert.x and RxJava integration.

5.4.2   *RxJava and Vert.x*

The RxJava integration in Vert.x is available from the vertx-rx-java2 module. In Gradle (and similarly in Maven), the dependency can be added as

```
implementation("io.vertx:vertx-rx-java2:version")
```

All APIs from the projects in the official Vert.x stack have RxJava support. The RxJava APIs are automatically generated from those of the core APIs. There are several idiomatic conversion rules to RxJava APIs, but as a simple example, when you have

```
void foo(String s, Handler<AsyncResult<String>> callback)
```

the translation to RxJava is

```
Single<String> foo(String s)
```

The RxJava APIs are in subpackages of `io.vertx.reactivex`. For instance, the RxJava version of `AbstractVerticle` is `io.vertx.reactivex.core.AbstractVerticle`.

Let's look at an example verticle using the RxJava APIs.

Listing 5.26   RxJava and Vert.x APIs

```
public class VertxIntro extends AbstractVerticle {          │ rxStart notifies of deployment
  @Override                                                 │ success using a Completable
  public Completable rxStart() {           ◄────────────────┘ rather than a Future.

    Observable
      .interval(1, TimeUnit.SECONDS, RxHelper.scheduler(vertx))    ◄───
      .subscribe(n -> System.out.println("tick"));
                                                       The scheduler enforces the
    return vertx.createHttpServer()                     Vert.x threading model.
      .requestHandler(r -> r.response().end("Ok"))
      .rxListen(8080)             ◄─────────
      .ignoreElement();      ◄─────────┐      This is an RxJava variant
  }                                    │      of listen(port, callback).
}                    This returns a Completable
                          from a Single.
```

This example opens a classic HTTP server that replies `Ok` to any request. The interesting part is that the RxJava variant of `AbstractVerticle` has an `rxStart` (and `rxStop`) method that notifies of deployment success. In our case, the verticle has been successfully deployed when the HTTP server has started, so we return a `Completable` object. You can check that methods prefixed with `rx` correspond to generated methods for supporting RxJava. If you inspect the RxJava APIs, you will note that the original methods (including callbacks) are still present.

The other interesting part of this example is the observable that emits events every second. It behaves essentially as a Vert.x timer would. There are several operator methods in the RxJava APIs that accept a scheduler object, because they need to defer asynchronous tasks. By default, they call back from an internal worker-thread pool that they manage, which breaks the Vert.x threading model assumptions. We can always pass a Vert.x scheduler to ensure that events are still being called back on the original context event loop.

5.4.3   *Collector service in RxJava*

We can now go back to our edge service example and rewrite the `CollectorService` verticle class with RxJava.

To begin, we'll update the imports to use the `io.vertx.reactivex.*` packages. Since the verticle starts an HTTP server, we can take advantage of `rxStart` as follows.

Listing 5.27   RxJava collector service preamble

```
@Override
public Completable rxStart() {
  webClient = WebClient.create(vertx);
  return vertx.createHttpServer()
    .requestHandler(this::handleRequest)      ←───┐ A Single<HttpServer>
    .rxListen(8080)                           ←────┘
    .ignoreElement();                  ←───┐ A Completable
}                                          └──
```

The next step is to write a method for fetching temperatures in parallel, and then to assemble the responses as a JSON object. Just like the callbacks version, we can have a method to fetch a single temperature. The code is shown in the following listing.

Listing 5.28   Fetching temperature with RxJava

```
private Single<HttpResponse<JsonObject>> fetchTemperature(int port) {
  return webClient
    .get(port, "localhost", "/")
    .expect(ResponsePredicate.SC_SUCCESS)
    .as(BodyCodec.jsonObject())
    .rxSend();                    ←──── This returns a Single.
}
```

Again, the difference from the callbacks versions is that we use rxSend (which returns a Single) instead of send (which uses a callback).

The next listing shows a method that composes parallel asynchronous HTTP requests and assembles a JSON object based on the responses.

Listing 5.29   Collecting temperatures requests with RxJava

```
private Single<JsonObject> collectTemperatures() {
  Single<HttpResponse<JsonObject>> r1 = fetchTemperature(3000);
  Single<HttpResponse<JsonObject>> r2 = fetchTemperature(3001);
  Single<HttpResponse<JsonObject>> r3 = fetchTemperature(3002);

  return Single.zip(r1, r2, r3, (j1, j2, j3) -> {   ←──┐ The zip operator composes
    JsonArray array = new JsonArray()                  │ three responses.
      .add(j1.body())
      .add(j2.body())
      .add(j3.body());
    return new JsonObject().put("data", array);   ←──┐ The value is the zip operator
  });                                                 │ response, boxed in a Single.
}
```

By using fetchTemperature to fetch individual responses, we obtain Single objects that observe individual HTTP responses. To compose the results, we use the zip operator, which takes severable sources and composes the result as another Single object. When all HTTP responses are available, the zip operator passes the values to a function that must produce a value (of any type). The returned value is then the `Single` object that the `zip` operator emits. Here we build a JSON array using the HTTP response bodies that the Vert.x web client has converted to JSON for us, and we then wrap the array in a JSON object.

Note that `zip` has many overloaded definitions with varying numbers of parameters to cope with two sources, three sources, and so on. When the code needs to handle an undefined number of sources, there is a variant taking a list of sources, and the function passed to `zip` accepts a list of values.

This leads us to the definition of the HTTP request handling method that collects the temperatures, posts to the snapshot service, and then responds to the requester. The code is in the following listing.

Listing 5.30   RxJava collector service HTTP handler

```
private void handleRequest(HttpServerRequest request) {
  Single<JsonObject> data = collectTemperatures();
  sendToSnapshot(data).subscribe(json -> {            We send data to the
    request.response()                                 snapshot service.
      .putHeader("Content-Type", "application/json")
      .end(json.encode());
  }, err -> {
    logger.error("Something went wrong", err);        We have a single
    request.response().setStatusCode(500).end();       point of error
  });                                                   management.
}
```

This method also performs the subscription: upon success JSON data is returned to the requester, and on failure an HTTP 500 error is returned. It is important to note that the subscription triggers the HTTP requests to the sensor services, then to the snapshot service, and so on. Until a subscription is made, RxJava observable pipelines are just "recipes" for processing events.

The last missing part is the method that sends data to the snapshot service.

Listing 5.31   Sending data to the snapshot service with RxJava

Once we have the JSON data,
we issue an HTTP request.

```
private Single<JsonObject> sendToSnapshot(Single<JsonObject> data) {
  return data.flatMap(json -> webClient
    .post(4000, "localhost", "")
    .expect(ResponsePredicate.SC_SUCCESS)      This sends a JSON object, then reports
    .rxSendJsonObject(json)                     on the HTTP request response.
    .flatMap(resp -> Single.just(json)));
}                                              This allows us to give back the JSON object
                                                rather than the HTTP request response.
```

This method introduces the `flatMap` operator, which is well known to functional programming enthusiasts. Don't worry if `flatMap` sounds cryptic to you; in the case of composing sequential asynchronous operations, you can just read "flatmap" as "and then."

Since `data` emits a JSON object, the `flatMap` operator allows us to issue an HTTP request with the web client once that JSON object has been emitted. We need another (nested) `flatMap` after the HTTP request to the snapshot service has succeeded. Indeed, `rxSendJsonObject` gives a single observable that emits an HTTP response. However, we need the JSON object because it has to be returned to the requester after sending to the snapshot service has succeeded, so the second `flatMap` allows us to do that and re-inject it into the pipeline. This is a very common pattern with RxJava.

Running the RxJava version of the edge service is no different from running the callback version. All we need to do is change the deployment of the `CollectorService` to the following:

```
vertx.deployVerticle("chapter5.reactivex.CollectorService");
```

Interacting with the service yields the same results as with the callback version.

The difference between `map` and `flatMap`

`flatMap` comes from the "flatten" and "map" operators. To better understand how it works, let's illustrate `flatMap` with JavaScript arrays (you can test it using `node` or directly from a web browser console).

With `let a = [1, 2, 3]`, a is an array with values 1, 2, and 3. Now suppose that for each value, we want to have the value multiplied by 10 and 100. With `map`, we could write `let b = a.map(x => [x * 10, x * 100])`, which gives us an array of arrays: `[ [ 10, 100 ], [ 20, 200 ], [ 30, 300 ] ]`.

This is not very convenient if we just want the values rather than nested arrays, so we can "flatten" b, `b.flat()`, which gives us `[ 10, 100, 20, 200, 30, 300 ]`. You can get the same result directly with `a.flatMap(x => [x * 10, x * 100])`.

This translates directly to other operations, like HTTP client requests or database calls, as `flatMap` avoids nested observables of observables.

5.5 *Kotlin coroutines*

The last asynchronous programming model to explore is that of *coroutines* in the Kotlin programming language. (For more information about Kotlin, see Dmitry Jemerov and Svetlana Isakova's *Kotlin in Action* [Manning, 2017]).

Coroutines are interesting to explore, as in many cases they allow us to write asynchronous code that looks like regular non-asynchronous code. Also, Kotlin has a solid implementation of coroutines that is very easy for Java developers to understand, and since we said that Vert.x was polyglot, this book had to show Vert.x without Java at some point!

5.5.1   *What is a coroutine?*

The term *coroutines* first appeared in a paper from Melvin Conway in 1963 about the design of a COBOL compiler.[4] Many languages have support for coroutines, or some form of coroutines: Python (generators), C# (async/await operators), Go (goroutines), and more. Implementations for Java using bytecode instrumentation exist, and a future version of Java will have support for coroutines thanks to Project Loom (https://openjdk.java.net/projects/loom/).

A coroutine can have its execution suspended and resumed at a later point in time. It can be seen as a function with multiple entry and exit points and whose execution stack can be resumed. Coroutines fit well with an asynchronous model, as they can be suspended when the result of an asynchronous operation is needed and resumed when it is available.

To make things more concrete, let's look at using coroutines in Kotlin. First, consider the following code.

Listing 5.32   Coroutines hello world

```
import kotlinx.coroutines.*

suspend fun hello(): String {        ◁──┘  This function can
  delay(1000)                ◁──              be suspended.
  return "Hello!"
}                                    This function is suspending and
                                     will not block the caller thread.

fun main() {
  runBlocking {          ◁──┐
    println(hello())            This allows waiting for
  }                            coroutines code to complete.
}
```

The call to `delay` does not block the caller thread because that method can be suspended. The method is called again when the time has elapsed, and it resumes executing at the next line, which returns a string. In a callback world, the `delay` function would have taken a callback parameter, which would have had to pass the returned string to the caller, probably using another callback.

Here is a more elaborated example.

Listing 5.33   Coroutines example

```
fun main() = runBlocking {
  val job1 = launch { delay(500) }    ◁──── Starts a job

  fun fib(n: Long): Long = if (n < 2) n else fib(n - 1) + fib(n - 2)
  val job2 = async { fib(42) }        ◁──┐
                                          Starts a job that returns a value
```

----

[4]Melvin E. Conway, "Design of a separable transition-diagram compiler," *Communications of the ACM* 6, 7 (July 1963), 396–408, http://mng.bz/4B4V.

```
job1.join()                    ◁——— Waits for the job to complete
println("job1 has completed")
println("job2 fib(42) = ${job2.await()}")    ◁——┐ Gets the value when
}                                                │ the job completes
```

In this example, `job1` is created using `launch`, which executes some code in parallel. It waits for 500 ms. The same applies to `job2`, except that `async` is for code blocks that return a value. It computes the Fibonacci value of 42, which takes some time. The `join` and `await` methods on the jobs allow us to wait for these jobs to complete. Last but not least, the `main` function is wrapped in a `runBlocking` call. This is because suspended methods are being called, so the execution must wait for all coroutines to complete.

We only scratched the surface of Kotlin and coroutines, but this should be enough to look at the Vert.x integration. To dive deeper into Kotlin, you may also want to read Pierre-Yves Saumont, *The Joy of Kotlin* (Manning, 2019).

5.5.2 *Vert.x and Kotlin coroutines*

Vert.x offers first-class support for Kotlin coroutines. To use them in a Gradle project, you'll need the dependencies and configuration shown in the following listing.

Listing 5.34 Vert.x Kotlin coroutine dependencies and configuration excerpt

```
import org.jetbrains.kotlin.gradle.tasks.KotlinCompile

plugins {
  kotlin("jvm") version "kotlinVersion"     ◁——┐ Replace kotlinVersion with
}                                                the current Kotlin version
                                                 (they are released often).

dependencies {
  // (...)                                        Replace vertxVersion with
  implementation("io.vertx:vertx-lang-kotlin:${vertxVersion}")    the current Vert.x version.
  implementation("io.vertx:vertx-lang-kotlin-coroutines:${vertxVersion}")  ◁—
  implementation(kotlin("stdlib-jdk8"))     ◁——┐
}                                                This brings JDK 8 Kotlin APIs.

val compileKotlin: KotlinCompile by tasks      By default, Kotlin compiles to
compileKotlin.kotlinOptions.jvmTarget = "1.8"  ◁—┤ JDK 6 bytecode for Android
// (...)                                           compatibility purposes. The
                                                   JDK 8 bytecode is better.
```

Again, the coroutine bindings are generated from the callback APIs. The convention is that for any method having a callback, a Kotlin suspending method is generated with the suffix `Await`. Given

```
void foo(String s, Handler<AsyncResult<String>> callback)
```

the following method will exist in the Kotlin coroutines binding:

```
suspend fun String fooAwait(String s)
```

There is a verticle base class called `io.vertx.kotlin.coroutines.CoroutineVerti-cle` where the `start` and `stop` methods are suspending, so you can use coroutines directly from them. By using `CoroutineVerticle`, you also get to execute coroutines on the verticle event-loop thread rather than on threads of a worker pool, like the default Kotlin coroutines do.

> **TIP**   If you write Vert.x code in Kotlin, you can also directly use RxJava from Kotlin. There is also a helper RxKotlin library that makes some RxJava APIs even more idiomatic from Kotlin.

5.5.3   *Edge service with coroutines*

Let's look at an implementation of the edge service using Kotlin coroutines. The preamble is given in the following listing.

Listing 5.35   Coroutine collector service preamble

```
class CollectorService : CoroutineVerticle() {
  private val logger = LoggerFactory.getLogger(CollectorService::class.java)
  private lateinit var webClient: WebClient    ◁──────┐  lateinit indicates that the field will
                                                       │  not be initialized in a constructor.
  override suspend fun start() {
    webClient = WebClient.create(vertx)
    vertx.createHttpServer()
      .requestHandler(this::handleRequest)
      .listenAwait(8080)              ◁──────┐  This awaits for the HTTP server to
  }                                           │  be started; otherwise it throws
  // (...)                                    │  an exception with the error.
}
```

Compared to the other implementations, there is not much difference except that the `start` method is suspending, and the HTTP server is started using `listenAwait`. Since that method call is suspending, the execution resumes when the HTTP server is running, and the method returns the HTTP server instance, which we simply ignore here.

The next listing shows the code for the `fetchTemperature` and `sendToSnapshot` methods adapted to coroutines.

Listing 5.36   HTTP requests and coroutines

```
private suspend fun fetchTemperature(port: Int): JsonObject {
  return webClient
    .get(port, "localhost", "/")
    .expect(ResponsePredicate.SC_SUCCESS)
    .`as`(BodyCodec.jsonObject())     ◁──────┐  "as" is a keyword in Kotlin, so it has to be
    .sendAwait()                              │  escaped when used as a method name.
```

```
      .body()
}

private suspend fun sendToSnapshot(json: JsonObject) {
  webClient
    .post(4000, "localhost", "/")
    .expect(ResponsePredicate.SC_SUCCESS)
    .sendJsonAwait(json)
}
```

Both methods now look like more classical imperative code. `fetchTemperature` returns a value (a JSON object), albeit asynchronously because the execution in the method is suspended when calling `sendAwait`.

The illusion of "asynchronous operations that do not look like asynchronous operations" is even more apparent in the following listing, which contains the core logic of the edge service.

Listing 5.37   Coroutines collector HTTP handler

```
private fun handleRequest(request: HttpServerRequest) {
  launch {
    try {
      val t1 = async { fetchTemperature(3000) }      ◁──┐ Fetching each temperature
      val t2 = async { fetchTemperature(3001) }          is asynchronous.
      val t3 = async { fetchTemperature(3002) }

                                                         Waiting for all values
      val array = Json.array(t1.await(), t2.await(), t3.await())   ◁──
      val json = json { obj("data" to array) }   ◁──┐
                                                     Vert.x has a small Kotlin DSL
      sendToSnapshot(json)                           to ease JSON object creation.
      request.response()
        .putHeader("Content-Type", "application/json")
        .end(json.encode())
                                                  Error management with a
    } catch (err: Throwable) {        ◁──────────  classic try/catch structure
      logger.error("Something went wrong", err)
      request.response().setStatusCode(500).end()
    }
  }
}
```

This code expresses very naturally that temperatures are fetched asynchronously, their values are collected in a JSON object, the snapshot service is called, and the result is eventually sent to the requester. Still, there are many suspension points with asynchronous operations. Also, the error management is a familiar `try/catch` structure.

You may have noticed the `launch` function call that wraps the whole method code. This is because while the `start` method is suspending, the HTTP request handler is not a suspending function type, and it will be called outside of a Kotlin coroutine context. Calling `launch` ensures a coroutine context is created, so suspending methods can be called. Also, the coroutine is automatically attached to a context that ensures events run on the verticle event-loop thread (thanks to the internals of `CoroutineVerticle`).

> **NOTE** Coroutines are not magic, and their implementation requires special compiler and runtime library support. A suspending function is split into many functions by the Kotlin compiler. The split points are the suspending function calls where the rest of the function ends up in another function (called a "continuation"). There is then a finite state machine that determines what split function to call when the suspended function resumes. The design proposal for Kotlin coroutines is on GitHub at http://mng.bz/Qxvj.

5.6   *Which model should I use?*

We just covered three different asynchronous programming models that are generally better than callbacks. There is no definite answer to which model you should be using to write Vert.x applications. Opting for one model or the other depends essentially on what you are trying to achieve.

This is the great thing about Vert.x: you can write a verticle with RxJava because it makes the code straightforward for the functional requirements of that verticle, and you can use Kotlin coroutines for another verticle. You can mix and match models within the same application.

Futures and promises are a simple and effective model for composing asynchronous operations. They are built into the Vert.x core APIs starting from version 4, and they offer the essential tools for dealing with asynchronous results: transforming values (`map`), recovering from errors (`recover/otherwise`), chaining (`flatMap`), and composition (`CompositeFuture`). They also provide interoperability with `CompletionStage` from the JDK.

RxJava allows you to reason about streams of events in a *functional* and *declarative* fashion. It is especially very powerful in terms of error management and recovery. There are operators for retrying failed operations, handling timeouts, and switching the processing to another value or pipeline in case of errors. There is, however, an inherent risk of "monad hell" when building a long chain of (sometimes nested) operators, and the code becomes harder to read. Splitting processing into multiple methods is a good strategy. Operators like `zip`, `flatMap`, and `concatMap` are not necessarily meaningful if you are not very familiar with functional programming idioms. Also, not all processing is easy to express as pipelines, especially when conditional branching is involved.

Kotlin coroutines have the advantage of producing code that doesn't look like asynchronous code. Simple error management cases can be expressed with familiar `try/catch` blocks. Although it wasn't mentioned here, Kotlin coroutines support channels and selectors in the style of the Go programming language, which allows message-passing between coroutines. That being said, more sophisticated error management, such as retries, needs to be expressed manually. Last but not least, it remains important to be aware of how coroutines and asynchronous programming work.

Again, there is no definite answer, as all models have their pros and cons, but with your own experience and preferences you will likely recognize which model you should use for a given situation. In the remainder of this book, we will use different models depending on the examples that we write, but this does not mean that you cannot rewrite them with a model that you prefer.

Summary

- Callbacks have expressiveness limitations when it comes to composing asynchronous operations, and they can render code harder to comprehend without proper care.
- Parallel and sequential asynchronous operations can be composed with other asynchronous programming models: futures and promises, reactive extensions, and coroutines.
- Reactive extensions have a rich set of composable operators, and they are especially well suited for event streams.
- Futures and promises are great for simple chaining of asynchronous operations.
- Kotlin coroutines provide language-level support for asynchronous operations, which is another interesting option.
- There is no universally good asynchronous programming model as they all have their preferred use cases. The good thing about Vert.x is that you can mix and match these models according to your problem domains.

Beyond the event bus

The event bus is a fundamental tool for articulating event processing in Vert.x, but there is more to it! Event-bus services are useful for exposing typed interfaces rather than plain messaging, especially when multiple message types are expected at an event-bus destination. Testing is also an important concept, and we'll look at what is different in testing asynchronous Vert.x code compared to traditional testing.

In this chapter we will revisit an earlier example, refactor it into an event-bus service, and test it.

6.1 Revisiting heat sensors with a service API

In chapter 3 we used heat sensors as an example. We had a `SensorData` verticle that kept the last observed values for each sensor and compute their average using request/reply communication on the event bus. The following listing shows the code we used to compute the temperature average.

Listing 6.1 Event-bus-based average computation API

```
private void average(Message<JsonObject> message) {          ◄──     We receive an
    double avg = lastValues.values().stream()                        event from the
        .collect(Collectors.averagingDouble(Double::doubleValue));   event bus.
    JsonObject json = new JsonObject().put("average", avg);
    message.reply(json);                    ◄──
}                                             |  We reply to the event.
```

This code is tightly coupled with the Vert.x event-bus APIs, as it needs to receive a message and reply to it. Any software component willing to call average has to send a message over the event bus and expect a response.

But what if we could have a regular Java interface with methods to call, rather than having to send and receive messages over the event bus? The interface proposed in the next listing would be completely agnostic of the event bus.

Listing 6.2 Heat sensor API as a Java interface

Asynchronously ask for a sensor value.
```
                                          Asynchronously ask for the average.
public interface SensorDataService {
    void valueFor(String sensorId, Handler<AsyncResult<JsonObject>>
    void average(Handler<AsyncResult<JsonObject>> handler);    ◄──
}
```

The proposed interface has methods with trailing callback parameters so the caller will be notified asynchronously of responses and errors. The Handler<AsyncResult<T>> type is commonly used for callbacks in Vert.x APIs, where T can be anything but is typically a JSON type.

The interface of listing 6.2 is what we are aiming for with event-bus services. Let's revise the heat sensor example, replacing event-bus interactions with a SensorDataService typed Java interface.

6.2 Return of the RPCs (remote procedure calls)

You may already be familiar with *remote procedure calls*, a popular abstraction in distributed computing.[1] RPCs were introduced to hide network communications when you're calling functions running on another machine (the server). The idea is that a local function acts as a proxy, sending a message with the call arguments over the network to the server, and the server then calls the *real* function. The response is then sent back to the proxy, and the client has the illusion of having called a regular, local function.

Vert.x event-bus services are a form of *asynchronous RPC*:

- A service encapsulates a set of operations, like SensorDataService in listing 6.2.
- A service is described by a regular Java API with methods for exposed operations.
- Neither the requester nor the implementation need to directly deal with event-bus messages.

[1]Bruce Jay Nelson, "Remote Procedure Call," PhD dissertation, Carnegie Mellon Univ., Pittsburgh, PA, USA. AAI8204168.

Figure 6.1 illustrates the various components at stake when invoking the `average` method of the `SensorDataService` interface. The client code invokes the `average` method on a service proxy. This is an object that implements the `SensorDataService` interface and then sends a message on the event bus to the `sensor.data-service` destination (this can be configured). The message body contains the method call parameter values, so because `average` only takes a callback, the body is empty. The message also has an `action` header that indicates which method is being called.

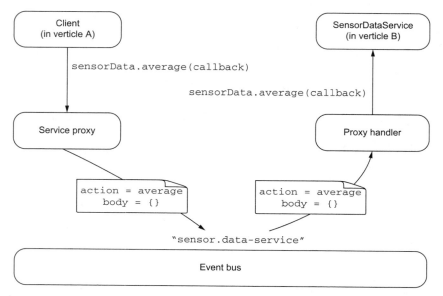

Figure 6.1 How service proxies work

A proxy handler listens to the `sensor.data-service` destination and dispatches method calls based on the message's action header and body. The actual `SensorData-Service` implementation is used here, and the `average` method is called. The proxy handler then replies to the event-bus message with a value passed through the `average` method callback. In turn, the client receives the reply through the service proxy, which passes the reply to the callback from the call on the client side.

This model can simplify dealing with the event bus, especially when many operations need to be exposed. It thus makes sense to define a Java interface as an API rather than manually dealing with messages.

6.3   *Defining a service interface*

Listing 6.2 has the interface that we want for `SensorDataService`, but there is a little more code to add. To develop an event-bus service, you need to

- Write a Java interface that respects a few conventions
- Write an implementation

Vert.x does not rely on magic through bytecode engineering or reflection at runtime, so service proxies and handlers need to be written and compiled. Fortunately, Vert.x comes with code generators, so you will generate both the service proxies and handlers at compilation time rather than write them yourself.

The complete `SensorDataService` interface is detailed in the following listing.

Listing 6.3   Sensor data service

```
@ProxyGen                                      ◁         This annotation is used to
public interface SensorDataService {                     generate an event-bus proxy.

  static SensorDataService create(Vertx vertx) {    ◁    Factory method for
    return new SensorDataServiceImpl(vertx);              creating a service instance
  }

  static SensorDataService createProxy(Vertx vertx, String address) {   ◁
    return new SensorDataServiceVertxEBProxy(vertx, address);            Factory method for
  }                                                                      creating a proxy

  void valueFor(String sensorId, Handler<AsyncResult<JsonObject>> handler);   ◁

  void average(Handler<AsyncResult<JsonObject>> handler);      Operation that
}                                                              takes a parameter
                                                               and a callback
Operation that takes no
parameter and a callback
```

The `@ProxyGen` annotation is used to mark an event-bus service interface so as to generate the proxy code.

You will also need to define a `package-info.java` file and annotate the package definition with `@ModuleGen` to enable the annotation processor, as shown in the next listing.

Listing 6.4   Package info file and enabling code generation

```
@ModuleGen(groupPackage = "chapter6", name = "chapter6")   ◁     Enable a module with
package chapter6;                                                code generation.

import io.vertx.codegen.annotations.ModuleGen;
```

The methods in a service interface need to adhere to a few conventions, notably that of having a callback as the last parameter. You will be tempted to use return values rather than callbacks, but remember that we are dealing with asynchronous operations, so we need callbacks! It is idiomatic for service interfaces to have factory methods for both the service implementations (`create`) and proxies (`createProxy`). These methods greatly simplify the code for either getting a proxy or publishing a service.

The `SensorDataServiceVertxEBProxy` class is generated by the Vert.x code generator, and if you peek into it, you will see event-bus operations. There is also a `Sensor-DataServiceVertxProxyHandler` class that's generated, but only Vert.x will use it, not your code.

Let's now look at the actual service implementation in the `SensorDataService-Impl` class.

6.4   *Service implementation*

The following service implementation is a direct adaptation of the code from chapter 3.

Listing 6.5   Implementation of `SensorDataService`

We pass the Vert.x context.

```
class SensorDataServiceImpl implements SensorDataService {

  private final HashMap<String, Double> lastValues = new HashMap<>();

  SensorDataServiceImpl(Vertx vertx) {
    vertx.eventBus().<JsonObject>consumer("sensor.updates", message -> {
      JsonObject json = message.body();
      lastValues.put(json.getString("id"), json.getDouble("temp"));
    });
  }
```

To get notified of sensor updates, we still need to subscribe to the event bus.

```
  @Override
  public void valueFor(String sensorId, Handler<AsyncResult<JsonObject>>
      handler) {
    if (lastValues.containsKey(sensorId)) {
      JsonObject data = new JsonObject()
        .put("sensorId", sensorId)
        .put("value", lastValues.get(sensorId));
      handler.handle(Future.succeededFuture(data));
    } else {
      handler.handle(Future.failedFuture("No value has been observed for " +
        sensorId));
    }
  }
```

Instead of passing messages for replies, we use asynchronous results.

```
  @Override
  public void average(Handler<AsyncResult<JsonObject>> handler) {
    double avg = lastValues.values().stream()
      .collect(Collectors.averagingDouble(Double::doubleValue));
    JsonObject data = new JsonObject().put("average", avg);
    handler.handle(Future.succeededFuture(data));
  }
}
```

Compared to the code of chapter 3, we have mostly replaced the event-bus code with passing asynchronous results via completed future objects. This code is also free from references to the service proxy handler code, which is being generated.

> **TIP**   The code in listing 6.5 is free of asynchronous operations. In more elaborated services, you will quickly stumble upon cases where you issue asynchronous calls to some other component like a database, an HTTP service, a message broker, or even another service over the event bus. Once you have a response ready, you will pass the result or an error to the method callback, just like we did in `SensorDataServiceImpl`.

6.5   *Enabling proxy code generation*

Service proxy generation is done using `javac` and `apt` annotation processing at compilation time. Two Vert.x modules are required: `vertx-service-proxy` and `vertx-codegen`.

To make the Vert.x code generation work with annotation processing in Gradle, you will need a configuration similar to the following.

Listing 6.6   Gradle configuration for code generation

```
dependencies {
    implementation("io.vertx:vertx-core:$version")
    implementation("io.vertx:vertx-codegen:$version")
    implementation("io.vertx:vertx-service-proxy:$version")

    annotationProcessor("io.vertx:vertx-service-proxy:$version")
    annotationProcessor("io.vertx:vertx-codegen:$version:processor")
    // (...)
}

tasks.getByName<JavaCompile>("compileJava") {
    options.annotationProcessorGeneratedSourcesDirectory =
    ➡ File("$projectDir/src/main/generated")
}
```

This is the scope for annotation processing.

This allows you to customize where the files are being generated.

Now whenever the Java classes are being compiled, the proxy classes are generated. You can see the files in the src/main/generated folder of your project.

If you look into the code of `SensorDataServiceVertxProxyHandler`, you'll see a `switch` block in the `handle` method, where the `action` header is being used to dispatch the method call to the service implementation methods. Similarly, in the `average` method of `SensorDataServiceVertxEBProxy` you will see the code that sends a message over the event bus to invoke that method. The code of both `SensorDataService-VertxProxyHandler` and `SensorDataServiceVertxEBProxy` is really what you would write if you had to implement your own event-bus service system.

6.6   *Deploying event-bus services*

Event-bus services need to be deployed to verticles, and event-bus addresses need to be defined. The following listing shows how to deploy a service.

Listing 6.7   Deploying a service

```
public class DataVerticle extends AbstractVerticle {

    @Override
    public void start() {
        new ServiceBinder(vertx)
            .setAddress("sensor.data-service")
            .register(SensorDataService.class, SensorDataService.create(vertx));
    }
}
```

The event-bus address for the service

Binds a service to an address

We expose a service implementation.

Deploying is as simple as binding to an address and passing a service implementation. We can use the factory `create` methods from the `SensorDataService` interface to do this.

You can deploy multiple services on a verticle. It makes sense to deploy event-bus services that are functionally related together, so a verticle remains a coherent event-processing unit.

Obtaining a service proxy to issue method calls is done by calling the corresponding factory method and passing the correct event-bus destination, as in the following listing.

Listing 6.8   Obtaining a service proxy

```
SensorDataService service = SensorDataService
  .createProxy(vertx, "sensor.data-service");

service.average(ar -> {
  if (ar.succeeded()) {
    System.out.println("Average = " + ar.result());
  } else {
    ar.cause().printStackTrace();
  }
});
```

The service interface follows the callbacks model, as this is the canonical definition for (asynchronous) service interfaces.

6.7   *Service proxies beyond callbacks*

We explored asynchronous programming models other than callbacks in the previous chapter, but we designed event-bus services with callbacks. The good news is that you can leverage code generation to get, say, RxJava or Kotlin coroutine variants for your service proxies. Even better, you do not need much extra work!

To make this work, you need to add the `@VertxGen` annotation to your service interface, as follows.

Listing 6.9   Adding `@VertxGen` to a service interface

To generate service proxies
```
⌐> @ProxyGen                    To allow code
   @VertxGen          ⌐         generation
   public interface SensorDataService {
     // (...)
   }
```

When this annotation is present, code generation by a Vert.x Java annotation processor is enabled with all suitable code generators available at build time.

To generate RxJava bindings, we need to add the dependencies in the following listing.

Listing 6.10 Dependencies for RxJava code generation

```
dependencies {
  // (...)                              Vert.x RxJava 2 module    RxJava 2 Vert.x
  implementation("io.vertx:vertx-rx-java2:$version")◄──┘          code generator
  annotationProcessor("io.vertx:vertx-rx-java2-gen:$version")  ◄──┘
}
```

When we compile the project, a `chapter6.reactivex.SensorDataService` class is generated. This is a small shim that bridges the original callbacks API to RxJava. The class has all the methods from the original `SensorDataService` API (including `create` factory methods), plus rx-prefixed methods.

Given the `average` method that takes a callback, the RxJava code generator creates an `rxAverage` method with no parameter that returns a `Single` object. Similarly, `valueFor` gets translated to `rxValueFor`, a method that takes a `String` argument (the sensor identifier) and returns a `Single` object.

The next listing shows a sample use of the generated RxJava API.

Listing 6.11 Using the RxJava variant of `SensorDataService`

An instance of
chapter6.reactivex.SensorDataService

```
SensorDataService service = SensorDataService
  .createProxy(vertx, "sensor.data-service");    rxAverage() gives a
                                                 Single<JsonObject>.
service.rxAverage()                    ◄──
  .delaySubscription(3, TimeUnit.SECONDS, RxHelper.scheduler(vertx))
  .repeat()
  .map(data -> "avg = " + data.getDouble("average"))
  .subscribe(System.out::println);
```

The RxJava pipeline created here makes a new subscription every three seconds and extracts the average into a string that is then displayed on the standard output.

> **NOTE** You must always develop your event-bus services with the callbacks API for the interface and implementation. Code generators then turn it into other models.

Now that you know how to develop event-bus services, let's switch to the topic of testing verticles and services.

6.8 *Testing and Vert.x*

Automated testing is critical in designing software, and Vert.x applications also need to be tested. The main difficulty when testing Vert.x code is the asynchronous nature of operations. Other than that, tests are classical: they have a setup phase and a test execution and verification phase, followed by a tear-down phase.

A verticle is relatively well isolated from the rest of the system, thanks to the event bus. This is very useful in a test environment:

- The event bus allows you to send events to a verticle to put it in a desired state and to observe what events it produces.
- The configuration passed to a verticle when it is deployed allows you to tune some parameters for a test-centric environment (e.g., using an in-memory database).
- It is possible to deploy mock verticles with controlled behaviors to substitute for verticles with lots of dependencies (e.g., databases, connecting to other verticles, etc.).

As such, testing verticles is more integration testing than unit testing, regardless of whether the verticles under test are being deployed within the same JVM or in cluster mode. We need to see verticles as opaque boxes that we communicate with via the event bus, and possibly by connecting to network protocols that verticles expose. For instance, when a verticle exposes an HTTP service, we are likely going to issue HTTP requests in tests to check its behavior.

In this book, we will only focus on the Vert.x-specific aspects of testing. If you lack experience with the broader topic of testing, I recommend reading a book like *Effective Unit Testing* by Lasse Koskela (Manning, 2013).

6.8.1   Using JUnit 5 with Vert.x

Vert.x supports both the classic JUnit 4 test framework as well as the more recent one for JUnit 5. Vert.x provides a module called `vertx-junit5` with support for version 5 of the JUnit framework (https://junit.org/junit5/). To use it in a Vert.x project, you need to add the `io.vertx:vertx-junit5` dependency, and possibly some JUnit 5 libraries.

In a Gradle project, the `dependencies` section needs to be updated as in the following listing.

Listing 6.12   Using JUnit 5 with Vert.x for a Gradle build

The JUnit 5 APIs replace $junit5Version with a current JUnit 5 version.

```
dependencies {
  // (...)
  testCompile("org.junit.jupiter:junit-jupiter-api:$junit5Version")
  testCompile("io.vertx:vertx-junit5:$vertxVersion")
  testCompile("org.assertj:assertj-core:3.11.1")
  testRuntimeOnly("org.junit.jupiter:junit-jupiter-engine:$junit5Version")
}

tasks.named<Test>("test") {
  useJUnitPlatform()
}
```

The Vert.x JUnit 5 support library

This is used by Gradle for running tests.

This enables JUnit 5 support in Gradle.

The `vertx-junit5` library already has a dependency on `junit-jupiter-api`, but it is a good practice to fix the version in the build. The `junit-jupiter-engine` module needs to be present in the `testRuntime` scope for Gradle. Finally, JUnit 5 can be used with any assertion API, including its built-in one, and AssertJ is a popular one.

6.8.2 *Testing DataVerticle*

We need two test cases to check the behavior of `DataVerticle`, and by extension that of `SensorDataService`:

- When no sensor is present, the average should be 0, and requesting a value for any sensor identifier must raise an error.
- When there are sensors, we need to check the average value and individual sensor values.

Figure 6.2 shows the interactions for the test environment. The test case has a proxy reference to make calls to `SensorDataService`. The actual `DataVerticle` verticle is deployed at the `sensor.data-service` destination. It can issue `valueFor` and `average` method calls from tests. Since `DataVerticle` receives messages from sensors on the event bus, we can send arbitrary messages rather than deploying actual `HeatSensor` verticles over which we have no control. Mocking a verticle is often as simple as sending the type of messages it would send.

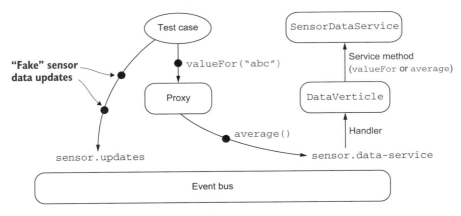

Figure 6.2   Isolating `SensorDataService`

The following listing shows the test class preamble.

Listing 6.13   Preamble of `SensorDataServiceTest`

```
@ExtendWith(VertxExtension.class)    ⟵——— JUnit 5 extension for Vert.x
class SensorDataServiceTest {

    private SensorDataService dataService;    ⟵——— Our service proxy reference
```

```
@BeforeEach                                    ←—— Setup method, executed before each test
void prepare(Vertx vertx, VertxTestContext ctx) {
   vertx.deployVerticle(new DataVerticle(), ctx.succeeding(id -> {   ←—┐
      dataService = SensorDataService.createProxy(vertx,
      "sensor.data-service");
      ctx.completeNow();       ←——┐
   }));
}
// (,,,)
```

We get a proxy reference. →

We notify that the setup has completed.

We deploy the verticle that internally exposes a service, and we expect a successful deployment (succeeding).

JUnit 5 supports extensions to give additional functionality. In particular, extensions can inject parameters into test methods, and they can intercept life-cycle events such as before and after a test method is called. The `VertxExtension` class simplifies writing test cases by doing the following:

- Injecting ready-to-use instances of `Vertx` with default configuration
- Injecting a `VertxTestContext` object to deal with the asynchronous nature of Vert.x code
- Ensuring awaiting for the `VertxTestContext` to either succeed or fail

The `prepare` method is executed before each test case, to prepare the test environment. We use it here to deploy the `DataVerticle` verticle and then fetch the service proxy and store it in the `dataService` field. Since deploying a verticle is an asynchronous operation, the `prepare` method is injected with a `Vertx` context and a `VertxTestContext` object to notify when it has completed.

TIP Users of JUnit before version 5 may be surprised that the class and test methods are package-private; this is idiomatic with JUnit 5.

You can see the first test case, when no sensors are deployed, in the following listing.

Listing 6.14 Test case without sensors

VertxTestContext allows you to deal with asynchronous operations in tests to report success and failures.

A checkpoint is mainly used to ensure that an asynchronous operation passed at a certain line.

failing is a helper for Handler<AsyncResult>, and verify wraps assertions.

```
@Test
void noSensor(VertxTestContext ctx) {
   Checkpoint failsToGet = ctx.checkpoint();   ←——┘
   Checkpoint zeroAvg = ctx.checkpoint();

   dataService.valueFor("abc", ctx.failing(err -> ctx.verify(() -> {   ←—
      assertThat(err.getMessage()).startsWith("No value has been observed");
      failsToGet.flag();
   })));

   dataService.average(ctx.succeeding(data -> ctx.verify(() -> {
      double avg = data.getDouble("average");
      assertThat(avg).isCloseTo(0.0d, withPercentage(1.0d));
      zeroAvg.flag();
   })));
}
```

This test case assumes that no sensor has been deployed, so trying to get any sensor value must fail. We check this behavior by looking for the temperature value of sensor abc, which doesn't exist. We then check that the average value is 0.

Checkpoints are flagged to mark that the test execution reached certain lines. When all declared checkpoints have been flagged, the test completes successfully. The test fails when an assertion fails, when an unexpected exception is thrown, or when a (configurable) delay elapses and not all checkpoints have been flagged.

Why asynchronous testing is different

Testing asynchronous operations is slightly different from the regular testing you may be familiar with. The default contract in test executions is that a test runner thread calls test methods, and they fail when exceptions are thrown. Assertion methods throw exceptions to report errors.

Since operations like `deployVerticle` and `send` are asynchronous, the test runner thread exits the method before they have any chance to complete. The `VertxExtension` class takes care of that by waiting for `VertxTestContext` to report either a success or a failure. To avoid having tests wait forever, there is a timeout (30 seconds by default).

Finally, we have a test case for when there are sensors.

Listing 6.15 Test case with sensors

```
@Test
void withSensors(Vertx vertx, VertxTestContext ctx) {
  Checkpoint getValue = ctx.checkpoint();
  Checkpoint goodAvg = ctx.checkpoint();
                                                         Messages to mock sensors
  JsonObject m1 = new JsonObject().put("id", "abc").put("temp", 21.0d);  ⟵
  JsonObject m2 = new JsonObject().put("id", "def").put("temp", 23.0d);

  vertx.eventBus()                    ⟵——— We send the messages.
    .publish("sensor.updates", m1)
    .publish("sensor.updates", m2);

  dataService.valueFor("abc", ctx.succeeding(data -> ctx.verify(() -> {
    assertThat(data.getString("sensorId")).isEqualTo("abc");
    assertThat(data.getDouble("value")).isEqualTo(21.0d);
    getValue.flag();
  })));

  dataService.average(ctx.succeeding(data -> ctx.verify(() -> {
    assertThat(data.getDouble("average")).isCloseTo(22.0,
    ➡ withPercentage(1.0d));            ⟵
    goodAvg.flag();                               AssertJ has assertions for floating-point
  })));                                           values with error margins.
}
```

This test simulates two sensors with identifiers `abc` and `def` by sending fake sensor data updates over the event bus, just like a sensor would do. We then have determinism in our assertions, and we can check the behavior for both `valueFor` and `average` methods.

6.8.3   *Running the tests*

The tests can be run from your IDE. You can also run them using Gradle: `gradlew test`.

Gradle generates a human-readable test report in build/reports/tests/test/index.html. When you open the file in a web browser, you can check that all tests passed, as shown in figure 6.3.

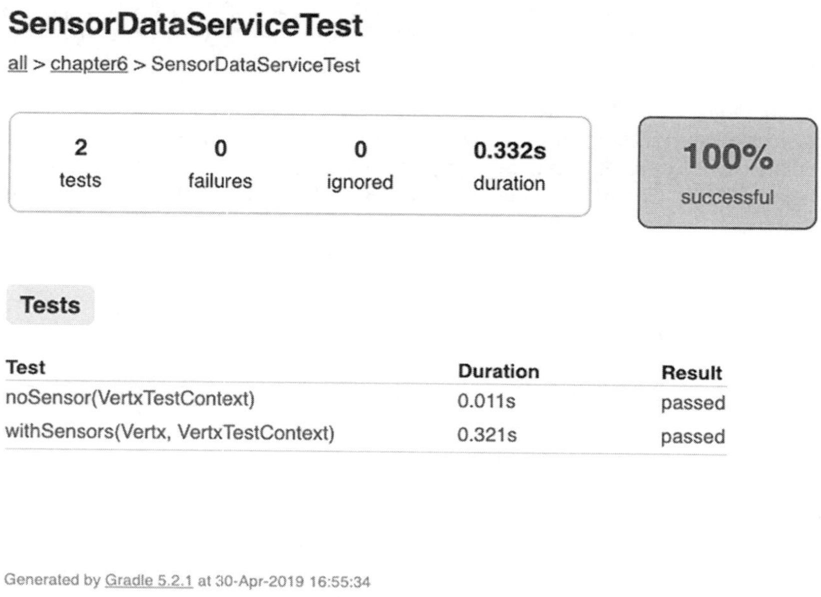

SensorDataServiceTest

<u>all</u> > <u>chapter6</u> > SensorDataServiceTest

2	0	0	0.332s	100%
tests	failures	ignored	duration	successful

Tests

Test	Duration	Result
noSensor(VertxTestContext)	0.011s	passed
withSensors(Vertx, VertxTestContext)	0.321s	passed

Generated by <u>Gradle 5.2.1</u> at 30-Apr-2019 16:55:34

Figure 6.3   Test report

Note that the Gradle `test` task is a dependency of `build`, so the tests are always executed when the project is fully built.

Summary

- Event-bus services and proxies abstract from event-bus communications by providing an asynchronous service interface.
- It is possible to generate bindings other than callbacks for event-bus services: RxJava, Kotlin coroutines, etc.
- Testing asynchronous code and services is more challenging than in the traditional imperative cases, and Vert.x comes with dedicated support for JUnit 5.

Part 2

Developing reactive services with Vert.x

Congratulations, you are now familiar with asynchronous programming with Vert.x and its core APIs! It's now time to dive into the main pieces of the Vert.x stack and to explore the modules for building advanced HTTP APIs and using databases, authentication, messaging, and more.

We will develop a reactive application on top of multiple event-driven microservices across these chapters. Chapter 12 is where we will make reactive a reality: we wrote scalable services in the previous chapters, but we also need to make the application resilient and responsive even when failures happen. You will be exposed to a methodology that uses load and chaos testing to observe how services behave, and we will discuss different failure mitigation strategies.

Last but not least, we will conclude the book by deploying to containers and Kubernetes clusters.

Designing a reactive application

7

This chapter covers

- What a reactive application is
- Introducing the reactive application scenario used throughout part 2

The first part of this book taught you asynchronous programming with Vert.x. This is key to writing scalable and resource-efficient applications.

It is now time to explore what makes an application *reactive*, as we strive for both scalability and dependability. To do that, we will focus the following chapters on developing a fully reactive application out of several event-driven microservices. In this chapter, we'll specify these services.

7.1 What makes an application reactive

In previous chapters we covered some elements of reactive:

- Back-pressure, as a necessary ingredient in asynchronous stream processing to regulate event throughput
- Reactive programming as a way to compose asynchronous operations

It is now time to explore the last facet: *reactive applications.* In chapter 1 I summarized *The Reactive Manifesto,* which declares that reactive applications are responsive, resilient, elastic, and message-driven.

The key property of reactive applications is that they remain responsive under demanding workloads and when they face the failure of other services. By "responsive," we mean that latency for service response remains under control. A good responsiveness example would be a service that responds within 500 ms in the 99% percentile, provided that 500 ms is a good number given the service's functional requirements and operational constraints.

An increasing workload will almost always degrade latency, but in the case of a reactive application, the goal is to avoid latency explosion when the service is under stress. Part 1 of this book mostly taught you asynchronous programming with Vert.x, which is the key ingredient for facing growing workloads. You saw that asynchronous processing of events allowed you to multiplex thousands of open network connections on a single thread. This model (when implemented correctly!) is much more resource-friendly and scalable than the traditional "1 thread per connection" model.

So Vert.x gives us a foundation for asynchronous programming on top of the JVM in order to meet demanding workloads, but what about dealing with failure? This is the other core challenge that we have to meet, and the answer is not a magic tool we can pick off the shelf. Suppose we have a service that talks to a database that becomes irresponsive because of an internal problem, like a deadlock. Some time will elapse before our service is notified of an error, perhaps in the form of a TCP connection timeout. In such a case, the latency explodes. By contrast, if the database is down, we get an immediate TCP connection error: latency is very good, but since the service cannot talk to its database, it is unable to process a request.

You will see in the last chapter of this part how to experiment with "what happens when things go wrong," and we'll discuss possible solutions for keeping services responsive. You might be tempted to enforce strict timeouts on all calls to other services (including databases), or to use *circuit-breakers* (more on that in the last chapter) everywhere, but a more analytical approach will help you see which solution to use, if any, and when. It is also important to see failure in the light of a service's functional requirements and application domain: the response to failure may not always be an error. For instance, if we can't get the latest temperature update from a sensor, we may serve the last known value and attach a timestamp to it, so the requester has all the necessary context attached to the data.

It is now time to build a reactive application, both to explore some elements of the Vert.x stack and to learn how to concretely build responsive applications.

7.2 *The 10k steps challenge scenario*

The application that we will implement in the upcoming chapters supports a (not so) fictional fitness-tracker challenge. Suppose we want to build an application to track and score users' steps, as illustrated in figure 7.1.

Challenge application

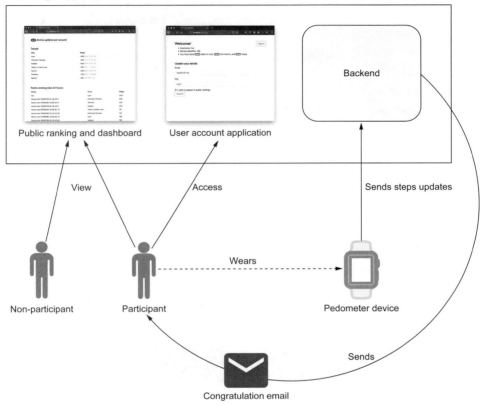

Figure 7.1   10k steps challenge application and actors overview

The application described in figure 7.1 would work as follows:

- Users sport connected pedometers that track how many steps they take.
- The pedometers regularly send step-count updates to the application that manages the challenge.
- The goal is to walk at least 10,000 steps each day, and users are greeted by an email every day when they do so.
- Users may choose to be publicly listed in rankings of step counts over the last 24 hours.
- Participants can also connect to a web application to see their data and update their information, such as their city and whether they want to appear in public rankings.

The web application allows new users to register by providing their device identifier as well as some basic information, such as their city and whether they intend to appear in public rankings (figure 7.2).

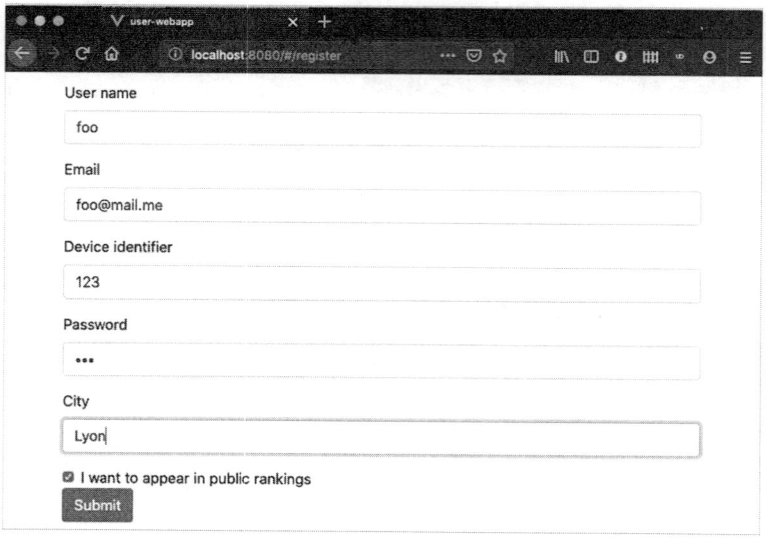

Figure 7.2   Screenshot of the user web application registration form

Once connected, a user can update some basic details and get reminded of their total steps, monthly steps, and daily steps (figure 7.3).

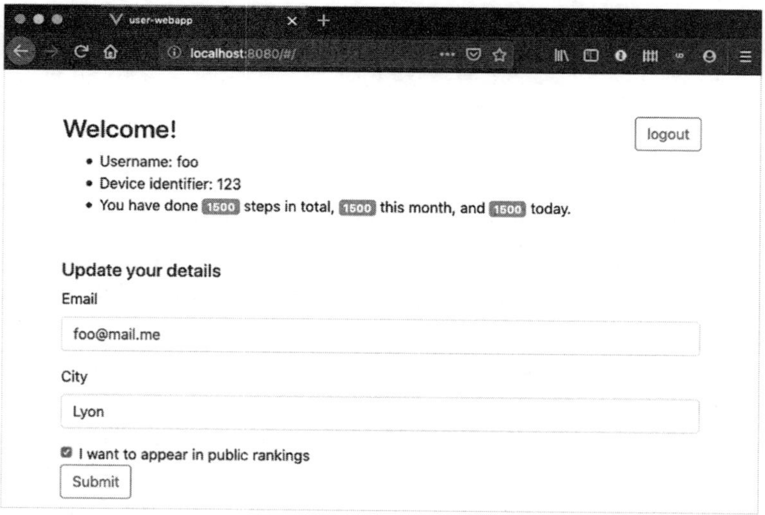

Figure 7.3   Screenshot of the user web application user-details page

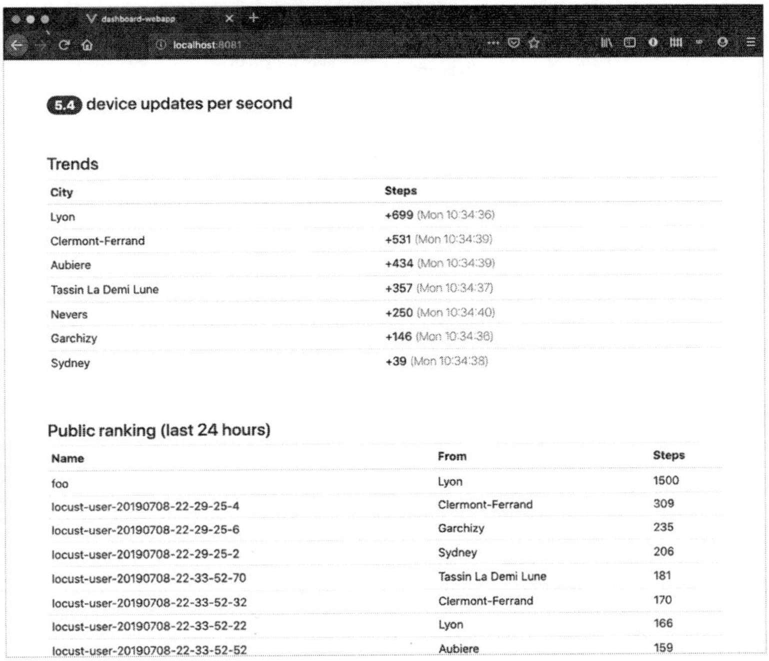

Figure 7.4   Screenshot of the public dashboard web application

There is also a separate web application that offers a public dashboard (figure 7.4).

The dashboard offers a ranking of public profiles over the last 24 hours, the current pedometer device update throughput, and trends by city. All the information displayed in the dashboard is updated live.

7.3   *One application, many services*

The application is decomposed as a set of (micro) services that interact with each other as in figure 7.5. Each service fulfills a single functional purpose and could well be used by another application. There are four public services: two user-facing web applications, one service for receiving pedometer device updates, and one service to expose a public HTTP API. The public API is used by the user web application, and we could similarly have mobile applications connect to it. There are four internal services: one to manage user profiles, one to manage activity data, one to congratulate users over email, and one to compute various stats over continuous events.

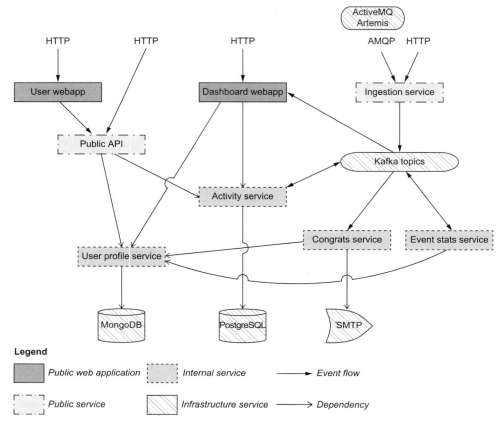

Figure 7.5   Overview of the application architecture

NOTE You may have heard of *command query responsibility segregation* (CQRS) and *event-sourcing*, which are patterns found in event-driven architectures.[1] CQRS structures how to read and write information, while event sourcing is about materializing the application state as a sequence of facts. Our proposed application architecture relates to both notions, but because it's not strictly faithful to the definitions, I prefer to just call it an "event-driven microservices architecture."

All services are powered by Vert.x, and we also need some third-party middleware, labelled "infrastructure services" in figure 7.5. We'll use two different types of databases: a document-oriented database (MongoDB) and a relational database (PostgreSQL). We need an SMTP server to send emails, and Apache Kafka is used for event-stream processing between some services. Because the ingestion service may receive updates from HTTP and AMQP, we'll also use an ActiveMQ Artemis server.

[1]For an introduction, see Martin Fowler's articles on CQRS (https://martinfowler.com/bliki/CQRS.html) and event sourcing (https://martinfowler.com/eaaDev/EventSourcing.html).

There are two types of arrows in figure 7.5. Event flows show important event exchanges between services. For instance, the ingestion service sends events to Kafka, whereas the event stats service both consumes and produces Kafka events. I also denoted dependencies: for example, the public API service depends on the user profile and activities services, which in turn depend on their own databases for data persistence.

We can illustrate one example of interactions between services by looking at how a device update impacts the dashboard web application's city trends ranking, as in figure 7.6.

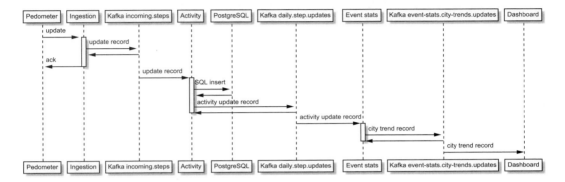

Figure 7.6   From a device update to a city trend update

It all starts with a pedometer sending an update to the ingestion service, which verifies that the update contains all required data. The ingestion service then sends the update to a Kafka topic, and the pedometer device is acknowledged so it knows that the update has been received and will be processed. The update will be handled by multiple consumers listening on that particular Kafka topic, and among them is the activity service. This service will record the data to the PostgreSQL database and then publish another record to a Kafka topic with the number of steps recorded by the pedometer on that day. This record is picked up by the event stats service, which observes updates over windows of five seconds, splits them by city, and aggregates the number of steps. It then posts an update with the increment in steps observed for a given city as another Kafka record. This record is then consumed by the dashboard web application, which finally sends an update to all connected web browsers, which in turn update the display.

About the application architecture

As you dig through the specifications and implementations of the services, you may find the decomposition a bit artificial at times. For instance, the user profile and activity services could well be just one, saving some requests to join data from the two services. Remember that the decomposition was made for pedagogical reasons, and to show relevant elements from the Vert.x stack.

(continued)

Making an application from (micro) services requires some compromises, especially as some services may be pre-existing, and you have to deal with them as they are, or you have limited ability to evolve them.

You may also find that the proposed architecture is not a nicely layered one, with some services nicely decoupled and some others having stronger dependencies on others. Again, this is done intentionally for pedagogical purposes. More often than not, real-world applications have to make compromises to deliver working software rather than pursue the quest for architectural perfection.

7.4 *Service specifications*

Let's discuss the functional and technical specifications of the application services. For each service, we'll consider the following elements:

- Functional overview
- API description, if any
- Technical points of interest, including crash recovery
- Scaling and deployment considerations

7.4.1 *User profile service*

The user profile service manages the profile data for a unique user. A user is identified by the following information:

- A username (must be unique)
- A password
- An email address
- A city
- A pedometer device identifier (must be unique)
- Whether the user wants to appear in public rankings or not

The service exposes an HTTP API and persists data in a MongoDB database (see figure 7.7).

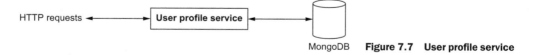

HTTP requests ◄────────► **User profile service** ◄────────► MongoDB   **Figure 7.7   User profile service**

The service falls into the category of CRUD (for *create*, *read*, *update*, and *delete*) services that sit on top of a database. Table 7.1 identifies the different elements of the HTTP API.

This service is not to be publicly exposed; it is meant to be consumed by other services. There is no authentication mechanism in place. The service is here to provide a

Table 7.1 User profile HTTP API

Purpose	Path	Method	Data	Response	Status code
Register a new user	/register	POST	Registration JSON document	N/A	200 on success, 409 when the username or device identifier already exists, 500 for technical errors
Get a user's details	/\<username>	GET	N/A	User data in JSON	200 on success, 404 if the username does not exist, 500 for technical errors
Update some user details	/\<username>	PUT	User data in JSON	N/A	200 on success, 500 for technical errors
Credentials validation	/authenticate	POST	Credentials in JSON	N/A	200 on success, 401 when authentication fails
Reverse lookup of a user by their device	/owns/\<deviceId>	GET	N/A	JSON data with the username owning the device	200 on success, 404 if the device does not exist, 500 for technical errors

facade for operations on top of the database. Both the service and the database can be scaled independently.

NOTE The API described in table 7.1 does not follow the architectural principles of *representational state transfer* (REST) interfaces. A *RESTful* interface would expose user resources as, say, /user/\<username>, and instead of registering new users through a POST request at /register, we would do so on the /user resource. Both faithful REST structures and more liberal HTTP API structures are valid choices.

7.4.2 Ingestion service

The ingestion service collects pedometer device updates and forwards records with update data to a Kafka stream for other services to process the events. The service receives device updates from either an HTTP API or an AMQP queue, as illustrated in figure 7.8. The service is a form of *protocol adapter* or *mediator*, as it converts events from one protocol (HTTP or AMQP) to another protocol (Kafka record streams).

A device update is a JSON document with the following entries:

- The device identifier
- A synchronization identifier, which is a monotonically increasing long integer that the device updates for each successful synchronization
- The number of steps since the last synchronization

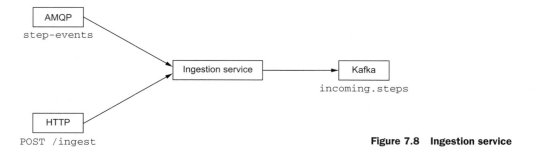

Figure 7.8   Ingestion service

The HTTP API supports a single operation, as shown in table 7.2.

Table 7.2   Ingestion service HTTP API

Purpose	Path	Method	Data	Response	Status code
Ingest a pedometer update	/ingest	POST	JSON document	N/A	200 on success, 500 for technical errors

The AMQP client receives messages from the step-events address. The JSON data is the same in both the HTTP API and AMQP client.

The service is meant to be publicly exposed so that it can receive pedometer updates. We assume that some reverse proxy will be used, offering encryption and access control. For instance, device updates over HTTPS could make use of client certificate checks to filter out unauthorized or unpatched devices.

AMQP and HTTP clients only get acknowledgements when records have been written to Kafka. In the case of HTTP, this means that a device cannot consider the synchronization to be successful until it has received an HTTP 200 response. The service does not check for duplicates, so it is safe for a device to consider the ingestion operation idempotent. As you will see, it is the role of the activity service to keep data consistent, and not that of the ingestion service.

The service can be scaled independently of the AMQP and the Kafka servers/clusters. If the service crashes before some form of acknowledgement has been made, a client can always safely retry because of idempotency.

7.4.3   *Activity service*

The activity service keeps track of step-activity updates sent by the pedometers. The service stores events to a PostgreSQL database and offers an HTTP API to gather some statistics, such as daily, monthly, and total step counts for a given device. Updates are received from a Kakfa topic, which is fed by the ingestion service (see figure 7.9).

The activity service also publishes events with the number of steps for a device on the current day. This way, other services can subscribe to the corresponding Kafka topic and be notified rather than having to regularly poll the activity service for updates.

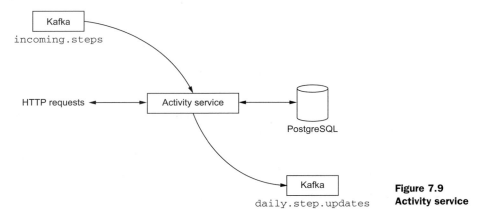

Figure 7.9
Activity service

The HTTP API is shown in table 7.3.

Table 7.3   Activity service HTTP API

Purpose	Path	Method	Data	Response	Status code
Total step count for a device	/\<device id>/total	GET	N/A	JSON document	200 on success, 404 if the device does not exist, 500 for technical errors
Step count for a device in a particular month	/\<device id>/\<year>/\<month>	GET	N/A	JSON document	200 on success, 404 if the device does not exist, 500 for technical errors
Step count for a device on a particular day	/\<device id>/\<year>/\<month>/\<day>	GET	N/A	JSON document	200 on success, 404 if the device does not exist, 500 for technical errors
Ranking of the devices in decreasing number of steps over the last 24 hours	/ranking-last-24-hours	GET	N/A	JSON document	200 on success, 500 for technical errors

Most of the operations are queries for a given device. As you will see in another chapter, the last operation provides an efficient query for getting a device's ranking, which is useful when the dashboard service starts.

The events sent to the daily.step.updates Kafka topic contain the following information in a JSON document:

- The device identifier
- A timestamp
- The number of steps recorded on the current day

For each incoming device update, there need to be three operations in this order:

- A database insert
- A database query to get the number of steps for the device on the current day
- A Kafka record write

Each of these operations may fail, and we don't have a distributed transaction broker in place. We ensure idempotency and correctness as follows:

- We only acknowledge the incoming device update records in Kafka after the last operation has completed.
- The database schema enforces some uniqueness constraints on the events being stored, so the insertion operation can fail if an event is being processed again.
- We handle a duplicate insertion error as a normal case to have idempotency, and we follow along with the next steps until they have all completed.
- Successfully writing a daily steps update record to Kafka allows us to acknowledge the initial device update record, and the system can make progress with the other incoming records.

The activity service is not meant to be publicly exposed, so just like the user profile service, there is no authentication in place. It can be scaled independently of the database.

7.4.4   Public API

This service exposes a public HTTP API for other services to consume. It essentially acts as a *facade* over the user profile and activity services, as shown in figure 7.10.

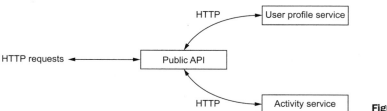

Figure 7.10   Public API

The service is a form of *edge service* or *API gateway* as it forwards and composes requests to other services. Since this is a public HTTP API, the service requires authentication for most of its operations. To do that we'll use *JSON web tokens* (https://tools .ietf.org/html/rfc7519), which we'll discuss in chapter 8, along with the service implementation. Since we want the public API to be usable from any HTTP client, including JavaScript code running in a web browser, we need to support *cross-origin resource sharing*, or CORS (https://fetch.spec.whatwg.org/#http-cors-protocol). Again we will dig into the details in due time. The HTTP API operations are described in table 7.4.

Table 7.4   Public API HTTP interface

Purpose	Path	Method	Data	Response	Status code
Register a new user and device	`/register`	POST	JSON document with registration data	N/A	200 on success, 502 otherwise
Get a JWT token to use the API	`/token`	POST	JSON document with credentials	JWT token (plain text)	200 on success, 401 otherwise
Get a user's data (requires a valid JWT)	`/<username>`	GET	N/A	JSON document	200 on success, 404 if not found, 502 otherwise
Update a user's data (requires a valid JWT)	`/<username>`	PUT	JSON document	N/A	200 on success, 404 if not found, 502 otherwise
Total steps of a user (requires a valid JWT)	`/<username>/total`	GET	N/A	JSON document	200 on success, 404 if not found, 502 otherwise
Total steps of a user in a month (requires a valid JWT)	`/<username>/<year>/<month>`	GET	N/A	JSON document	200 on success, 404 if not found, 502 otherwise
Total steps of a user on a day (requires a valid JWT)	`/<username>/<year>/<month>/<day>`	GET	N/A	JSON document	200 on success, 404 if not found, 502 otherwise

Note that the request paths will be prefixed with `/api/v1`, so requesting a token is a `POST` request to `/api/v1/token`. It is always a good idea to have some versioning scheme in the URLs of a public API. The JWT tokens are restricted to the username that was used to obtain it, so user B cannot perform, say, a request to `/api/v1/A/2019/07/14`.

The public API service can be scaled to multiple instances. In a production setting, a load-balancing HTTP proxy should dispatch requests to the instances. There is no state to maintain in the service, since it forwards and composes requests to the other services.

7.4.5   *User web application*

The user web application provides a way for a user to register, update their details, and check some basic data about their activity. As shown in figure 7.11, there is a backend to serve the web application's static assets to web browsers over HTTP.

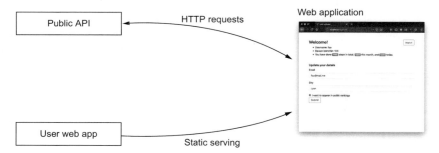

Figure 7.11   User web application

The frontend is a single-page application written in JavaScript and the Vue.JS framework. It is served by the user web application service, and all interactions with the application's backend happen through calls to the public API service.

As such, this service is more a Vue.JS application than a Vert.x application, although it is still interesting to see how Vert.x serves static content with minimal effort. We could have chosen other popular JavaScript frameworks, or even no framework at all. I find Vue.JS to be a simple and efficient choice. Also, since Vue.JS embraces *reactive idioms*, it makes for a fully reactive application from the backend API to the frontend.

The service itself just serves static files, so it can be scaled to multiple instances and put behind a load balancer in a production setting. There is no state on the server side, either in the service or in the public API in use. It is the frontend application that stores some state in users' web browsers.

7.4.6   *Event stats service*

The event stats service reacts to selected events from Kafka topics to produce statistics and publish them as Kafka records for other services to consume, as illustrated in figure 7.12.

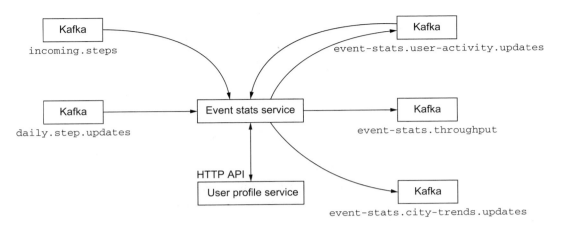

Figure 7.12 Event stats service

The service performs the following computations:

- Based on time windows of five seconds, it computes the throughput of device updates based on the number of events received on the `incoming.steps` topic, and it then emits a record to the `event-stats.throughput` topic.
- Events received on the `daily.step.updates` topic carry data on the number of steps from a device on the current day. This data lacks user data (name, city, etc.), so for each event the service queries the user profile service to enrich the original record with user data, and then sends it to the `event-stats.user-activity.updates` topic.
- The service computes city trends by processing the events from the `event-stats.user-activity.updates` topic over time windows of five seconds, and for each city it publishes an update with the aggregated number of steps for that city to the `event-stats.city-trends.updates` topic.

Kafka records can be acknowledged in an automatic fashion by batches, as there is little harm in processing a record again, especially for the throughput and city trends computations. To ensure that exactly one record is produced for an activity update, a manual acknowledgement is possible, although an occasional duplicate record should not impact a consuming service.

The event stats service is not meant to be public, and it does not offer any interface for other services. Finally, the service should be deployed as a single instance due to the nature of the computations.

7.4.7 *Congrats service*

The role of the congrats service is to monitor when a device reaches at least 10,000 steps on a day, and then to send a congratulation email to the owner, as shown in figure 7.13.

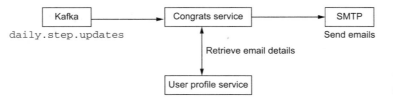

daily.step.updates

Figure 7.13   Congrats service

The service makes calls to the user profile service to get the email of the user associated with a device, and then it contacts an SMTP server to send an email.

Note that we could have reused the event-stats.user-activity.updates Kafka topic fed by the event stats service, as it enriches the messages received from daily.step.updates with user data, including an email address. An implementation detail in how Kafka record keys are being produced for both topics makes it simpler to enforce that at most one message is sent to a user each day by using the records from daily.step.updates and then getting the email from the user profile service. This does not add much network and processing overhead either, since a user must receive an email only for the first activity update with at least 10,000 steps on a given day.

This service is not to be publicly exposed, and it does not expose any API. A single instance should suffice in a production setting, but the service can be scaled to multiple instances sharing the same Kafka consumer group so that they can split the workload among them.

7.4.8   *Dashboard web application*

The dashboard web application offers live updates on the incoming updates throughput, city trends, and public user ranking. As seen in figure 7.14, the service consumes Kafka records emitted by the event stats service and regularly pushes updates to the web application.

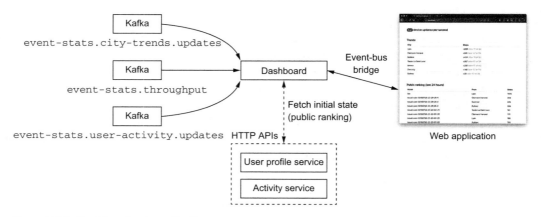

Figure 7.14   Dashboard web application

The web application is written using the Vue.JS framework, just like the user web application described earlier. The frontend and backend are connected using the Vert.x event bus, so both the Vert.x and Vue.JS code bases can communicate with the same programming model.

Throughput and city trend updates from Kafka topics are directly forwarded over the Vert.x event bus, so the connected web application client receives the updates in real time. The backend maintains in-memory data about the number of steps over the last 24 hours for all users who have made their profile public. The ranking is updated every 5 seconds, and the result is pushed to the web application over the event bus so that the ranking is updated in the connected web browsers.

Since the backend is event-driven over Kafka topics, a good question is what happens when the service starts (or when it recovers from a crash). Indeed, on a fresh start we do not have all the step data from the last 24 hours, and we will only receive updates from the service's start time.

We need a *hydration* phase when the service starts, where we query the activity service and get the rankings over the last 24 hours. We then need to query the user profile service for each entry of the ranking, since we need to correlate each device with a user profile. This is a potentially costly operation, but it shouldn't happen very often.

Note that waiting for the hydration to complete does not prevent the processing of user activity updates, as eventually only the most recent value from either a Kafka record or the hydration data will prevail when updating the in-memory data.

The dashboard web application service is meant to be publicly exposed. It can be scaled to multiple instances if need be, and it can be put behind an HTTP proxy load balancer.

7.5 *Running the application*

To run the application, you need to run all the infrastructure services and all the microservices. The complete source code of the application can be found in the part2-steps-challenge folder of the source code repository.

First of all, Docker must be installed on your machine, because building the application requires containers to be started while executing test suites. The application can be built with Gradle using the `gradle assemble` command, or with `gradle build` if you also want to run the tests as part of the build and have Docker running.

Once the application services have been built, you will need to run all infrastructure services like PostgreSQL, MongoDB, Apache Kafka, and so on. You can greatly simplify the task by running them from Docker containers. To do that, the `docker-compose.yml` file describes several containers to be run with Docker Compose, a simple and effective tool for managing several containers at once. Running `docker-compose up` will start all the containers, and `docker-compose down` will stop and remove them all. You can also press `Ctrl+C` in a terminal running Docker Compose, and it will stop the containers (but not remove them, so they can be started with the current state again).

TIP   On macOS and Windows, I recommend installing Docker Desktop. Most Linux distributions offer Docker as a package. Note that `docker` needs to run as `root`, so on Linux you may need to add your user to a special group to avoid using `sudo`. The official Docker documentation provides troubleshooting instructions (https://docs.docker.com/engine/install/linux-postinstall/). In all cases, make sure that you can successfully run the `docker run hello-world` command as a user.

The container images that we will need to run are the following:

- MongoDB with an initialization script to prepare a collection and indexes
- PostgreSQL with an initialization script to create the schema
- Apache Kafka with Apache ZooKeeper from the Strimzi project images (see https://strimzi.io)
- ActiveMQ Artemis
- MailHog, an SMTP server suitable for integration testing (https://github.com/mailhog/MailHog)

All microservices are packaged as self-contained executable JAR files. For example, you can run the activity service as follows:

```
$ java -jar activity-service/build/libs/activity-service-all.jar
```

That being said, starting all services manually is not very convenient, so the project also contains a `Procfile` file to run all the services. The file contains lines with service names and associated shell commands. You can then use the Foreman tool to run the services (https://github.com/ddollar/foreman) or a compatible tool like Hivemind (https://github.com/DarthSim/hivemind):

```
$ foreman start
```

This is very convenient, as you can run all the services from two terminal panes, as illustrated in figure 7.15.

Foreman can also generate various system service descriptors from a Procfile: initab, launchd, systemd, and more. Finally, Foreman is written in Ruby, but there are also ports to other languages listed on the project page.

TIP   Foreman simplifies running all services, but you don't have to use it. You can run each individual service on the command line. The content of Procfile will show you the exact command for each service.

The next chapters will illustrate the challenges of implementing a reactive application by building on top of a set of (imperfect!) microservices that cover the topics of web, APIs, messaging, data, and continuous stream processing. In the next chapter, we'll explore the web stack used to implement some of the services described in this chapter.

Figure 7.15 Running the microservices and infrastructure services with Docker Compose and Foreman

Summary

- A reactive application focuses on controlling latency under various workloads and in the presence of failures from other services.
- A reactive application can be decomposed as a set of independently scaled event-driven microservices.

The web stack

This chapter covers

- The construction of an edge service and a public API
- The Vert.x web client
- JSON web tokens (JWT) and cross-origin resource sharing (CORS)
- Serving and integrating a Vue.js reactive application with Vert.x
- Testing an HTTP API with REST Assured

Reactive applications often use HTTP because it is such a versatile protocol, and Vert.x offers comprehensive support for web technologies. The Vert.x web stack provides many tools for building web application backends. These include advanced routing, authentication, an HTTP client, and more. This chapter will guide you through exposing an HTTP API with *JSON web tokens* (JWT) for access control, making HTTP requests to other services, and building a reactive single-page application that connects to the HTTP API.

> **NOTE** This book does not cover the following noteworthy elements from the Vert.x web stack that are not needed to build the application in this part of the book: routing with regular expressions, cookies, server-side sessions, server-side template rendering, and cross-site request forgery protection. You can get more details about those topics in the official documentation at https://vertx.io/.

8.1 Exposing a public API

Let's start with a reminder of what the public API service does, as illustrated in figure 8.1. This service is an edge service (or service gateway, depending on how you prefer to name it) as it exposes an HTTP API, but it essentially composes functionality found in other services. In this case, the user profile and activity services are being used. These two services are internal to the application and are not publicly exposed. They also lack any form of authentication and access control, which is something the public API cannot afford for most operations.

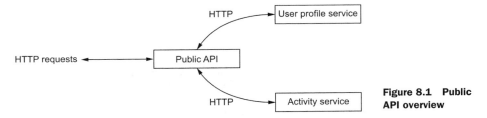

Figure 8.1 Public API overview

The following Vert.x modules are needed to implement the public API:

- `vertx-web`, to provide advanced HTTP request-processing functionality
- `vertx-web-client`, to issue HTTP requests to the user profile and activity services
- `vertx-auth-jwt`, to generate and process JSON web tokens and perform access control

The complete source code of the public API service can be found in the part2-steps-challenge/public-api folder of the book's source code repository.

We'll start with the Vert.x web router.

8.1.1 Routing HTTP requests

Vert.x core provides a very low-level HTTP server API, where you need to pass a request handler for all types of HTTP requests. If you just use Vert.x core, you need to manually check the requested path and method. This is fine for simple cases, and it's what we did in some earlier chapters, but it can quickly become complicated.

The `vertx-web` module provides a *router* that can act as a Vert.x HTTP server request handler, and that manages the dispatch of HTTP requests to suitable handlers based on request paths (e.g., `/foo`) and HTTP methods (e.g., `POST`). This is illustrated in figure 8.2.

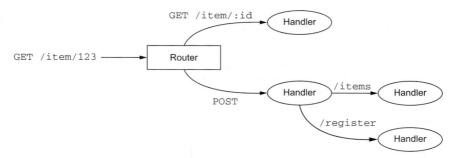

Figure 8.2   Routing HTTP requests

The following listing shows how to initialize and then set up a router as an HTTP request handler.

Listing 8.1   Initializing and using a router as an HTTP request handler

```
Router router = Router.router(vertx);
// (...)                          ◁──────── Define routes

vertx.createHttpServer()
  .requestHandler(router)         ◁──────── A router is just another
  .listen(8080);                            HTTP request handler.
```

The `Router` class provides a fluent API to describe routes based on HTTP methods and paths, as shown in the following listing.

Listing 8.2   Defining routes

BodyHandler is a predefined handler that extracts HTTP request body payloads.

Here bodyHandler is called for all HTTP POST and PUT requests.

```
BodyHandler bodyHandler = BodyHandler.create();
router.post().handler(bodyHandler);     ◁
router.put().handler(bodyHandler);

String prefix = "/api/v1";

router.post(prefix + "/register").handler(this::register);   ◁
router.post(prefix + "/token").handler(this::token);
// (...) defines jwtHandler, more later

router.get(prefix + "/:username/:year/:month")   ◁
  .handler(jwtHandler)          ◁
  .handler(this::checkUser)          Handlers can be chained.
  .handler(this::monthlySteps);
// (...)
```

The register method handles /api/v1/register POST requests.

We can extract path parameters by prefixing elements with ":".

An interesting property of the Vert.x router is that handlers can be chained. With the definitions from listing 8.2, a POST request to /api/v1/register first goes through a

`BodyHandler` instance. This handler is useful for easily decoding an HTTP request body payload. The next handler is the `register` method.

Listing 8.2 also defines the route for GET requests to `monthlySteps`, where the request first goes through `jwtHandler`, and then `checkUser`, as illustrated in figure 8.3. This is useful for decomposing an HTTP request, processing concerns in several steps: `jwtHandler` checks that a valid JWT token is in the request, `checkUser` checks that the JWT token grants permissions to access the resource, and `monthlySteps` checks how many steps a user has taken in a month.

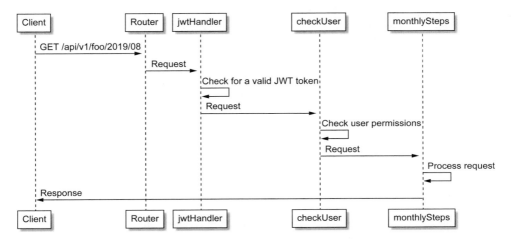

Figure 8.3   Routing chain for the monthly steps endpoint

Note that both `checkUser` and `jwtHandler` will be discussed in section 8.2.

> **TIP** The `io.vertx.ext.web.handler` package contains useful utility handlers including `BodyHandler`. It especially provides handlers for HTTP authentication, CORS, CSRF, favicon, HTTP sessions, static files serving, virtual hosts, and template rendering.

8.1.2   Making HTTP requests

Let's now dive into the implementation of a handler. Since the public API service forwards requests to the user profile and activity services, we need to use the Vert.x web client to make HTTP requests. As noted previously, the Vert.x core APIs offer a low-level HTTP client, whereas the `WebClient` class from the `vertx-web-client` module offers a richer API.

Creating a web client instance is as simple as this:

```
WebClient webClient = WebClient.create(vertx);
```

A `WebClient` instance is typically stored in a private field of a verticle class, as it can be used to perform multiple concurrent HTTP requests. The whole application uses the RxJava 2 bindings, so we can take advantage of them to compose asynchronous operations. As you will see in later examples, the RxJava bindings sometimes bring additional functionality for dealing with error management.

The following listing shows the implementation of the `register` route handler.

Listing 8.3   Using the Vert.x web client in a route handler

Methods match the HTTP methods (GET, POST, etc.).

HTTP headers can be passed.

This converts the request from a Vert.x Buffer to a JsonObject.

Subscription in RxJava triggers the request.

```
private void register(RoutingContext ctx) {
  webClient
    .post(3000, "localhost", "/register")
    .putHeader("Content-Type", "application/json")
    .rxSendJson(ctx.getBodyAsJson())
    .subscribe(
      response -> sendStatusCode(ctx, response.statusCode()),
      err -> sendBadGateway(ctx, err));
}

private void sendStatusCode(RoutingContext ctx, int code) {
  ctx.response().setStatusCode(code).end();
}

private void sendBadGateway(RoutingContext ctx, Throwable err) {
  logger.error("Woops", err);
  ctx.fail(502);
}
```

This example demonstrates both how to handle an HTTP request with a router, and how to use the web client. The `RoutingContext` class encapsulates details about the HTTP request and provides the HTTP response object via the `response` method. HTTP headers can be set in both requests and responses, and the response is sent once the `end` method has been called. A status code can be specified, although by default it will be `200` (OK).

You can see that `getBodyAsJson` transforms the HTTP request body to a `Json-Object`, while `rxSendJson` sends an HTTP request with a `JsonObject` as the body. By default, Vert.x `Buffer` objects carry bodies in both requests and responses, but there are helper methods to convert from or to `String`, `JsonObject`, and `JsonArray`.

The next listing offers another router handler method for HTTP `GET` requests to `/api/v1/:username`, where `:username` is a path parameter.

Listing 8.4   Fetching and forwarding a user's details

Extracts a path parameter

```
private void fetchUser(RoutingContext ctx) {
  webClient
    .get(3000, "localhost", "/" + ctx.pathParam("username"))
```

```
      .as(BodyCodec.jsonObject())        ◁──┐  Converts the response
      .rxSend()                             │  to a JsonObject
      .subscribe(
        resp -> forwardJsonOrStatusCode(ctx, resp),
        err -> sendBadGateway(ctx, err));
}

private void forwardJsonOrStatusCode(RoutingContext ctx,
⇒ HttpResponse<JsonObject> resp) {
  if (resp.statusCode() != 200) {
    sendStatusCode(ctx, resp.statusCode());
  } else {
    ctx.response()
      .putHeader("Content-Type", "application/json")
      .end(resp.body().encode());        ◁──┐
  }                                          │  Ends the response with some content
}
```

This example shows the as method that converts HTTP responses to a type other than
Buffer using a BodyCodec. You can also see that the HTTP response's end method can
take an argument that is the response content. It can be a String or a Buffer. While it
is often the case that the response is sent in a single end method call, you can send
intermediary fragments using the write method until a final end call closes the HTTP
response, as shown here:

```
response.write("hello").write(" world").end();
```

8.2   *Access control with JWT tokens*

JSON Web Token (JWT) is an open specification for securely transmitting JSON-
encoded data between parties (https://tools.ietf.org/html/rfc7519). JWT tokens are
signed with either a symmetric shared secret or an asymmetric public/private key pair,
so it is always possible to verify that the information that they contain has not been
modified. This is very interesting, as a JWT token can be used to hold claims such as
identity and authorization grants. JWT tokens can be exchanged as part of HTTP
requests using the Authorization HTTP header.

Let's look at how to use JWT tokens, what data they contain, and how to both vali-
date and issue them with Vert.x.

> **TIP** JWT is only one protocol supported by Vert.x. Vert.x offers the vertx-
> auth-oauth2 module for OAuth2, which is a popular protocol among public
> service providers like Google, GitHub, and Twitter. You will be interested in
> using it if your application needs to integrate with such services (such as when
> accessing a user's Gmail account data), or when your application wants to
> grant third-party access through OAuth2.

8.2.1 *Using JWT tokens*

To illustrate using JWT tokens, let's interact with the public API and authenticate as
user `foo` with password `123`, and get a JWT token. The following listing shows the
HTTP response.

Listing 8.5   Getting a JWT token

```
$ http :4000/api/v1/token username=foo password=123      ◁
HTTP/1.1 200 OK                                                Authenticating as user
Content-Type: application/jwt                                  foo with password 123
content-length: 496
```

```
eyJ0eXAiOiJKV1QiLCJhbGciOiJSUzI1NiJ9.eyJkZXZpY2VJZCI6ImExYjIiLCJpYXQiOjE1NjUx
Njc0NzUsImV4cCI6MTU2NTc3MjI3NSwiaXNzIjoiMTBrLXN0ZXBzLWFwaSIsInN1YiI6ImZvb
yJ9.J_tn2BjMNYE6eFSHwSJ9e8DoCEUr_xMSlYAyBSy1-E_pouvDq4lp8QjG51cJoa5Gbrt1bg
tDHinJsLncG1RIsGr_cz1rQw8_GlI_-GdhqFBw8dVjlsgykSf5tfaiiRwORmz7VH_AAk-935aV
1xMg4mxkbOvN4YDxRLhLb4Y78TA47F__ivNsM4gLD8CHzOUmTEta_pjpZGzsErmYvzDOV6F7rO
ZcRhZThJxLvR3zskrtx83iaNHTwph53bkHNOQzC66wxNMar_T4HMRWzqnnr-sFIcOwLFsWJKow
c1rQuadjv-ew541YQLaVmkEcai6leZLwCfCTcsxMX9rt0AmOFg
```

A JWT token has the MIME type `application/jwt`, which is plain text. We can pass
the token to make a request as follows.

Listing 8.6   Using a JWT token to access a resource

```
http :4000/api/v1/foo Authorization:'Bearer
eyJ0eXAiOiJKV1QiLCJhbGciOiJSUzI1NiJ9.eyJkZXZpY2VJZCI6ImExYjIiLCJpYXQiOjE1NjUx
Njc0NzUsImV4cCI6MTU2NTc3MjI3NSwiaXNzIjoiMTBrLXN0ZXBzLWFwaSIsInN1YiI6ImZvb
yJ9.J_tn2BjMNYE6eFSHwSJ9e8DoCEUr_xMSlYAyBSy1-E_pouvDq4lp8QjG51cJoa5Gbrt1bg
tDHinJsLncG1RIsGr_cz1rQw8_GlI_-GdhqFBw8dVjlsgykSf5tfaiiRwORmz7VH_AAk-935a
V1xMg4mxkbOvN4YDxRLhLb4Y78TA47F__ivNsM4gLD8CHzOUmTEta_pjpZGzsErmYvzDOV6F7
rOZcRhZThJxLvR3zskrtx83iaNHTwph53bkHNOQzC66wxNMar_T4HMRWzqnnr-sFIcOwLFsWJK
owc1rQuadjv-ew541YQLaVmkEcai6leZLwCfCTcsxMX9rt0AmOFg'
```

```
HTTP/1.1 200 OK                ◁
Content-Type: application/json      We can access the resource, because
content-length: 90                  we have a valid token for user foo.

{
    "city": "Lyon",
    "deviceId": "a1b2",
    "email": "foo@bar.com",
    "makePublic": true,
    "username": "foo"
}
```

TIP The token value fits on a single line, and there is only a single space
between `Bearer` and the token.

The token is passed with the `Authorization` HTTP header, and the value is prefixed
with `Bearer`. Here the token allows us to access the resource `/api/v1/foo`, since the

token was generated for user `foo`. If we try to do the same thing without a token, or if we try to access the resource of another user, as in the following listing, we get denied.

> **Listing 8.7 Accessing a resource without a matching JWT token**

```
http :4000/api/v1/abc Authorization:'Bearer
eyJ0eXAiOiJKV1QiLCJhbGciOiJSUzI1NiJ9.eyJkZXZpY2VJZCI6ImExYjIiLCJpYXQiOjE1NjUx
  Njc0NzUsImV4cCI6MTU2NTc3MjI3NSwiaXNzIjoiMTBrLXN0ZXBzLWFwaSIsInN1YiI6ImZv
  yJ9.J_tn2BjMNYE6eFSHwSJ9e8DoCEUr_xMS1YAyBSy1-E_pouvDq4lp8QjG51cJoa5Gbrt1b
  gtDHinJsLncG1RIsGr_cz1rQw8_GlI_-GdhqFBw8dVjlsgykSf5tfaiiRwORmz7VH_AAk-935
  aV1xMg4mxkbOvN4YDxRLhLb4Y78TA47F__ivNsM4gLD8CHzOUmTEta_pjpZGzsErmYvzDOV6F
  7rOZcRhZThJxLvR3zskrtx83iaNHTwph53bkHNOQzC66wxNMar_T4HMRWzqnrr-sFIcOwLFsW
  JKowc1rQuadjv-ew541YQLaVmkEcai6leZLwCfCTcsxMX9rt0AmOFg'
HTTP/1.1 403 Forbidden              ◁──────┐
content-length: 0                          │  We are denied access to a resource of
                                           │  user abc because we passed a (valid)
                                           │  token for user foo.
```

8.2.2 What is in a JWT token?

So far so good, but what is in the token string?

If you look closely, you will see that a JWT token string is a big line with three parts, each separated by a dot. The three parts are of the form `header.payload.signature`:

- `header` is a JSON document specifying the type of token and the signature algorithm being used.
- `payload` is a JSON document containing *claims*, which are JSON entries where some are part of the specification and some can be free-form.
- `signature` is the signature of the header and payload with either a shared secret or a private key, depending on what algorithm you chose.

The header and payload are encoded with the Base64 algorithm. If you decode the JWT token obtained in listing 8.5, the header contains the following:

```
{
  "typ": "JWT",
  "alg": "RS256"
}
```

This is what the payload contains:

```
{
  "deviceId": "a1b2",
  "iat": 1565167475,
  "exp": 1565772275,
  "iss": "10k-steps-api",
  "sub": "foo"
}
```

Here, `deviceId` is the device identifier for user `foo`, `sub` is the subject (user `foo`), `iat` is the date when the token was issued, `exp` is the token expiration date, and `iss` is the token issuer (our service).

The signature allows you to check that the content of both the header and payload have been signed by the issuer and have not been modified, as long as you know the public key. This makes JWT tokens a great option for authorization and access control in APIs; a token with all needed claims is self-contained and does not require you to make checks for each request against an identity management service like an LDAP/OAuth server.

It is important to understand that anyone with a JWT token can decode its content, because Base64 is not an encryption algorithm. You must never put sensitive data like passwords in tokens, even if they are transmitted over secure channels like HTTPS. It is also important to set token expiration dates, so that a compromised token cannot be used indefinitely. There are various strategies for dealing with JWT token expiration, like maintaining a list of compromised tokens in the backend, and combining short expiration deadlines with frequent validity extension requests from clients, where the issuer resends the token, but with an extended exp claim.

8.2.3   *Handling JWT tokens with Vert.x*

The first thing we need in order to issue and check tokens is a pair of public and private RSA keys, so we can sign JWT tokens. You can generate these using the shell script in the following listing.

Listing 8.8   Generating RSA 2048 public and private keys

```
#!/bin/bash
openssl genrsa -out private.pem 2048
openssl pkcs8 -topk8 -inform PEM -in private.pem -out
➥ private_key.pem -nocrypt
openssl rsa -in private.pem -outform PEM -pubout -out public_key.pem
```

The next listing shows a helper class to read the PEM files as a string.

Listing 8.9   Helper to read RSA keys

```
class CryptoHelper {

  static String publicKey() throws IOException {
    return read("public_key.pem");
  }

  static String privateKey() throws IOException {
    return read("private_key.pem");
  }

  private static String read(String file) throws IOException {
    Path path = Paths.get("public-api", file);
    if (!path.toFile().exists()) {
      path = Paths.get("..", "public-api", file);
    }
    return String.join("\n", Files.readAllLines(path, StandardCharsets.UTF_8));
  }
}
```

This allows us to run the service from either the service folder or the application project root.

Joins all lines, separating them with a newline character

Note that the code in `CryptoHelper` uses blocking APIs. Since this code is run once at initialization, and PEM files are small, we can afford a possible yet negligible blocking of the event loop.

We can then create a Vert.x JWT handler as follows.

Listing 8.10 Creating a JWT handler

```
String publicKey = CryptoHelper.publicKey();
String privateKey = CryptoHelper.privateKey();

jwtAuth = JWTAuth.create(vertx, new JWTAuthOptions()      ◁─┤ jwtAuth is a private
  .addPubSecKey(new PubSecKeyOptions()                         field of type JWTAuth.
    .setAlgorithm("RS256")
    .setBuffer(publicKey))
  .addPubSecKey(new PubSecKeyOptions()
    .setAlgorithm("RS256")                           Vert.x router handler for
    .setBuffer(privateKey)));                          JWT authentication

JWTAuthHandler jwtHandler = JWTAuthHandler.create(jwtAuth);      ◁─┘
```

The JWT handler can be used for routes that require JWT authentication, as it decodes the `Authorization` header to extract JWT data.

The following listing recalls a route with the handler in its handlers chain.

Listing 8.11 JWT handler in a route

```
router.get(prefix + "/:username/:year/:month")
  .handler(jwtHandler)              ◁──┐
  .handler(this::checkUser)            │ The JWT handler
  .handler(this::monthlySteps);
```

The JWT handler supports the common authentication API from the `vertx-auth-common` module, which offers a unified view across different types of authentication mechanisms like databases, OAuth, or Apache `.htdigest` files. The handler puts authentication data in the routing context.

The following listing shows the implementation of the `checkUser` method where we check that the user in the JWT token is the same as the one in the HTTP request path.

Listing 8.12 Checking that a valid JWT token is present

```
private void checkUser(RoutingContext ctx) {
  String subject = ctx.user().principal().getString("sub");    ◁─┐ User name
  if (!ctx.pathParam("username").equals(subject)) {   ◁─┐          from the
    sendStatusCode(ctx, 403);                            │          JWT token
  } else {                              User name specified in
    ctx.next();    ◁─┐                  the HTTP request path
  }                  │ Pass to the
}                    │ next handler
}
```

This provides a simple separation of concerns, as the `checkUser` handler focuses on access control and delegates to the next handler in the chain by calling `next` if access is granted, or ends the request with a 403 status code if the wrong user is trying to access a resource.

Knowing that access control is correct, the `monthlySteps` method in the following listing can focus on making the request to the activity service.

Listing 8.13   Getting monthly steps data

```
private void monthlySteps(RoutingContext ctx) {
  String deviceId = ctx.user().principal().getString("deviceId");   ◁┐  From the
  String year = ctx.pathParam("year");                                 │  JWT token
  String month = ctx.pathParam("month");
  webClient
    .get(3001, "localhost", "/" + deviceId + "/" + year + "/" + month)
    .as(BodyCodec.jsonObject())
    .rxSend()
    .subscribe(
      resp -> forwardJsonOrStatusCode(ctx, resp),
      err -> sendBadGateway(ctx, err));
}
```

The device identifier is extracted from the JWT token data and passed along to the web client request.

8.2.4   *Issuing JWT tokens with Vert.x*

Last, but not least, we need to generate JWT tokens. To do that, we need to make two requests to the user profile service: first we need to check the credentials, and then we gather profile data to prepare a token.

The following listing shows the handler for the `/api/v1/token` route.

Listing 8.14   JWT token-creation router handler

```
private void token(RoutingContext ctx) {
  JsonObject payload = ctx.getBodyAsJson();              ◁┐  We extract the
  String username = payload.getString("username");         │  credentials from the
  webClient                                                │  request to /api/v1/token.
    .post(3000, "localhost", "/authenticate")     ◁┐  We first issue an
    .expect(ResponsePredicate.SC_SUCCESS)            │  authentication request.
    .rxSendJson(payload)
    .flatMap(resp -> fetchUserDetails(username))    ◁┐  On success, we make
    .map(resp -> resp.body().getString("deviceId"))    │  another request to get
    .map(deviceId -> makeJwtToken(username, deviceId)) ◁┘ the profile data.
    .subscribe(
      token -> sendToken(ctx, token),     We prepare the token.
      err -> handleAuthError(ctx, err));
}

private void sendToken(RoutingContext ctx, String token) {
```

```
    ctx.response().putHeader("Content-Type", "application/jwt").end(token);
}

private void handleAuthError(RoutingContext ctx, Throwable err) {
  logger.error("Authentication error", err);
  ctx.fail(401);
}
```

This is a typical RxJava composition of asynchronous operations with flatMap to chain requests. You can also see the declarative API of the Vert.x router, where we can specify that we expect the first request to be a success.

The following listing shows the implementation of fetchUserDetails, which gets the user profile data after the authentication request has succeeded.

Listing 8.15 Fetching user details

```
private Single<HttpResponse<JsonObject>> fetchUserDetails(String username) {
  return webClient
    .get(3000, "localhost", "/" + username)
    .expect(ResponsePredicate.SC_OK)          <──── We expect a success.
    .as(BodyCodec.jsonObject())
    .rxSend();
}
```

Finally, the next listing shows how to prepare a JWT token.

Listing 8.16 Preparing a JWT token

```
private String makeJwtToken(String username, String deviceId) {
  JsonObject claims = new JsonObject()       <─┐
    .put("deviceId", deviceId);                 │ Our custom claims
  JWTOptions jwtOptions = new JWTOptions()
    .setAlgorithm("RS256")
    .setExpiresInMinutes(10_080) // 7 days
    .setIssuer("10k-steps-api")            <─┐  A claim that is in the
    .setSubject(username);                    │  JWT specification
  return jwtAuth.generateToken(claims, jwtOptions);
}
```

The JWTOptions class offers methods for the common claims from the JWT RFC, such as the issuer, expiration date, and subject. You can see that we did not specify when the token was issued, although there is a method for that in JWTOptions. The jwtAuth object does the right thing here and adds it on our behalf.

8.3   Cross-origin resource sharing (CORS)

We have a public API that forwards requests to internal services, and this API uses JWT tokens for authentication and access control. I also demonstrated on the command line that we can interact with the API. In fact, *any* third-party application can talk to our API over HTTP: a mobile phone application, another service, a desktop application, and so on. You might think that web applications could also talk to the API from JavaScript code running in web browsers, but it is (fortunately!) not that simple.

8.3.1   What is the problem?

Web browsers enforce security policies, and among them is the *same-origin policy*. Suppose we load app.js from https://my.tld:4000/js/app.js:

- app.js is allowed to make requests to https://my.tld:4000/api/foo/bar.
- app.js is not allowed to make requests to https://my.tld:4001/a/b/c because a different port is not the same origin.
- app.js is not allowed to make requests to https://other.tld/123 because a different host is not the same origin.

Cross-origin resource sharing (CORS) is a mechanism by which a service can allow incoming requests from other origins (https://fetch.spec.whatwg.org/). For instance, the service exposing https://other.tld/123 can specify that cross-origin requests are allowed from code served from https://my.tld:4000, or even from *any* origin. This allows web browsers to proceed with a cross-origin request when the request origin allows it; otherwise it will deny it, which is the default behavior.

When a cross-origin request is triggered, such as to load some JSON data, an image, or a web font, the web browser sends a request to the server with the requested resource, and passes an `Origin` HTTP header. The server then responds with an `Access-Control-Allow-Origin` HTTP header with the allowed origin, as illustrated in figure 8.4.

A value of `"*"` means that any origin can access the resource, whereas a value like `https://my.tld` means that only cross-origin requests from https://my.tld are allowed. In figure 8.4, the request succeeds with the JSON payload, but if the CORS policy forbids the call, the app.js code would get an error while attempting to make a cross-origin request.

Depending on the type of cross-origin HTTP request, web browsers do *simple* or *preflighted* requests. The request in figure 8.4 is a simple one. By contrast, a `PUT` request

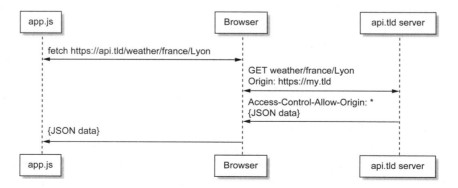

Figure 8.4   Example CORS interaction

would need a preflighted request, as it can potentially have side effects (PUT implies modifying a resource), so a preflight OPTIONS HTTP request to the resource must be made to check what the CORS policy is, followed by the actual PUT request when allowed. Preflighted requests provide more detail, such as the allowed HTTP headers and methods, because a server can, for example, have a CORS policy of forbidding doing DELETE requests or having an ABC header in the HTTP request. I recommend reading Mozilla's "Cross-Origin Resource Sharing (CORS)" document (http://mng .bz/X0Z6), as it provides a detailed and approachable explanation of the interactions between browsers and servers with CORS.

8.3.2 Supporting CORS with Vert.x

Vert.x comes with a ready-to-use CORS handler with the CorsHandler class. Creating a CorsHandler instance requires three settings:

- The allowed origin pattern
- The allowed HTTP headers
- The allowed HTTP methods

The following listing shows how to install CORS support in a Vert.x router.

Listing 8.17 Installing CORS support in a router

```
Set<String> allowedHeaders = new HashSet<>();         ◁──┐  The set of allowed
allowedHeaders.add("x-requested-with");                   │  HTTP headers
allowedHeaders.add("Access-Control-Allow-Origin");
allowedHeaders.add("origin");
allowedHeaders.add("Content-Type");
allowedHeaders.add("accept");
allowedHeaders.add("Authorization");

Set<HttpMethod> allowedMethods = new HashSet<>();     ◁──┐  The set of allowed
allowedMethods.add(HttpMethod.GET);                       │  HTTP methods
allowedMethods.add(HttpMethod.POST);
allowedMethods.add(HttpMethod.OPTIONS);
allowedMethods.add(HttpMethod.PUT);

router.route().handler(CorsHandler         ◁──┐  A CORS handler
  .create("*")                                 │  for all origins
  .allowedHeaders(allowedHeaders)
  .allowedMethods(allowedMethods));
```

The HTTP methods are those supported in our API. You can see that we don't support DELETE, for instance. The CORS handler has been installed for all routes, since they are all part of the API and should be accessible from any kind of application, including web browsers. The allowed headers should match what your API needs, and also what clients may pass, like specifying a content type, or headers that could be injected by proxies and for distributed tracing purposes.

We can check that CORS is properly supported by making an HTTP `OPTIONS` pre-flight request to one of the routes supported by the API.

> **Listing 8.18   Checking CORS support**

```
$ http OPTIONS :4000/api/v1/token Origin:'http://foo.tld'
HTTP/1.1 405 Method Not Allowed
access-control-allow-origin: *
content-length: 0
```

By specifying an `origin` HTTP header, the CORS handler inserts an `access-control-allow-origin` HTTP header in the response. The HTTP status code is 405, since the `OPTION` HTTP method is not supported by the specific route, but this is not an issue as web browsers are only interested in the CORS-related headers when they do a pre-flight request.

8.4   *A modern web frontend*

We have discussed the interesting points in the public API: how to make HTTP requests with the Vert.x web client, how to use JWT tokens, and how to enable CORS support. It is now time to see how we can expose the user web application (defined in chapter 7), and how that application can connect to the public API.

The application is written with the Vue.js JavaScript framework. Vert.x is used to serve the application's compiled assets: HTML, CSS, and JavaScript.

The corresponding source code is located in the part2-steps-challenge/user-webapp folder of the book's source code repository.

8.4.1   *Vue.js*

Vue.js deserves a book by itself, and we recommend that you read Erik Hanchett and Benjamin Listwon's *Vue.js in Action* (Manning, 2018) if you are interested in learning this framework. I'll provide a quick overview here, since we're using Vue.js as the JavaScript framework for the two web applications developed as part of the larger 10k steps application.

Vue.js is a modern JavaScript frontend framework, like React or Angular, for building modern web applications, including single-page applications. It is *reactive* as changes in a component model trigger changes in the user interface. Suppose that we display a temperature in a web page. When the corresponding data changes, the temperature is updated, and Vue.js takes care of (most) of the plumbing for doing that.

Vue.js supports components, where an HTML template, CSS styling, and JavaScript code can be grouped together, as in the following listing.

> **Listing 8.19   Canvas of a Vue.js component**

```
<template>
  <div id="app">
    {{ hello }}          ◁──┐ Replaced by the value
                            │ of the hello property
```

```
      </div>
</template>
                               CSS rules local to
<style scoped>        ◁────┘    the component
   div {
      border: solid 1px black;
   }
</style>

<script>
   export default {
      data() {
         return {                    The initial definition
            hello: "Hello, world!"  ◁────┘ of the hello property
         }
      }
   }
</script>
```

A Vue.js project can be created using the Vue.js command-line interface (https://cli
.vuejs.org/):

```
$ vue create user-webapp
```

The yarn build tool can then be used to install dependencies (yarn install), serve the
project for development with automatic live-reload (yarn run serve), and build a production version of the project HTML, CSS, and JavaScript assets (yarn run build).

8.4.2 *Vue.js application structure and build integration*

The user web application is a single-page application with three different screens: a
login form, a page with user details, and a registration form.

The key Vue.js files are the following:

- src/main.js—The entry point
- src/router.js—The Vue.js router that dispatches to the components of the three
  different screens
- src/DataStore.js—An object to hold the application store using the web
  browser local storage API, shared among all screens
- src/App.vue—The main component that mounts the Vue.js router
- src/views—Contains the three screen components: Home.vue, Login.vue, and
  Register.vue

The Vue.js router configuration is shown in the following listing.

Listing 8.20   Vue.js router configuration

```
import Vue from 'vue'
import Router from 'vue-router'
import Home from './views/Home.vue'
```

```
import Login from './views/Login.vue'
import Register from './views/Register.vue'

Vue.use(Router)

export default new Router({
  routes: [
    {
      path: '/',          ⟵──── Component path
      name: 'home',
      component: Home      ⟵──── Component reference
    },
    {
      path: '/login',
      name: 'login',
      component: Login
    },
    {
      path: '/register',
      name: 'register',
      component: Register
    },
  ]
})
```

Component name (label pointing to `name: 'home'`)

The application code is colocated in the same module as the Vert.x application that serves the user web application, so you will find the usual Java source files under src/main/java and a Gradle build.gradle.kts file. The Vue.js compiled assets (yarn build) must be copied to src/main/resources/webroot/assets for the Vert.x-based service to serve them.

This makes for two build tools in a single project, and fortunately they can coexist peacefully. In fact, it is very easy to call yarn from Gradle, as the com.moowork.node Gradle plugin provides a self-contained Node environment. The following listing shows the Node-related configuration of the user web application Gradle build file.

Listing 8.21   Using the com.moowork.node Gradle plugin

Uses the Node plugin · **Creates a task to call yarn** · **Adds a dependency on running yarn install first**

```
import com.moowork.gradle.node.yarn.YarnTask
apply(plugin = "com.moowork.node")
tasks.register<YarnTask>("buildVueApp") {
  dependsOn("yarn_install")
  // (...)
  args = listOf("build")
}
tasks.register<Copy>("copyVueDist") {
  dependsOn("buildVueApp")
  from("$projectDir/dist")
  into("$projectDir/src/main/resources/webroot/assets")
}
```

Gradle caching instructions that you can find in the full source code

Calls yarn build

Task to copy the compiled assets

```
val processResources by tasks.named("processResources") {
    dependsOn("copyVueDist")
}
val clean by tasks.named<Delete>("clean") {
    delete("$projectDir/dist")
    delete("$projectDir/src/main/resources/webroot/assets")
}
// (...)
```

Make sure building the project also builds the Vue.js application.

Extra clean task to be done for the Vue.js compiled assets

The buildVueApp and copyVueDist tasks are inserted as part of the regular project build tasks, so the project builds both the Java Vert.x code and the Vue.js code. We also customize the clean task to remove the generated assets.

8.4.3 Backend integration illustrated

Let's look at one of the Vue.js components: the login screen shown in figure 8.5.

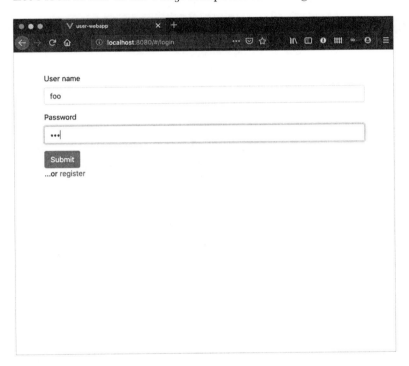

Figure 8.5 Screenshot of the login screen

The file for this component is src/views/Login.vue. The component shows the login form, and when submitted it must call the public API to get a JWT token. On success, it must store the JWT token locally and then switch the view to the home component. On error, it must stay on the login form and display an error message.

The HTML template part of the component is shown in the following listing.

Listing 8.22   Login component HTML template

```
<template>
  <div>
    <div class="alert alert-danger" role="alert"
    ➥ v-if="alertMessage.length > 0">
      {{ alertMessage }}
    </div>
    <form v-on:submit="login">
      <div class="form-group">
        <label for="username">User name</label>
        <input type="username" class="form-control" id="username"
        ➥ placeholder="somebody123" v-model="username">
      </div>
      <div class="form-group">
        <label for="password">Password</label>
        <input type="password" class="form-
  control" id="password" placeholder="abc123" v-model="password">
      </div>
      <button type="submit" class="btn btn-primary">Submit</button>
    </form>
    <div>
      <p>...or <router-link to="/register">register</router-link></p>
    </div>
  </div>
</template>
```

Conditionally display the div block depending on the value of the alertMessage component data.

Template syntax to render the value of alertMessage

Call the login method on form submit.

v-model binds the field value to the username component data.

<router-link> allows linking to another component.

The JavaScript part of the component provides the component data declaration as well as the `login` method implementation. We use the Axios JavaScript library to make HTTP client calls to the public API. The following listing provides the component JavaScript code.

Listing 8.23   Login component JavaScript code

```
import DataStore from '../DataStore'
import axios from 'axios'

export default {
  data() {
    return {
      username: '',
      password: '',
      alertMessage: ''
    }
  },
  methods: {
    login: function () {
      if (this.username.length === 0 || this.password.length === 0) {
        return
      }
```

Component data declaration

Component methods declaration

If either of the fields is empty, there is no point in trying to authenticate against the public API.

```
      axios                                              Issue an
        .post("http://localhost:4000/api/v1/token", {   authentication
          username: this.username,                       request with the
          password: this.password                        credentials as a
        })                                               JSON payload.
Tell the   .then(response => {
router to    DataStore.setToken(response.data)           In case of success, store
change       DataStore.setUsername(this.username)        the token and username
component.   this.$router.push({name: 'home'})           from the response.
        })
        .catch(err => this.alertMessage = err.message)
      }
    }
  }
```

Triggers the error message to be reactively
displayed when the value of alertMessage changes

The component data properties are updated as the user types text in the username and password fields, and the `login` method is called on form submit. If the call succeeds, the application moves to the `home` component.

The next listing is from the code of the Home.vue component, and it shows how you can use the JWT token to fetch the user's total number of steps.

Listing 8.24 Using the JWT token with Axios

```
axios
  .get(`http://localhost:4000/api/v1/${DataStore.username()}/total`, {
    headers: {
      'Authorization': `Bearer ${DataStore.token()}`       Pass the token from
    }                                                       the value fetched by
  })                                                        the login component.
  .then(response => this.totalSteps = response.data.count)
  .catch(err => {                              Update the component data,
    if (err.response.status === 404) {         triggering a view refresh.
      this.totalSteps = 0
    } else {
      this.alertMessage = err.message
    }
  })
```

Let's now see how we can serve the web application assets with Vert.x.

8.4.4 Static content serving with Vert.x

The Vert.x code does not have much to do beyond starting an HTTP server and serving static content. The following listing shows the content of the `rxStart` method of the `UserWebAppVerticle` class.

Listing 8.25 Serving static content with Vert.x

```
@Override
public Completable rxStart() {
  Router router = Router.router(vertx);
```

```
router.route().handler(StaticHandler.create("webroot/assets"));
router.get("/*").handler(ctx -> ctx.reroute("/index.html"));

return vertx.createHttpServer()
  .requestHandler(router)
  .rxListen(HTTP_PORT)
  .ignoreElement();
}
```

Alias /* to /index.html.

Resolve static content against webroot/assets in the classpath.

The StaticHandler caches files in memory, unless configured otherwise in the call to the create method. Disabling caching is useful in development mode, because you can modify static assets' content and see changes by reloading in a web browser without having to restart the Vert.x server. By default, static files are resolved from the webroot folder in the classpath, but you can override it as we did by specifying webroot/assets.

Now that we've discussed how to use the Vert.x web stack, it is time to focus on testing the services that compose the reactive application.

8.5   *Writing integration tests*

Testing is a very important concern, especially as there are multiple services involved in the making of the 10k steps challenge reactive application. There is no point in testing that the user web application service delivers static content properly, but it is crucial to have tests covering interactions with the public API service. Let's discuss how to write integration tests for this service.

The public API source code reveals an IntegrationTest class. It contains several ordered test methods that check the API behavior:

1 Register some users.
2 Get a JWT token for each user.
3 Fetch a user's data.
4 Try to fetch the data of another user.
5 Update a user's data.
6 Check some activity stats for a user.
7 Try to check the activity of another user.

Since the public API service depends on the activity and user profile services, we either need to mock them with *fake* services that we run during the tests' execution, or deploy them along with all their dependencies, like databases. Either approach is fine. In the chapters in this part we will sometimes create a fake service for running our integration tests, and sometimes we will just deploy the real services.

In this case, we are going to deploy the real services, and we need to make this from JUnit 5 in a self-contained and reproducible manner. We first need to add the project dependencies, as in the following listing.

Listing 8.26 Test dependencies to run the integration tests

Dependency on another project module

This is used to insert data in PostgreSQL. More on that later.

```
testImplementation(project(":user-profile-service"))
testImplementation(project(":activity-service"))
testImplementation("io.vertx:vertx-pg-client:$vertxVersion")
testImplementation("org.testcontainers:junit-jupiter:$testContainersVersion")

testImplementation("org.junit.jupiter:junit-jupiter-api:$junit5Version")
testImplementation("io.vertx:vertx-junit5:$vertxVersion")
testImplementation("io.vertx:vertx-junit5-rx-java2:$vertxVersion")
testImplementation("io.rest-assured:rest-assured:$restAssuredVersion")
testImplementation("org.assertj:assertj-core:$assertjVersion")
```

A nice DSL library for testing HTTP services

This is to run Docker containers.

These dependencies bring us two useful tools for writing tests:

- Testcontainers is a project for running Docker containers in JUnit tests, so we will be able to use infrastructure services like PostgreSQL or Kafka (www.test containers.org).
- REST Assured is a library focusing on testing HTTP services, providing a convenient fluent API for describing requests and response assertions (http://rest-assured.io).

The preamble of the test class is shown in the following listing.

Listing 8.27 Preamble of the integration test class

Use the Vert.x JUnit 5 support.

Test methods must be run in order.

```
@ExtendWith(VertxExtension.class)
@TestMethodOrder(OrderAnnotation.class)
@TestInstance(TestInstance.Lifecycle.PER_CLASS)
@DisplayName("Integration tests for the public API")
@Testcontainers
class IntegrationTest {

  @Container
  private static final DockerComposeContainer CONTAINERS =
    new DockerComposeContainer(new File("../docker-compose.yml"));

  // (...)
}
```

Use Testcontainers support.

Start containers from a Docker Compose file.

Testcontainers gives lots of choices for starting one or many containers. It supports generic Docker images, specialized classes for common infrastructure (PostgreSQL, Apache Kafka, etc.), and Docker Compose. Here we reuse the Docker Compose descriptor for running the whole application (docker-compose.yml), and the containers described in the file are started before the first test is run. The containers are destroyed when all tests have executed. This is very interesting—we get to write integration tests against the real infrastructure services that would be used in production.

The `prepareSpec` method is annotated with `@BeforeAll` and is used to prepare the tests. It inserts some data in the PostgreSQL database for the activity service and then deploys the user profile and activity verticles. It also prepares a `RequestSpecification` object from REST Assured, as follows.

> **Listing 8.28 Preparing a REST Assured request specification**

All requests and responses will be logged, which is useful for tracking errors.

```
requestSpecification = new RequestSpecBuilder()
    .addFilters(asList(new ResponseLoggingFilter(), new RequestLoggingFilter()))
    .setBaseUri("http://localhost:4000/")
    .setBasePath("/api/v1")
    .build();
```

This avoids repeating the base path of all URLs in requests.

This object is shared among all tests methods, as they all have to make requests to the API. We enable logging of all requests and responses for easier debugging, and we set `/api/v1` as the base path for all requests.

The test class maintains a hash map of users to register and later use in calls, as well as a hash map of JWT tokens.

> **Listing 8.29 Utility hash maps for the integration test**

```
private final HashMap<String, JsonObject> registrations = new
    HashMap<String, JsonObject>() {
  {
    put("Foo", new JsonObject()
      .put("username", "Foo")
      .put("password", "foo-123")
      .put("email", "foo@email.me")
      .put("city", "Lyon")
      .put("deviceId", "a1b2c3")
      .put("makePublic", true));
    // (...)
  }
};

private final HashMap<String, String> tokens = new HashMap<>();
```

Users

JWT tokens, once retrieved

The following listing is the first test, where the users from the `registrations` hash map are registered.

> **Listing 8.30 Test for registering users**

```
@Test
@Order(1)
@DisplayName("Register some users")
void registerUsers() {
```

```
registrations.forEach((key, registration) -> {
  given(requestSpecification)
    .contentType(ContentType.JSON)          We encode the JSON
    .body(registration.encode())            data to a string.
    .post("/register")
    .then()                                 HTTP POST to /api/v1/register
    .assertThat()
    .statusCode(200);                       Assert that the status
});                                         code is a 200.
}
```

The REST Assured fluent API allows us to express our request and then do an assertion on the response. It is possible to extract a response as text or JSON to perform
further assertions, as in the next listing, which is extracted from the test method that
retrieves JWT tokens.

Listing 8.31   Test code for retrieving JWT tokens

```
JsonObject login = new JsonObject()
  .put("username", key)
  .put("password", registration.getString("password"));

String token = given(requestSpecification)
  .contentType(ContentType.JSON)
  .body(login.encode())
  .post("/token")
  .then()
  .assertThat()
  .statusCode(200)                      Assert that the content-type
  .contentType("application/jwt")       header is in the response and
  .extract()                            matches that of JWT tokens.
  .asString();
                                        Extract the response.
assertThat(token)
  .isNotNull()                          AssertJ assertions
  .isNotBlank();                        on a String

tokens.put(key, token);
```

The test fetches a token and then asserts that the token is neither a `null` value or a
blank string (empty or with spaces). Extracting JSON data is similar, as shown next.

Listing 8.32   Extracting JSON with REST Assured

```
JsonPath jsonPath = given(requestSpecification)
  .headers("Authorization", "Bearer " + tokens.get("Foo"))    Pass a JWT
  .get("/Foo/total")                                          token.
  .then()
  .assertThat()
  .statusCode(200)
  .contentType(ContentType.JSON)
```

```
.extract()
.jsonPath();
```
Work with a JSON representation.

```
assertThat(jsonPath.getInt("count")).isNotNull().isEqualTo(6255);
```

The test fetches the total number of steps for user `Foo`, extracts the JSON response, and then checks that the step count (the `count` key in the JSON response) is equal to 6255.

The integration test can be run with Gradle (`./gradlew :public-api:test`) or from a development environment, as shown in figure 8.6.

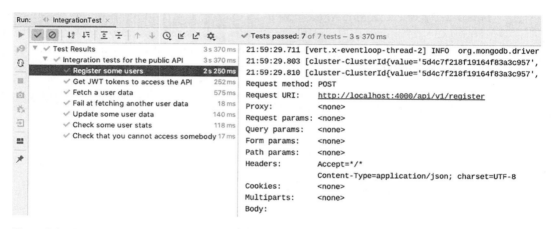

Figure 8.6   Running the integration tests from IntelliJ IDEA

You now have a good understanding of using the Vert.x web stack both for exposing endpoints and consuming other services. The next chapter focuses on the messaging and event streaming stack of Vert.x.

Summary

- The Vert.x web module makes it easy to build an edge service with CORS support and HTTP calls to other services.
- JSON web tokens are useful for authorization and access control in a public API.
- Vert.x does not have a preference regarding frontend application frameworks, but it is easy to integrate a Vue.js frontend application.
- By combining Docker containers managed from Testcontainers and the Rest Assured library, you can write integration tests for HTTP APIs.

Messaging and event
streaming with Vert.x

This chapter covers
- Messaging with AMQP
- Event streaming with Apache Kafka
- Sending emails
- Integration testing with messaging and event-streaming middleware

Reactive applications are a good fit for messaging and event-streaming technologies. So far we have mostly looked at services that expose HTTP APIs. But although HTTP is a versatile and effective protocol for interacting with a service, it should not be the only choice.

There are several options for integrating Vert.x-based services using messaging and event streaming. This chapter introduces AMQP message brokers and Apache Kafka. We will also discuss sending email using an SMTP server.

In this chapter we'll dive into the implementation of the ingester and congratulation services. The ingester receives step updates from devices over HTTP and AMQP, and it forwards them into the system as Kafka events. The congratulation

179

service listens for certain Kafka events to spot when a user has reached 10,000 steps in a day, and it sends a congratulation email.

9.1 *Event-driven services beyond HTTP with Vert.x*

HTTP is a sensible choice as a networked interface for an event-driven service, especially when a service offers an API. Messaging and event-streaming middleware offer useful tools for decoupling and integrating services. They are also typically better suited than HTTP for exchanging lots of events between services.

9.1.1 *What Vert.x provides*

Vert.x provides clients for message brokers, event streaming with Apache Kafka, and a general-purpose TCP protocol for the event bus.

MESSAGE BROKERS

Messaging middleware can be more effective than HTTP for service-to-service communications with better throughput, and it can also provide durability guarantees when a consumer or producer service is temporarily unavailable. Vert.x provides several modules for doing integration work with messaging middleware:

- An *Advanced Message Queuing Protocol* (AMQP) client
- A *Simple Text Oriented Messaging Protocol* (STOMP) client
- A RabbitMQ client
- A *Message Queuing Telemetry Transport* (MQTT) client

AMQP is a standard protocol for messaging middleware, and it's implemented by a large number of brokers such as Apache ActiveMQ, JBoss A-MQ, Windows Azure Service Bus, RabbitMQ, and more. Vert.x provides a dedicated client for RabbitMQ and its extensions. Note that it is also possible to use the Vert.x AMQP client with RabbitMQ, since it exposes an AMQP server alongside the RabbitMQ-specific server.

STOMP is a text-based protocol for messaging middleware. It has fewer features than AMQP, but they may be enough for simple messaging. It is supported by popular message brokers.

MQTT is a protocol designed for machine-to-machine publish/subscribe interactions. It is quite popular for embedded/Internet of Things devices because it uses low bandwidth.

KAFKA EVENT STREAMING

Vert.x provides support for Apache Kafka, a popular implementation of event-streaming middleware.

At first glance, event-streaming middleware resembles messaging systems, but it allows for interesting architectural patterns because different services can consume the same set of events at their own pace. Message brokers support publish/subscribe mechanisms for multiple services to consume the same events, but event-streaming middleware also has the ability to replay events at will. Rewinding event streams is a distinctive feature. Event-streaming middleware also allows new services to be plugged into the processing pipeline without impacting other services.

You can use event-streaming middleware just like messaging middleware, but there is more to it than just passing events between services.

EVENT-BUS TCP BRIDGE

Last but not least, Vert.x provides an event-bus bridge over a simple TCP protocol, with binding in JavaScript, Go, C#, C, and Python. This allows us to use the event bus to connect with non-Java applications. We will not cover this event-bus bridge in the book, but you can easily learn how to use it from the official Vert.x documentation. From the Vert.x side, this is really just the event bus, except that some of the events can be produced and consumed outside of the JVM.

9.1.2 *The middleware and services that we'll use*

The 10k steps challenge application allows us to explore AMQP for messaging, Kafka for event streaming, and sending email with an SMTP server:

- AMQP is used by the ingestion service because it receives pedometer device updates over either HTTP or AMQP.
- Kafka is used to convey events between many services of the application.
- SMTP is used to send congratulation emails to users.

As in the previous chapter, Docker Compose can be used to start the required middleware services for local development purposes: Apache Kafka (which also requires Apache ZooKeeper), Apache ActiveMQ Artemis, and MailHog (a test-friendly SMTP server). You can, of course, install and run each service by yourself if you want to, but starting disposable containers with Docker offers a simplified development experience.

On the Vert.x side, we'll use the following modules to build our services:

- `vertx-amqp-client`—The AMQP client
- `vertx-kafka-client`—The Apache Kafka client
- `vertx-mail-client`—The SMTP client that will send emails

9.1.3 *What is AMQP (and a message broker)?*

The *Advanced Message Queuing Protocol* (AMQP) is a widely used network protocol for messaging middleware backed by an open specification. The protocol itself is binary, based on TCP, and it supports authentication and encryption. We'll use Apache ActiveMQ in the project, and it supports AMQP.

Message brokers are a classic form of service integration, as they typically support message queues and publish/subscribe communications. They allow services to communicate through message passing, and the broker ensures message durability.

Figure 9.1 shows the interactions between a device, an AMQP queue that collects step events, and the ingestion service.

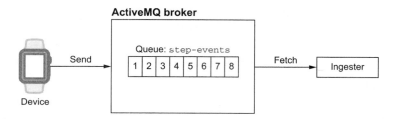

Figure 9.1 Overview
of an AMQP queue

Messages can be made *durable*, so that they are not lost if the broker crashes. Producers and consumers can use acknowledgements to ensure that a message has been properly sent or retrieved and then processed. Brokers also offer various quality-of-service features, such as expiration dates and advanced routing. Depending on the broker, messages can be transformed from one representation to another, such as converting from a binary format to JSON. Some brokers also support aggregating multiple messages into one, or conversely splitting one message to produce many.

> **NOTE** If you are new to ActiveMQ, I suggest reading *ActiveMQ in Action* by Bruce Snyder, Dejan Bosanac, and Rob Davies (Manning, 2011).

9.1.4 *What is Kafka?*

Apache Kafka is event-streaming middleware based on distributed logs. While that may sound complicated, all you really need to understand is that Kafka offers streams of event records, where producers can append new records and consumers can walk back and forth along streams. For instance, incoming pedometer step updates form a stream where each event is an update sent by a device, and the ingestion service produces these events. On the other hand, various consumers can look at the events on that stream to populate databases, compute statistics, and so on. Events remain in a stream for some amount of time, or until the stream is too big and has to discard its oldest records.

Kafka supports publish/subscribe interactions between distributed services, as illustrated in figure 9.2. In a Kafka cluster, events are *published* and *consumed* from *topics* that group related events. Topics are split into *replicated partitions*, which are ordered sequences of events. Each event is identified by its *offset* position in the event log that materializes its partition.

Consumers pull events from partitions. They can keep track of the last offset that they have consumed, but it is also possible to arbitrarily seek any random position in a partition, or even to replay all events since the beginning. Also, *consumer groups* can divide work by reading from different partitions and parallelizing event processing.

It is easy to think that Kafka is a *messaging* system like ActiveMQ, and in some cases Kafka is very fine messaging middleware, but it should still be considered *streaming* middleware.

In a message broker, messages disappear when they have been consumed from a queue, or when they expire. Kafka partitions eventually evict records, either using a partition size limit (such as 2 GB) or using some eviction delay (such as two weeks).

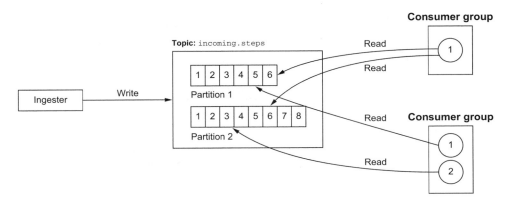

Figure 9.2 Overview of a Kafka topic

Kafka records should be considered "semi-durable" as they will eventually disappear. It is possible to configure the partitions in a topic to keep events forever, but this is quite rare as events are expected to produce durable effects when consumed. For instance, the ingestion service produces incoming step update records, and the activity service turns these records into long-term facts in a database. Another interesting feature of Kakfa is that topics can be replayed at will, so new services can join and consume a stream at their own pace.

> **NOTE** I suggest reading Dylan Scott's *Kafka in Action* (Manning, 2017) if you are new to Apache Kafka.

Let's now dive into the ingestion service.

9.2 *Reliably ingesting messages over HTTP and AMQP*

Everything begins with the ingestion service, as it receives step count updates from the pedometers. In our (fictitious) application, we can expect that several types of pedometers will be available, and that they have different communication capabilities. For example, some devices may directly talk to the ingestion service over the internet, while others may need to reach a gateway that forwards updates to the ingestion service.

This is why we offer two interfaces for ingesting device updates:

- A device can connect to the HTTP API provided by the ingestion service.
- A device can forward an update to a message broker, and the ingestion service receives the updates from the broker.

Once an update has been received, it must be validated and then sent to a Kafka topic. It is interesting to explore both the AMQP and HTTP interfaces, as we can see similarities in their implementations but also differences in acknowledging device updates.

9.2.1   *Ingesting from AMQP*

We'll start with the AMQP ingestion. We first need to create an AMQP client that connects to the broker. The following listing shows the client configuration code.

Listing 9.1   AMQP client configuration

```
private AmqpClientOptions amqpConfig() {
  return new AmqpClientOptions()
    .setHost("localhost")
    .setPort(5672)
    .setUsername("artemis")            ◁    The credentials are
    .setPassword("simetraehcapa");          the default ones from
}                                            the Docker image.
// (...)

AmqpClientOptions amqpOptions = amqpConfig();
AmqpReceiverOptions receiverOptions = new AmqpReceiverOptions()
    .setAutoAcknowledgement(false)     ◁
▷  .setDurable(true);                       We will manually acknowledge
                                            incoming messages.
   We want durable messaging.
```

The `amqpConfig` method that we use here provides a configuration with hardcoded values. This is great for the testing we do in this book, but for production you would, of course, resolve credentials, hostnames, and port numbers from some external source. These could be environment variables or a registry service, such as Apache ZooKeeper or Consul. We also set up the connection for durable messaging and declare manual acknowledgment, as we want to retry message processing if writing to a Kafka topic fails.

The next step is to set up the event-processing pipeline for incoming AMQP messages. We use RxJava to dispatch messages to a processing function, log errors, and recover from errors, as shown in the following listing.

Listing 9.2   AMQP event-processing pipeline

```
   Create an AMQP client.
                                                    Create a message receiver from
└▷ AmqpClient.create(vertx, amqpOptions)                the step-events destination.
    .rxConnect()
    .flatMap(conn -> conn.rxCreateReceiver("step-events", receiverOptions)) ◁
    .flatMapPublisher(AmqpReceiver::toFlowable)       ◁
    .doOnError(this::logAmqpError)       ◁── Error logging    Create a Flowable
    .retryWhen(this::retryLater)        ◁                     of AMQP messages.
▷   .subscribe(this::handleAmqpMessage);  │ Retry logic
   Subscription that dispatches
   incoming messages
```

This pipeline is interesting as it is purely declarative. It starts with the creation of a client, and then it obtains a receiver for the `step-events` durable queue and a flow of messages. From there we declare what to do upon receiving a message or an error. We also keep the code short and clean by using Java method references rather than lambdas. But what do the `logAmqpError`, `retryLater`, and `handleAmqpMessage` methods do?

Logging messages is not very complicated.

Listing 9.3   Logging AMQP errors

```
private void logAmqpError(Throwable err) {         Log the error
  logger.error("Woops AMQP", err);           ◁——|  and stack trace.
}
```

Errors happen. For instance, we can lose the connection to the AMQP broker. In this case, an error passes along the pipeline, and `logAmqpError` logs it, but `doOnError` lets the error propagate to subscribers.

We then need to retry connecting to the AMQP broker and resume receiving events, which translates to resubscribing to the source in RxJava. We can do that with the `retryWhen` operator, as it allows us to define our own policy. If you just want to retry a number of times, or even always, then `retry` is simpler. The following listing shows how we introduce a 10-second delay before resubscribing.

Listing 9.4   Recovering from errors with a delayed resubscription

```
private Flowable<Throwable> retryLater(Flowable<Throwable> errs) {
  return errs.delay(10, TimeUnit.SECONDS, RxHelper.scheduler(vertx));   ◁——
}
                         It is important to use the scheduler parameter
                            to process events on a Vert.x event loop.
```

The `retryLater` operator works as follows:

- It takes a `Flowable` of errors as its input, since we are in a `Flowable` of AMQP messages.
- It returns a `Flowable` of *anything*, where
  - Emitting `onComplete` or `onError` does not trigger a resubscription.
  - Emitting `onNext` (no matter what the value is) triggers a resubscription.

To delay the resubscription by 10 seconds, we use the `delay` operator. It will eventually emit a value, so `onNext` will be called and a resubscription will happen. You can, of course, think of more elaborate handlers, like limiting the number of retries or using an exponential back-off strategy. We will use this pattern a lot, as it greatly simplifies the error-recovery logic.

9.2.2   *Translating AMQP messages to Kafka records*

The following listing contains the method that handles incoming AMQP messages, validates them, and then pushes them as Kafka records.

Listing 9.5   Handling AMQP messages

```
private void handleAmqpMessage(AmqpMessage message) {
  if (!"application/json".equals(message.contentType()) ||
    invalidIngestedJson(message.bodyAsJsonObject())) {        Check for a valid
    logger.error("Invalid AMQP message (discarded): {}",      JSON message.
      message.bodyAsBinary());
    message.accepted();
    return;
  }
  JsonObject payload = message.bodyAsJsonObject();
  KafkaProducerRecord<String, JsonObject> record = makeKafkaRecord(payload);
  updateProducer.rxSend(record).subscribe(
    ok -> message.accepted(),                                 Prepare a
    err -> {                                                  Kafka record.
Acknowledge  logger.error("AMQP ingestion failed", err);
the AMQP       message.rejected();
message.    });                           Reject the AMQP message.
  }
```

The `handleAmqpMessage` method first performs some validation on the incoming
AMQP message and then prepares a Kafka record. The AMQP message is acknowledged when the Kafka record is written, and it is rejected if the record could not be
written.

> **TIP** In listing 9.5 and all subsequent services, we will directly work with `Json-`
> `Object` data representation. There is little point in converting the JSON rep-
> resentation to Java domain classes (such as an `IngestionData` class) given
> that we mostly copy and transform data. You can, of course, perform such
> mapping if you have to do some more complex business logic and the cost of
> abstraction is justified.

The `invalidIngestedJson` method checks that the JSON data contains all required
entries, as follows.

Listing 9.6   Checking for valid JSON data

```
private boolean invalidIngestedJson(JsonObject payload) {
  return !payload.containsKey("deviceId") ||
    !payload.containsKey("deviceSync") ||      Checking for JSON entries
    !payload.containsKey("stepsCount");
}
```

The `makeKafkaRecord` method in the following listing converts the AMQP message
JSON to a Kafka record aimed at the `incoming-steps` topic.

Listing 9.7   Preparing a Kafka record

```
private KafkaProducerRecord<String, JsonObject> makeKafkaRecord(JsonObject
  payload) {
  String deviceId = payload.getString("deviceId");
```

```
    JsonObject recordData = new JsonObject()          ◁──── We copy JSON data.
      .put("deviceId", deviceId)
      .put("deviceSync", payload.getLong("deviceSync"))
      .put("stepsCount", payload.getInteger("stepsCount"));
    return KafkaProducerRecord.create("incoming.steps", deviceId, recordData); ◁┐
}                                                                              │
```
                                                                                Record with key
                                                                     deviceId and JSON data

We could avoid copying all JSON entries manually and just pass the JSON from the AMQP message to the Kafka record. This, however, helps ensure that no extra data ends up in the Kafka record.

The `updateProducer` field is of type `KafkaProducer<String, JsonObject>` because it produces messages with string keys and JSON payloads. Instances of `KafkaProducer` are created by passing configuration from a `Map` as follows.

Listing 9.8   Configuring a Kafka producer

```
Map<String, String> kafkaConfig() {
  Map<String, String> config = new HashMap<>();              Class to serialize
  config.put("bootstrap.servers", "localhost:9092");        values from strings
  config.put("key.serializer",
    ➥ "org.apache.kafka.common.serialization.StringSerializer");  ◁─────┘
  config.put("value.serializer",
    ➥ "io.vertx.kafka.client.serialization.JsonObjectSerializer");  ◁────┐
  config.put("acks", "1");                                  Class to serialize values from
  return config;                                               Vert.x JsonObject
}
// (...)


// in rxStart()
updateProducer = KafkaProducer.create(vertx, kafkaConfig());  ◁─┐ Create a Vert.x
                                                                │ Kafka producer.
```

The configuration especially specifies the *serializer* (or *deserializer*) classes, as Kafka records need to be mapped to Java types. `StringSerializer` comes from the Kafka client library, and it serializes Java strings to Kafka data, whereas `JsonObjectSerializer` comes from Vert.x and serializes `JsonObject` data. You need to specify correct serializer classes for both your keys and values. Similarly, you will need to configure deserializers when reading from Kafka topics.

> **TIP** The Vert.x Kafka module wraps the Java client from the Apache Kafka project, and all configuration key/value pairs match those from the Kafka Java client documentation.

9.2.3   Ingesting from HTTP

The code to ingest from HTTP is very similar to that of ingesting with AMQP. The most notable difference is that an HTTP status code needs to be set, so that the device that sent an update knows that ingestion has failed and must be retried later.

We first need an HTTP server and router.

Listing 9.9   HTTP server for ingestion

```
Router router = Router.router(vertx);
router.post().handler(BodyHandler.create());              ◁——    BodyHandler decodes
router.post("/ingest").handler(this::httpIngest);                 HTTP request bodies.

return vertx.createHttpServer()
  .requestHandler(router)
  .rxListen(HTTP_PORT)
  .ignoreElement();
```

The `httpIngest` method is shown in the next listing, and it's quite similar to `handleAmqpMessage`.

Listing 9.10   Ingesting updates from HTTP

```
private void httpIngest(RoutingContext ctx) {
  JsonObject payload = ctx.getBodyAsJson();          |—  Check the JSON entries.
  if (invalidIngestedJson(payload)) {           ◁——'
    logger.error("Invalid HTTP JSON (discarded): {}", payload.encode());
    ctx.fail(400);        ◁——┐  Bad JSON; let the
    return;                  |  requester know that.
  }
  KafkaProducerRecord<String, JsonObject> record = makeKafkaRecord(payload);
  updateProducer.rxSend(record).subscribe(
    ok -> ctx.response().end(),          ◁—— Successful ingestion
    err -> {
      logger.error("HTTP ingestion failed", err);
      ctx.fail(500);     ◁——┐  The ingestion failed; let
    });                     |  the requester know that.
}
```

HTTP status codes are important for letting the client know if the payload is incorrect (400), if the ingestion failed due to some (temporary) error (500), or if the ingestion succeeded (200).

The ingestion service is a good example of integration using different input protocols. Let's now explore more of Apache Kafka with Vert.x through the congratulation service.

9.3   *Sending congratulation emails*

While the ingestion service *produces* Kafka events, the congratulation service *consumes* Kafka events.

The activity service generates daily step events whenever a device update has been received. Each event contains the number of steps recorded for the originating device on the current day. The congratulation service can observe these events as they are sent to the `daily.step.updates` Kafka topic, and it can target the events where the number of steps is above 10,000.

9.3.1 Listening for daily step update events

The events sent to the `daily.step.updates` Kafka topic are JSON data with the following content:

- `deviceId` is the device identifier.
- `timestamp` is the timestamp when the event was produced in the activity service.
- `stepsCount` is the number of steps for the current day.

The Kafka records also have a key, which is the concatenation of several parameters: `deviceId:year-month-day`. In this scheme, all records of device `1a2b` produced on October 6th 2019 have the key `1a2b:2019-10-06`. As you will shortly see, the key will be useful not just to ensure that events for a given device are consumed in order, but also to ensure that we don't send more than one congratulation email per day.

The pipeline for processing daily steps event is shown in figure 9.3.

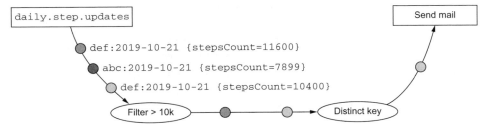

Figure 9.3 Pipeline from daily step counts to congratulation emails

Daily step updates flow from the `daily.step.updates` Kafka topic, and then

1. We discard events where the number of steps is less than 10,000.
2. We discard events for which an event with the same key has already been processed.
3. We send an email.

The following listing contains the corresponding RxJava pipeline.

Listing 9.11   Kafka RxJava pipeline for receiving and processing daily step updates

```
KafkaConsumer.<String, JsonObject>create(vertx,              Subscribe to the Kafka topic.
    KafkaConfig.consumerConfig("congrats-service"))
  .subscribe("daily.step.updates")            ◁           Filter out events with
  .toFlowable()                                           less than 10,000 steps.
  .filter(this::above10k)              ◁                  Discard events for which a
  .distinct(KafkaConsumerRecord::key)       ◁             previous event with the same
  .flatMapSingle(this::sendmail)       ◁                  key has been processed.
  .doOnError(err -> logger.error("Woops", err))
  .retryWhen(this::retryLater)                   Asynchronous operation to send an email
  .subscribe(mailResult -> logger.info("Congratulated {}",
    mailResult.getRecipients()));      ◁
                                            Log each successful
  Retry on error.                           congratulation.
```

The preceding listing uses the RxJava binding to subscribe to a Kafka topic as a `Flow-able` for Kafka records. We then use the `filter` combinator to filter out records with less than 10,000 steps, and use the predicate method in the following listing.

Listing 9.12   Predicate for events with at least 10,000 steps

```
private boolean above10k(KafkaConsumerRecord<String, JsonObject> record) {
  return record.value().getInteger("stepsCount") >= 10_000;    <─┐ Predicate on
}                                                                 JSON data.
```

The `distinct` combinator in listing 9.11 ensures that only one event for each Kafka record key is retained, right after `filter`. This is to avoid sending more than one congratulation email to a user on a given day, as we could easily have a first event with, say, 10,100 steps, followed later by another event with 10,600 steps, and so on. Note that this design is not 100% bulletproof, as it requires storing already-processed key values in memory, and upon a service restart we could accidentally send a second email. This is a reasonable trade-off in our example, compared to using a persistent data store just to keep track of when an email was last sent to a user.

The rest of the pipeline uses similar event processing and `retryWhen` logic to resubscribe on errors. The `sendmail` method is an asynchronous operation to send an email—let's look at how it works.

9.3.2 Sending emails

The `vertx-mail-client` module offers an SMTP client. The following listing shows how to create such a client.

Listing 9.13   Creating an SMTP client

```
MailClient mailClient = MailClient.createShared(vertx, MailerConfig.config());  <─┐
                                                           Create a shared instance.
```

As with many other Vert.x clients, we obtain an instance through a factory method, passing a `Vertx` context as well as some parameters.

The `MailerConfig` class provides a method to retrieve configuration data, as shown next.

Listing 9.14   Mail client configuration

```
class MailerConfig {
  static MailConfig config() {
    return new MailConfig()
      .setHostname("localhost")    <──── Server host
      .setPort(1025);              <─┐
  }                                   Server port
}
```

Again, these hardcoded values are fine for testing purposes and for keeping our code simple. The values are for connecting to MailHog, the testing SMTP server that we're using from a Docker container. The `MailConfig` class supports more configuration options like SSL, authentication method, credentials, and so on.

A daily-steps update Kafka event applies to a device; it does not contain the name of the owner or the email address. Before we can send an email, we must first fetch the missing information (name and email) from the user profile service. We thus need two requests to that service:

- A request of the form `/owns/deviceId` to get the user name
- A request of the form `/username` to get the user profile and retrieve the email address

The `sendmail` method is shown in the following listing.

Listing 9.15 Implementation of the `sendmail` method

Extract the device identifier.

```
private Single<MailResult> sendmail(KafkaConsumerRecord<String, JsonObject>
  record) {
  String deviceId = record.value().getString("deviceId");
  Integer stepsCount = record.value().getInteger("stepsCount");
  return webClient
    .get(3000, "localhost", "/owns/" + deviceId)
    .as(BodyCodec.jsonObject())
    .rxSend()
    .map(HttpResponse::body)
    .map(json -> json.getString("username"))
    .flatMap(this::getEmail)
    .map(email -> makeEmail(stepsCount, email))
    .flatMap(mailClient::rxSendMail);
  }
```

Prepare a request to find who owns the device.

Extract the body, which is a JsonObject.

Extract the username value.

Asynchronous operation to fetch the email for the user

Prepare an email message.

Asynchronously send the email.

The `sendmail` method is another RxJava pipeline that composes asynchronous operations and data processing, illustrated in figure 9.4.

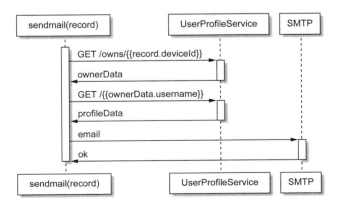

Figure 9.4 Asynchronous operations to prepare and then send a congratulation email

It starts by issuing an HTTP request to the user profile service and finding the user name of the device owner. It then prepares another request to fetch the user profile data to get the email address. The following listing provides the implementation of the getEmail method.

Listing 9.16   Request to retrieve the email address

```
private Single<String> getEmail(String username) {
  return webClient
    .get(3000, "localhost", "/" + username)
    .as(BodyCodec.jsonObject())
    .rxSend()                         ←——— Send the request.
    .map(HttpResponse::body)
    .map(json -> json.getString("email"));   ←——— Keep only the email address.
}
```

The next step is to prepare an email, enclosed in a MailMessage instance, as shown in the following implementation of the makeEmail method.

Listing 9.17   Preparing an email message

```
private MailMessage makeEmail(Integer stepsCount, String email) {
  return new MailMessage()
    .setFrom("noreply@tenksteps.tld")      ←——— Address of the sender
    .setTo(email)
    .setSubject("You made it!")      ←——| Subject
    .setText("Congratulations on reaching " + stepsCount + "
       steps today!\n\n- The 10k Steps Team\n");      ←——— Body
}
```

Recipient address → .setTo(email)

Note that for more advanced email formatting, you could use a template engine rather than text.

Now that you know how to do messaging and event streaming with Vert.x, let's not forget integration testing, to ensure that both the ingestion and congratulation services work correctly.

9.4   Integration tests

Testing the ingestion service involves sending device updates over AMQP and HTTP, and observing the Kafka topics. Conversely, testing the congratulation service involves sending events to Kafka topics, and observing the emails.

9.4.1   Ingestion testing

Testing the ingestion service requires sending a message over AMQP or HTTP, and then checking that a Kafka record has been emitted, as shown in figure 9.5.

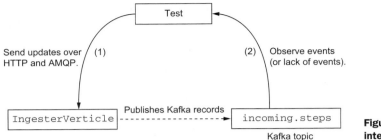

Figure 9.5 **Ingestion integration-test overview**

The `IntegrationTest` class in the ingestion service source code uses JUnit 5 and Docker containers to start an AMQP broker, Apache Kafka, and Apache ZooKeeper. The following listing shows the test preparation.

Listing 9.18 Ingestion test preparation

Kafka consumer

```
@BeforeEach
void setup(Vertx vertx, VertxTestContext testContext) {
  kafkaConsumer = KafkaConsumer.create(vertx, kafkaConfig());
  amqpClient = AmqpClient.create(vertx, amqClientOptions());
  KafkaAdminClient adminClient = KafkaAdminClient.create(vertx,
    kafkaConfig());
  vertx
    .rxDeployVerticle(new IngesterVerticle())
    .delay(500, TimeUnit.MILLISECONDS, RxHelper.scheduler(vertx))
    .flatMapCompletable(id ->
      adminClient.rxDeleteTopics(singletonList("incoming.steps")))
    .onErrorComplete()
    .subscribe(testContext::completeNow, testContext::failNow);
}
```

> **AMQP client**

> **Client to administer Kafka**

> **Deploy the ingestion verticle.**

> **Delete all incoming.steps topics if they exist.**

The preparation consists of deploying the `IngesterVerticle` verticle, and then deleting any existing `incoming.steps` topic. This ensures that tests do not pollute each other with remaining Kafka events. Note the `onErrorComplete` combinator: it ensures progress, because deleting topics raises an error when they don't exist. We want to run the tests when `incoming.steps` does not exist, which is typically the case of the first test being run. Of course, `onErrorComplete` can mask a deployment failure of `Ingester-Verticle`, but we will find that out in test executions.

The following listing shows the preamble of the test case where a well-formed AMQP message is being ingested.

Listing 9.19 AMQP ingestion test preamble

```
@Test
@DisplayName("Ingest a well-formed AMQP message")
void amqIngest(VertxTestContext testContext) {
```

```
JsonObject body = new JsonObject().put("deviceId", "123")    ← Open an AMQP
    .put("deviceSync", 1L).put("stepsCount", 500);              client connection.
amqpClient.rxConnect()                                       ←
    .flatMap(connection -> connection.rxCreateSender("step-events"))    ←
    .subscribe(sender -> {                                   Create a sender to the
        AmqpMessage msg = AmqpMessage.create()               step-events destination.
            .durable(true)
            .ttl(5000)
            .withJsonObjectAsBody(body).build();
        sender.send(msg);          ←
    },                                    Send the message.
    testContext::failNow);
// (...)
}
```

Create an AMQP message. (annotation pointing to `AmqpMessage msg = AmqpMessage.create()`)

The AMQP client sends a message that we know is well-formed, as its body contains all the required JSON entries.

Once this is done, we need to check that a Kafka record has been sent, as follows.

Listing 9.20   AMQP ingestion test: checking for a Kafka record

```
kafkaConsumer.subscribe("incoming.steps")    ← Subscribe to the
    .toFlowable()                               Kafka topic.
    .subscribe(
        record -> testContext.verify(() -> {    ←
            assertThat(record.key()).isEqualTo("123");          Perform assertions
            JsonObject json = record.value();                   on the Kafka record.
            assertThat(json.getString("deviceId")).isEqualTo("123");
            assertThat(json.getLong("deviceSync")).isEqualTo(1L);
            assertThat(json.getInteger("stepsCount")).isEqualTo(500);
            testContext.completeNow();    ←
        }),                                   The test passes.
        testContext::failNow);    ←
                                      Fail the test on any error.
```

Of course, we also need to test what happens when an incorrect message is sent, like an empty JSON document. We must check that no Kafka record is being emitted, as in the following listing.

Listing 9.21   Ingesting a bad JSON document

```
@Test
@DisplayName("Ingest a badly-
    formed AMQP message and observe no Kafka record")
void amqIngestWrong(Vertx vertx, VertxTestContext testContext) {
    JsonObject body = new JsonObject();    ← Empty JSON
    // (...)                               ←
                                              Send it (same code as in listing 9.20)
    kafkaConsumer.subscribe("incoming.steps")
        .toFlowable()
        .timeout(3, TimeUnit.SECONDS, RxHelper.scheduler(vertx))    ← Wait for three
        .subscribe(                                                    seconds.
```

```
record -> testContext.failNow(new
    IllegalStateException("We must not get a record")),
err -> {
    if (err instanceof TimeoutException) {        Check that this is the
        testContext.completeNow();                error we expected!
    } else {
        testContext.failNow(err);
    }
});
}
```

The timeout in the RxJava pipeline is important, as we need to let some time lapse to be sure that no Kafka record has been sent. The remainder of the `IntegrationTest` class is quite similar, with two test cases for the HTTP ingestion: one that checks what happens when a correct payload is sent, and one where the payload is an empty JSON document.

9.4.2 Congratulation email testing

Testing the behavior of the congratulation service is more involved than the ingestion, as there are more moving parts in the test environment, as illustrated in figure 9.6.

The goal is to send Kafka records and then observe the emails that have been sent (or not sent). Interestingly, MailHog is not just an SMTP server; it also provides a web interface and an HTTP API to simulate an email inbox. This allows us to perform tests by sending Kafka records, and then checking what emails have been received in the inbox.

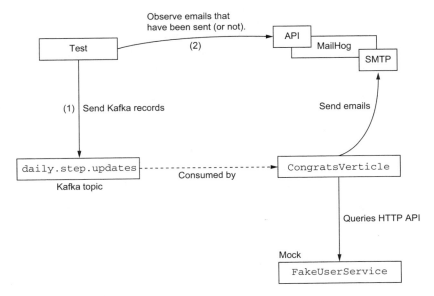

Figure 9.6   Congratulation service integration-test overview

The `CongratsTest` class features a `prepare` initialization method that creates a Kafka producer (to send Kafka events) and a Vert.x web client (to query the inbox). The steps in the `prepare` method to prepare the environment are shown in the following listing.

Listing 9.22   Preparing the congratulation service integration test

Delete Kafka topics.
```
KafkaAdminClient adminClient = KafkaAdminClient.create(vertx, conf);
adminClient
    .rxDeleteTopics(Arrays.asList("incoming.steps", "daily.step.updates"))
    .onErrorComplete()
    .andThen(vertx.rxDeployVerticle(new CongratsVerticle()))    ◁── Deploy the verticle.
    .ignoreElement()
    .andThen(vertx.rxDeployVerticle(new FakeUserService()))
    .ignoreElement()
    .andThen(webClient.delete(8025, "localhost", "/api/v1/messages").rxSend()) ◁┐
    .ignoreElement()
    .subscribe(testContext::completeNow, testContext::failNow);
```
Deploy a mock user account service.

Delete all messages from the inbox.

We first delete existing Kafka topics, and then we deploy the verticle under test. We also deploy a verticle to mock the user profile service and delete all messages from the inbox by making an HTTP DELETE query to the MailHog instance.

The `FakeUserService` verticle found in the test source exposes an HTTP service with the minimal level of functionality to replace the real user profile service in our tests. All requests to find out who owns a device point to user `Foo`, and retrieving the details of user `Foo` gives just the username and email. The following listing shows an excerpt with the code for answering a user details request with information for user `Foo` and just the JSON entries needed for `CongratsVerticle` to operate.

Listing 9.23   Excerpt from the `FakeUserService` class

```
router.get("/:username").handler(this::username);    ◁── Route for a user
//(...)                                                    profile info

private void username(RoutingContext ctx) {
  logger.info("User data request {}", ctx.request().path());
  JsonObject notAllData = new JsonObject()    ◁── JSON with just the required
    .put("username", "Foo")                        data for the service and test
    .put("email", "foo@mail.tld");
  ctx.response()
    .putHeader("Content-Type", "application/json")
    .end(notAllData.encode());
}
```

This way we have good isolation of the congratulation service for testing. We could also have deployed the real user profile service, but that would have involved preparing a database with some data. It is always better to replace dependent services with mock ones when you can.

The next listing shows the full test case for checking that no email is sent on a Kafka record with less than 10,000 steps.

```
@Test
@DisplayName("No email must be sent below 10k steps")
void checkNothingBelow10k(Vertx vertx, VertxTestContext testContext) {
  producer
    .rxSend(record("123", 5000))          ⬅── Kafka record for device
    .ignoreElement()                           123 and 5000 steps
    .delay(3, TimeUnit.SECONDS, RxHelper.scheduler(vertx))  ⬅── Wait for three seconds
    .andThen(webClient                                          after the message has
      .get(8025, "localhost", "/api/v2/search?kind=to&query=foo@mail.tld")  ⬅──
      .as(BodyCodec.jsonObject()).rxSend())
    .map(HttpResponse::body)                         Query all messages for
    .subscribe(                                      email foo@mail.tld.
      json -> {
        testContext.verify(() ->
        ➥ assertThat(json.getInteger("total")).isEqualTo(0));  ⬅── Check that there
        testContext.completeNow();                                 is no message.
      },
      testContext::failNow);
}
```

The MailHog API allows us to check what messages have been sent. The next listing checks whether an email was sent for more than 10,000 steps.

```
producer
  .rxSend(record("123", 11_000))     ⬅──── A record with 11,000 steps
  .ignoreElement()
  .delay(3, TimeUnit.SECONDS, RxHelper.scheduler(vertx))
  .andThen(webClient
    .get(8025, "localhost", "/api/v2/search?kind=to&query=foo@mail.tld")
    .as(BodyCodec.jsonObject()).rxSend())
  .map(HttpResponse::body)
  .subscribe(
    json -> {
      testContext.verify(() ->
      ➥ assertThat(json.getInteger("total")).isEqualTo(1));  ⬅── We must have
      testContext.completeNow();                                  one message.
    },
    testContext::failNow);
```

The last test case in the checkNotTwiceToday method checks that only one email was sent for two successive records with more than 10,000 steps. I haven't reproduced the code here due to its verbosity, but you can get it from the book's source code repository.

This concludes the design, implementation, and testing of two services that use messaging and event streaming. The next chapter focuses on Vert.x and data sources.

Summary

- AMQP is a standard protocol for message brokers, and you saw how to consume and produce AQMP messages with Vert.x and Apache ActiveMQ.
- Apache Kafka is event-streaming middleware that allows services to replay events at will. Vert.x provides efficient integration with Kafka.
- RxJava allows you to write event-processing pipelines in a declarative fashion, and with built-in error recovery.
- We explored strategies for writing integration tests with AMQP, Kafka, and test containers by sending messages from tests to replace external components.
- MailHog is a test-friendly SMTP server that exposes a convenient API for inspecting what emails have been sent.

10

Persistent state
management
with databases

This chapter covers

- Storing data and authenticating users with MongoDB
- Using PostgreSQL from Vert.x
- Testing strategies for integration testing of event-driven services that interact with databases

Reactive applications favor stateless designs, but state has to be managed somewhere.

Databases are essential in most applications, because data needs to be stored, retrieved, and queried. Databases can store all kinds of data, such as application state, facts, or user credentials. There are different types of databases on the market: some are generalist and others are specialized for certain types of use cases, access patterns, and data.

In this chapter we'll explore database and state management with Vert.x by diving into the implementation of the user and activity services. These services will allow us to use a document-oriented database (MongoDB) and a relational database (PostgreSQL). You will also see how you can use MongoDB for authenticating users, and how to write integration tests for data-driven services.

10.1 Databases and Vert.x

Vert.x offers a wide range of clients for connecting to data sources. These clients contain drivers that talk to servers, and that may offer efficient connection management, like connection pooling. This is useful for building all kinds of services, from APIs backed by a data source to integration services that mix data sources, messaging, and APIs.

10.1.1 What the Eclipse Vert.x stack provides

The Eclipse Vert.x project provides the data client modules listed in table 10.1.

Table 10.1   Data client modules supported by Eclipse Vert.x

Identifier	Description
`vertx-mongo-client`	MongoDB is a document-oriented database.
`vertx-jdbc-client`	Supports any relational database that offers a JDBC driver.
`vertx-pg-client` and `vertx-mysql-client`	Access PostgreSQL and MySQL relational databases through dedicated Vert.x reactive drivers.
`vertx-redis-client`	Redis is versatile data structure store.
`vertx-cassandra-client`	Apache Cassandra is a database tailored for very large volumes of data.

You can find drivers for other kinds of data sources in the larger Vert.x community. Those are beyond the scope of the project at the Eclipse Foundation.

MongoDB is a popular document-oriented database; it is a good match with Vert.x since it manipulates JSON documents. Redis is an in-memory data structure store with configurable on-disk data snapshots that can be used as a cache, as a database, and as a message broker. Apache Cassandra is a multinode, replicated database designed for storing huge amounts of data. Cassandra is well suited for databases where size is measured in hundreds of terabytes or even petabytes. You can, of course, use it for just a few terabytes, but a more traditional database may suffice in these cases.

Speaking of "traditional" relational databases, Vert.x can connect to *anything* for which there is a JDBC driver. That being said, JDBC is an older protocol based on a multithreaded design and blocking I/O. The JDBC support in Vert.x offloads database calls to worker thread pools, and it pushes results back to event-loop contexts. This is to avoid blocking event loops, since JDBC calls do block. This design limits scalability, as worker threads are needed, but for moderate workloads it should be fine.

If you use PostgreSQL or MySQL, Vert.x provides its own reactive drivers. These drivers implement the network protocols of each database server, and they are built in a purely asynchronous fashion using Netty, the networking foundation of Vert.x. The drivers offer excellent performance, both in terms of latency and concurrent connections. They are also very stable and implement the current protocols and features of the databases. You should prefer the Vert.x reactive driver clients for PostgreSQL and MySQL, and use the JDBC client when you need to connect to other databases.

If you are looking for a solid database, PostgreSQL is probably a good bet. PostgreSQL is versatile and has been used in all sorts of small and large-scale projects over the years. You can, of course, use it as a traditional relational database, but it also supports JSON documents as first-class objects, and geographic objects through the PostGIS extension.

10.1.2 *A note on data/object mapping, and why you may not always need it*

Before we dive into the user profile service design and implementation with MongoDB, I would like to quickly discuss certain established idioms of enterprise Java development, and explain why, in search of simplicity and efficiency, the code in this chapter deviates intentionally from supposed best practices.

The code of the 10k steps challenge may surprise you, because it does not perform object data mapping, where any data has to be mapped to some Java object model that represents the application domain, such as data transfer objects (DTOs).[1] For instance, some JSON data representing a pedometer update would be mapped to a `DeviceUpdate` Java class before any further processing was done. Here we will directly manipulate data in `JsonObject` instances as they flow between HTTP, Kafka, and database interfaces. We will not map, say, device update JSON data to `DeviceUpdate`; we will work with the `JsonObject` representation of that data instead.

Vert.x does allow you to do data mapping from and to Java classes, but unless the object model contains some significant business logic or can be leveraged by some processing in a third-party library, I see little value in doing any form of data binding. I advocate such a design for several reasons:

- It saves us from writing classes that have no functionality except exposing trivial getters and setters.
- It avoids unnecessary allocation of objects with typically short lifetimes (e.g., the lifespan of processing an HTTP request).
- Data is not always easy to map to an object model, and you may not be interested in all the data, but rather in some selected entries.
- In the case of relational databases, the object and the models have some well-known mismatches that can result in complex mappings and bad performance due to excessive queries.[2]
- It eventually leads to code that is more functional.

---

[1] For information on DTOs, see Martin Fowler's "Data Transfer Object" article at https://martinfowler.com/eaaCatalog/dataTransferObject.html.

[2] See Ted Neward, "The Vietnam of Computer Science," http://blogs.tedneward.com/post/the-vietnam-of-computer-science/.

If you're in doubt, always ask yourself whether you actually need an object model, or whether the data representation is good enough for the processing work that you are doing. If your object model consists of nothing but getters and setters, perhaps it's a good sign that (at least initially) you don't need it.

Let's now dive into using MongoDB in the user profile service.

10.2 *User profile service with MongoDB*

The user profile service manages user data such as name, email, and city, and it's also used to authenticate a user against login/password credentials. This service is used by other services that need to retrieve and correlate data against user information.

The user service makes use of MongoDB for two purposes:

- Storing user data: username, password, email, city, device identifier, and whether data should appear in public rankings
- Authenticating users against a username plus password combination

MongoDB is a good fit here because it is a document database; each user can be represented as a document. We will use the `vertx-mongo-client` module to connect to MongoDB instances, and we will use the `vertx-auth-mongo` module for authentication.

10.2.1 *Data model*

The `vertx-auth-mongo` module is a turnkey solution for doing user authentication on top of a MongoDB database, as it manages all the intricacies of properly storing and retrieving credentials. It implements the common authentication interface of module `vertx-auth-common`. It especially deals with storing cryptographic hashes of passwords with a *salt* value, because storing actual passwords is never a good idea. According to the conventions defined in the `vertx-auth-mongo` module, there is a document for each user in the target database with the following entries:

- `username`—A string for the username
- `salt`—A random data string used to secure the password
- `password`—A string made by computing the SHA-512 hash from the actual password plus the `salt` value
- `roles`—An array of strings defining *roles* (such as "administrator")
- `permissions`—An array of strings defining *permissions* (such as "can_access _beta").

In our case, we won't use roles and permissions, since all users will be equal, so these entries will be empty arrays. We will not have to deal with the subtleties of handling salts and password hashing, as this is taken care of by the authentication module.

While this data model is prescribed by `vertx-auth-mongo`, nothing precludes us from adding more fields to the documents that represent users. We can thus add the following entries:

- `city`—A string for the user's city
- `deviceId`—A string for the pedometer device identifier
- `email`—A string for the user's email address
- `makePublic`—A Boolean to indicate whether or not the user wants to appear in public rankings

We'll also enforce two integrity constraints with MongoDB indexes: both `username` and `deviceId` must be unique across all documents. This avoids duplicate user names as well as two users having the same device. This will pose a correctness challenge when registering new users, because we will not be able to use any transaction mechanism. We will need to roll back partial data inserts when the `deviceId` uniqueness constraint prevents a duplicate insert.

Let's now look at how we can use the Vert.x MongoDB client and Vert.x authentication support.

10.2.2 User profile API verticle and initialization

The `UserProfileApiVerticle` class exposes the HTTP API for the user profile service. It holds three important fields:

- `mongoClient`, of type `MongoClient`, is used to connect to a MongoDB server.
- `authProvider`, of type `MongoAuthentication`, is used to perform authentication checks using MongoDB.
- `userUtil`, of type `MongoUserUtil`, is used to facilitate new user creation.

We initialize these fields from the `rxStart` verticle initialization method (since we use RxJava), as shown in the following listing.

Listing 10.1 Initializing the MonbgoDB client and authentication provider

Create a client based on some configuration.

```
mongoClient = MongoClient.createShared(vertx, mongoConfig());

authProvider = MongoAuthentication.create(mongoClient,
    new MongoAuthenticationOptions());

userUtil = MongoUserUtil.create(mongoClient,
    new MongoAuthenticationOptions(), new MongoAuthorizationOptions());
```

Create an authentication provider on MongoDB.

Helper to create users in the MongoDB database

The authentication provider piggybacks on the MongoDB client instance, which is configured as in the next listing. We pass empty configuration options for the authentication provider as we follow the conventions of the Vert.x MongoDB authentication module. The same goes with the utility that will help us when adding users.

Listing 10.2   MongoDB client configuration method

```
private JsonObject mongoConfig() {          We will be testing locally.
  return new JsonObject()
    .put("host", "localhost")  ◄           profiles is the database
    .put("port", 27017)                     name, but we could equally
    .put("db_name", "profiles");  ◄         use something else.
}
```

Since we are exposing an HTTP API, we'll use a Vert.x web router to configure the various routes to be handled by the service, as shown in the following listing.

Listing 10.3   User profile service HTTP routing

```
Router router = Router.router(vertx);
BodyHandler bodyHandler = BodyHandler.create();
router.post().handler(bodyHandler);
router.put().handler(bodyHandler);
router.post("/register")                          The processing logic
  .handler(this::validateRegistration)  ◄         is split between two
  .handler(this::register);                        chained handlers.
router.get("/:username").handler(this::fetchUser);
router.put("/:username").handler(this::updateUser);
router.post("/authenticate").handler(this::authenticate);
router.get("/owns/:deviceId").handler(this::whoOwns);
```

Note that we use two chained handlers for the registration. The first handler is for data validation, and the second handler is for the actual processing logic. But what is in the validation logic?

10.2.3   *Validating user input*

Registration is a critical step, so we must ensure that the data is valid. We must check that the incoming data (a JSON document) contains all required fields, and that they are all valid. For instance, we need to check that an email is actually an email, and that a username is not empty and does not contain unwanted characters.

The `validateRegistration` method in the following listing delegates the validation to the helper methods `anyRegistrationFieldIsMissing` and `anyRegistration-FieldIsWrong`.

Listing 10.4   The registration validation method

```
private void validateRegistration(RoutingContext ctx) {
  JsonObject body = jsonBody(ctx);
  if (anyRegistrationFieldIsMissing(body) ||      Registration failed, so we end
  ⮑ anyRegistrationFieldIsWrong(body)) {          the HTTP request with status
    ctx.fail(400);  ◄                              code 400.
  } else {
    ctx.next();                    The next handler in
  }                                the chain is called.
}
```

When any validation steps fails, we respond with a 400 HTTP status code; otherwise, we call the next handler, which in our case will be the `register` method.

The implementation of the `anyRegistrationFieldIsMissing` method is quite simple. We check that the provided JSON document contains the required fields, as follows.

Listing 10.5 Checking for missing JSON fields

```
private boolean anyRegistrationFieldIsMissing(JsonObject body) {
    return !(body.containsKey("username") &&        Check that all fields are present.
        body.containsKey("password") &&
        body.containsKey("email") &&
        body.containsKey("city") &&
        body.containsKey("deviceId") &&
        body.containsKey("makePublic"));
}
```

The `anyRegistrationFieldIsWrong` method delegates checks to regular expressions, as in the following listing.

Listing 10.6 Validating specific fields

Regular expression for valid
usernames like abc, a-b-c, etc.

Regular expression matching

```
private final Pattern validUsername = Pattern.compile("\\w[\\w+|-]*");
// (...)
private boolean anyRegistrationFieldIsWrong(JsonObject body) {
    return !validUsername.matcher(body.getString("username")).matches() ||
        !validEmail.matcher(body.getString("email")).matches() ||
        body.getString("password").trim().isEmpty() ||
        !validDeviceId.matcher(body.getString("deviceId")).matches();
}
```

`trim` removes whitespace at the beginning and
end of the string and then checks for emptiness.

The `validDeviceId` regular expression is the same as `validUsername`. Validating an email address (`validEmail`) is a more sophisticated regular expression. I chose to use one of the safe regular expressions from the Open Web Application Security Project (OWASP) for that purpose (www.owasp.org/index.php/OWASP_Validation_Regex _Repository).

Now that we have validated the data, it is time to register the users.

10.2.4 Adding users in MongoDB

Inserting a new user in the database requires two steps:

1 We need to ask the helper to insert a new user, as it will also deal with other aspects like hashing passwords and having a salt value.
2 We need to update the user document to add extra fields that are not required by the authentication provider schema.

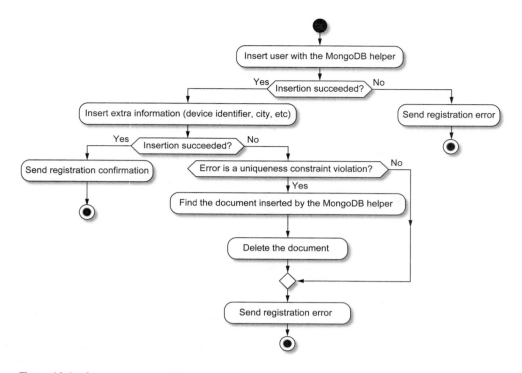

Figure 10.1   Steps to successfully add a user

Since this is a two-step data insert, and we cannot use any transaction management facility, we need to take care of the data integrity ourselves, as shown in figure 10.1.

Fortunately RxJava makes the error management declarative, so we won't have to deal with nested conditionals of asynchronous operations, which would be complicated to do with callbacks or promises/futures.

The `register` method starts by extracting the JSON payload from the HTTP request, and then the username and password of the user to create, as follows.

Listing 10.7   Preamble of the register method

```
private void register(RoutingContext ctx) {
    JsonObject body = jsonBody(ctx);                    ⟵—— Extract the JSON body.
    String username = body.getString("username");
    String password = body.getString("password");

    userUtil
        .rxCreateUser(username, password)              ⟵—— Insert a new user.
    // (...)
}
```

Remember that `register` is called after validation, so we expect the JSON data to be good. We pass the authentication provider the username and password. There is also a form where `rxCreateUser` accepts two extra lists for defining roles and permissions. Then the helper populates the database with a new document.

Next we have to run a query to update the newly created document and append new entries. The MongoDB query is shown in the following listing and is represented as a JSON object.

Listing 10.8 MongoDB query to update a new user

```
JsonObject extraInfo = new JsonObject()
  .put("$set", new JsonObject()                        ⟵  This is the $set operator
    .put("email", body.getString("email"))                 from MongoDB.
    .put("city", body.getString("city"))
    .put("deviceId", body.getString("deviceId"))
    .put("makePublic", body.getBoolean("makePublic")));
```

We must thus chain the `rxInsertUser` operation with a MongoDB update query, knowing that `rxInsertUser` returns a `Single<String>` where the value is the identifier of the new document. The following listing shows the complete user addition processing with RxJava.

Listing 10.9 Complete user addition processing with RxJava

```
userUtil
  .rxCreateUser(username, password)        ⟵  User insert query
  .flatMapMaybe(docId -> insertExtraInfo(extraInfo, docId))  ⟵ Update query
  .ignoreElement()
  .subscribe(
    () -> completeRegistration(ctx),       ⟵  HTTP 200
    err -> handleRegistrationError(ctx, err));  ⟵ Deal with the error
```

The `flatMapMaybe` operator allows us to chain the two queries.

The `insertExtraInfo` method is shown in the next listing and returns a `Maybe-Source`, because finding and updating a document may not hold a result if no matching document was found.

Listing 10.10 Implementation of the `insertExtraInfo` method

```
private MaybeSource<? extends JsonObject> insertExtraInfo(JsonObject
➥ extraInfo, String docId) {
  JsonObject query = new JsonObject().put("_id", docId);
  return mongoClient
    .rxFindOneAndUpdate("user", query, extraInfo)     ⟵  Find and update
    .onErrorResumeNext(err -> {                            a document.
      return deleteIncompleteUser(query, err);        ⟵  Manual rollback
    });
}
```

Note that the update query can fail; for example, if another user has already registered a device with the same identifier. In this case, we need to manually roll back and remove the document that was created by the authentication provider, because otherwise we would have an incomplete document in the database. The following listing holds the implementation of the deleteIncompleteUser method.

Listing 10.11   Implementation of the deleteIncompleteUser method

```
private boolean isIndexViolated(Throwable err) {
  return err.getMessage().contains("E11000");   ⟵─────  This is the technical code for
}                                                         an index constraint violation.

private MaybeSource<? extends JsonObject> deleteIncompleteUser(JsonObject
⇒ query, Throwable err) {
  if (isIndexViolated(err)) {
    return mongoClient
      .rxRemoveDocument("user", query)   ⟵───────  Remove the document.
      .flatMap(del -> Maybe.error(err));   ⟵──────  Replace the result with the original
  } else {                                           exception and propagate it.
    return Maybe.error(err);   ⟵──────
  }                              err is another kind of error,
}                                and we propagate it.
```

We need to rely on a technical code in an exception message to distinguish between index violation errors and other types of errors. In the first case, the previous data has to be removed because we want to deal with it and recover; in the second case, this is another error and we cannot do much, so we propagate it.

Finally, the handleRegistrationError method shown in the next listing needs to inspect the error to respond with the appropriate HTTP status code.

Listing 10.12   Implementation of the handleRegistrationError method

```
private void handleRegistrationError(RoutingContext ctx, Throwable err) {
  if (isIndexViolated(err)) {
    logger.error("Registration failure: {}", err.getMessage());
    ctx.fail(409);   ⟵──────
  } else {             The error is because the user provided an
    logger.error("Woops", err);   existing username or device identifier.
    ctx.fail(500);   ⟵──────
  }                    This is a technical error.
}
```

It is important to notify the requester if the request failed because the username or device identifier has already been taken, or if it failed due to some technical error. In one case, the error is the fault of the requester, and in the other case, the service is the culprit, and the requester can try again later.

10.2.5 Authenticating a user

Authenticating a user against a username and password is very simple. All we need to do is query the authentication provider, which returns an `io.vertx.ext.auth.User` instance on success. In our case, we are not interested in querying permissions or roles—all we want to do is check that authentication succeeded.

Assuming that an HTTP `POST` request sent to `/authenticate` has a JSON body with `username` and `password` fields, we can perform the authentication request as follows.

Listing 10.13 Authenticating a user

```
private void authenticate(RoutingContext ctx) {
  authProvider.rxAuthenticate(jsonBody(ctx))          ◄─── Authentication method
    .subscribe(
      user -> completeEmptySuccess(ctx),
      err -> handleAuthenticationError(ctx, err));
}

private void completeEmptySuccess(RoutingContext ctx) {
  ctx.response().setStatusCode(200).end();           ◄─── Success
}

private void handleAuthenticationError(RoutingContext ctx, Throwable err) {
  logger.error("Authentication problem {}", err.getMessage());
  ctx.response().setStatusCode(401).end();      ◄─┐ Report an
}                                                  │ authentication failure.
```

The result of an authentication request is a `User`, or an exception if it failed. Depending on the outcome, we end the HTTP request with a 200 or 401 status code.

10.2.6 Fetching a user's data

HTTP `GET` requests to `/username` must return the data associated with that user (e.g., `/foo`, `/bar`, etc.). To do that, we need to prepare a MongoDB query and return the data as a JSON response.

We need a MongoDB "find" query to locate a user document. To do that we need two JSON documents:

- A query document to find based on the value of the `username` field of the database documents
- A document to specify the fields that should be returned.

The following code performs such a query.

Listing 10.14 Fetching a user's data in MongoDB

```
JsonObject query = new JsonObject()     │ We want to match
  .put("username", username);      ◄─┘ exactly the username.

JsonObject fields = new JsonObject()    │ We don't want the
  .put("_id", 0)                   ◄─┘ document identifier.
```

```
    .put("username", 1)          ◁──┐  We want to repeat
    .put("email", 1)                │  the username.
    .put("deviceId", 1)
    .put("city", 1)
    .put("makePublic", 1);

mongoClient
    .rxFindOne("user", query, fields)     ◁──── Find one document.
    .toSingle()
    .subscribe(
      json -> completeFetchRequest(ctx, json),
      err -> handleFetchError(ctx, err));
```

It is important to specify which fields should be part of the response, and to be explicit about it. In our case, we don't want to reveal the document identifier, so we set it to 0 in the `fields` document. We also explicitly list the fields that we want to be returned with 1 values. This also ensures that other fields like the password and salt values from the authentication are not accidentally revealed.

The next listing shows the two methods that complete the fetch request and HTTP response.

Listing 10.15   Completing a user fetch request

```
private void completeFetchRequest(RoutingContext ctx, JsonObject json) {
  ctx.response()
    .putHeader("Content-Type", "application/json")
    .end(json.encode());                     ◁──┐  Complete successfully by
}                                               │  forwarding the JSON result.

private void handleFetchError(RoutingContext ctx, Throwable err) {
    if (err instanceof NoSuchElementException) {  ◁──┐
      ctx.fail(404);                                 │  Fail with a 404 if the user
    } else {                                         │  does not exist, or with a
      fail500(ctx, err);                             │  500 if a technical error
    }                                                │  was encountered.
}
```

It is important to properly deal with the error cases and to distinguish between a non-existing user and a technical error.

Let's now see the case of updating a user.

10.2.7 Updating a user's data

Updating a user's data is similar to fetching data, as we need two JSON documents: one to match documents, and one to specify what fields need to be updated. The following listing shows the corresponding code.

Listing 10.16 Updating a user's data with MongoDB

```
JsonObject query = new JsonObject().put("username", username);        ◄─┐ We want to
JsonObject updates = new JsonObject();                                   │ match by
if (body.containsKey("city")) {          ◄─────────────┐                 │ username.
  updates.put("city", body.getString("city"));         │
}                                                       │
if (body.containsKey("email")) {                        │ We selectively check each
  updates.put("email", body.getString("email"));        │ allowed field for updates.
}                                                       │
if (body.containsKey("makePublic")) {
  updates.put("makePublic", body.getBoolean("makePublic"));
}
                                                  ┌─ If no allowed field was
if (updates.isEmpty()) {        ◄─────────────────┘  specified, we quickly return.
  ctx.response().setStatusCode(200).end();
  return;
}
                                                         ┌─ The $set operator is used in
updates = new JsonObject().put("$set", updates);   ◄─────┘  MongoDB to update data.
mongoClient
  .rxFindOneAndUpdate("user", query, updates)      ◄──┐ We search and update
  .ignoreElement()                                    │ one document.
  .subscribe(
    () -> completeEmptySuccess(ctx),
    err -> handleUpdateError(ctx, err));
```

Since the update request is a JSON document coming from an HTTP request, there is always the possibility of an external attack if we are not careful. A malicious user could craft a JSON document in the request with updates to the password or username, so we test for the presence of each allowed field in updates: `city`, `email`, and `makePublic`. We then create a JSON document with updates just for these fields, rather than reusing the JSON document received over HTTP, and we make an update request to the Vert.x MongoDB client.

We have now covered the typical use of MongoDB in Vert.x, as well as how to use it for authentication purposes. Let's move on to PostgreSQL and the activity service.

10.3 Activity service with PostgreSQL

The activity service stores all the step updates as they are received from pedometers. It is a service that reacts to new step update events (to store data), and it can be queried by other services to get step counts for a given device on a given day, month, or year.

The activity service uses PostgreSQL to store activity data after device updates have been accepted by the ingestion service. PostgreSQL is well suited for this purpose because the SQL query language makes it easy to compute aggregates, such as step counts for a device on a given month.

The service is split into two independent verticles:

- `EventsVerticle` listens for incoming activity updates over Kafka and then stores data in the database.
- `ActivityApiVerticle` exposes an HTTP API for querying activity data.

We could have put all the code on a single verticle, but this decoupling renders the code more manageable, as each verticle has a well-defined purpose. `EventsVerticle` performs writes to the database, whereas `ActivityApiVerticle` performs the read operations.

10.3.1 Data model

The data model is not terribly complex and fits in a single relation `stepevent`. The SQL instructions for creating the `stepevent` table are shown in the following listing.

Listing 10.17 SQL instruction for creating the `stepevent` table

```
CREATE TABLE IF NOT EXISTS stepevent
(
  device_id VARCHAR,
  device_sync BIGINT,
  sync_timestamp timestamptz,       ◁──┘ A timestamp with a timezone
  steps_count INTEGER,
  PRIMARY KEY (device_id, device_sync)   ◁──── A composite primary key
);
```

The primary key uniquely identifies an activity update based on a device identifier (device_id) and a synchronization counter from the device (device_sync). The timestamp of the event is recorded (sync_timestamp), and finally the number of steps is stored (steps_count).

> **TIP** If you come from a background with a heavy use of *object-relational mappers* (ORMs), you may be surprised by the preceding database schema, and especially the fact that it uses a composite primary key rather than some auto-incremented number. You may want to first consider the proper design of your relational model with respect to normal forms, and only then see how to handle data in your code, be it with collections and/or objects that reflect the data. If you're interested in the topic, Wikipedia provides a good introduction to database normalization: https://en.wikipedia.org/wiki/Database_normalization.

10.3.2 Opening a connection pool

The `vertx-pg-client` module contains the `PgPool` interface that models a pool of connections to a PostgreSQL server, where each connection can be reused for subsequent queries. `PgPool` is your main access point in the client for performing SQL queries.

The following listing shows how to create a PostgreSQL connection pool.

Listing 10.18   Creating a PostgreSQL connection pool

```
PgPool pgPool = PgPool.pool(vertx, PgConfig.pgConnectOpts(),
    new PoolOptions());
// (...)                                    Create a connection pool.

public static PgConnectOptions pgConnectOpts() {        Configuration for
  return new PgConnectOptions()                          the connection
    .setHost("localhost")
    .setDatabase("postgres")
    .setUser("postgres")
    .setPassword("vertx-in-action");
}
```

The pool creation requires a Vert.x context, a set of connection options such as the host, database, and password, and pool options. The pool options can be tuned to set the maximum number of connections as well as the size of the waiting queue, but default values are fine here.

The `pool` object is then used to perform queries to the database, as you will see next.

10.3.3 Life of a device update event

The `EventsVerticle` is in charge of listening to Kafka records on the `incoming.steps` topic, where each record is an update received from a device through the ingestion service. For each record, `EventsVerticle` must do the following:

- Insert the record into the PostgreSQL database.
- Generate an updated record with the daily step count for the device of the record.
- Publish it as a new Kafka record to the `daily.step.updates` Kafka topic.

This is illustrated in figure 10.2.

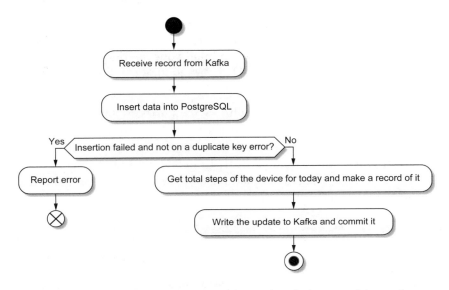

Figure 10.2   Steps for recording a device update and producing an update event

These steps are modeled by the RxJava pipeline defined in the following listing.

Listing 10.19 RxJava pipeline for processing updates in `EventsVerticle`

Subscribe to the Kafka topic.

```
eventConsumer                                    Insert a new record
  .subscribe("incoming.steps")                   in the database.
  .toFlowable()
  .flatMap(this::insertRecord)                    Query the database to
  .flatMap(this::generateActivityUpdate)          publish another record.
  .flatMap(this::commitKafkaConsumerOffset)
  .doOnError(err -> logger.error("Woops", err))   Commit the record to Kafka.
  .retryWhen(this::retryLater)
  .subscribe();
```

This RxJava pipeline is reminiscent of those we saw earlier in the messaging and eventing stack, as we compose three asynchronous operations. This pipeline reads from Kafka, inserts database records (`insertRecord`), produces a query to write to Kafka (`generateActivityUpdate`), and commits it (`commitKafkaConsumerOffset`).

10.3.4 *Inserting a new record*

The SQL query to insert a record is shown next.

Listing 10.20 SQL query to insert step events

```
static String insertStepEvent() {
  return "INSERT INTO stepevent VALUES($1, $2, current_timestamp, $3)";
}
```
                                    $n is the *n*th entry in the values tuple.

TIP Vert.x does not prescribe any object-relational mapping tool. Using plain SQL is a great option, but if you want to abstract your code from the particularities of databases and use an API to build your queries rather than using strings, I recommend looking at jOOQ (www.jooq.org/). You can even find a Vert.x/jOOQ integration module in the community.

We use a class with static methods to define SQL queries, as it is more convenient than plain string constants in our code. The query will be used as a prepared statement, where values prefixed by a $ symbol will be taken from a tuple of values. Since we use a prepared statement, these values are safe from SQL injection attacks.

The `insertRecord` method is called for each new Kafka record, and the method body is shown in the following listing.

Listing 10.21 Implementation of the `insertRecord` method

```
JsonObject data = record.value();          JSON body from the Kafka record

Tuple values = Tuple.of(          Tuple structure
```

```
         data.getString("deviceId"),
         data.getLong("deviceSync"),
         data.getInteger("stepsCount"));
```
→ Insert request

```
      return pgPool
         .preparedQuery(insertStepEvent())  ←┐
         .rxExecute(values)  ←
         .map(rs -> record)  ←┐
         .onErrorReturn(err -> {
            if (duplicateKeyInsert(err)) {
               return record;
            } else {
               throw new RuntimeException(err);
            }
         })
         .toFlowable();
```

Execute the request with parameters.

Remap the Kafka record for processing in the generateActivityUpdate method.

Handle duplicate inserts gracefully.

We first extract the JSON body from the record, and then prepare a tuple of values to pass as parameters to the SQL query in listing 10.20. The result of the query is a row set, but since this is not a SELECT query, we do not care about the result. Instead, we simply remap the result with the original Kafka record value, so the generateActivityUpdate method can reuse it.

The onErrorReturn operator allows us to handle duplicate inserts gracefully. It is possible that after a service restart we'll end up replaying some Kafka events that we had already processed, so the INSERT queries will fail instead of creating entries with duplicate primary keys.

The duplicateKeyInsert method in the following listing shows how we can distinguish between a duplicate key error and another technical error.

Listing 10.22 Detecting a duplicate key error

```
private boolean duplicateKeyInsert(Throwable err) {
   return (err instanceof PgException) &&
      "23505".equals(((PgException) err).getCode());  ←
}
```
Technical code error for a duplicate key insertion attempt

We again have to search for a technical error code in the exception message, and if it corresponds to a PostgreSQL duplicate key error, then onErrorReturn puts the original Kafka record in the pipeline rather than letting an error be propagated.

10.3.5 Generating a device's daily activity update

The next step in the RxJava processing pipeline after a record has been inserted is to query the database to find out how many steps have been taken on the current day. This is then used to prepare a new Kafka record and push it to the daily.step.updates Kafka topic.

The SQL query corresponding to that operation is specified by the stepsCount-ForToday method in the following listing.

Listing 10.23   SQL query to get the steps count for a device on the current day

Steps count will be 0 if there are no matching entries.

```
static String stepsCountForToday() {
  return "SELECT current_timestamp, coalesce(sum(steps_count), 0)
  FROM stepevent WHERE " +
    "(device_id = $1) AND" +
    "(date_trunc('day', sync_timestamp) = date_trunc('day',
    current_timestamp))";
}
```

Match records for the current day, truncating hours, minutes, and seconds.

This request computes the sum (or 0) of the steps taken on the current day for a given device identifier.

The next listing shows the implementation of the `generateActivityUpdate` method, picking up the original Kafka record forwarded by the `insertRecord` method.

Listing 10.24   Implementation of the `generateActivityUpdate` method

Extract the device identifier from the original Kafka record.

Key for the new Kafka record

```
String deviceId = record.value().getString("deviceId");
LocalDateTime now = LocalDateTime.now();
String key = deviceId + ":" + now.getYear() + "-" + now.getMonth() + "-" +
  now.getDayOfMonth();

return pgPool
  .preparedQuery(stepsCountForToday())
  .rxExecute(Tuple.of(deviceId))
  .map(rs -> rs.iterator().next())
  .map(row -> new JsonObject()
    .put("deviceId", deviceId)
    .put("timestamp", row.getTemporal(0).toString())
    .put("stepsCount", row.getLong(1)))
  .flatMap(json ->
    updateProducer.rxSend(KafkaProducerRecord.create("daily.step.updates",
    key, json)))
  .map(rs -> record)
  .toFlowable();
```

Prepared statement with a tuple of one value

We expect just one row.

Create a new JsonObject out of the row values.

Compose the Kafka send operation.

This code shows how we can manipulate rows following a SELECT query. The result of a query is `RowSet`, materialized here by the `rs` argument in the first `map` operator, and which can be iterated row by row. Since the query returns a single row, we can directly access the first and only row by calling `next` on the `RowSet` iterator. We then access the row elements by type and index to build a `JsonObject` that creates the Kafka record sent to the `daily.step.updates` topic.

10.3.6   *Activity API queries*

The `ActivityApiVerticle` class exposes the HTTP API for the activity service—all routes lead to SQL queries. I won't show all of them. We'll focus on the monthly steps for a device, handled through HTTP GET requests to `/:deviceId/:year/:month`. The SQL query is shown next.

> **Listing 10.25 Monthly step count SQL query**

```
static String monthlyStepsCount() {
  return "SELECT sum(steps_count) FROM stepevent WHERE" +
    "(device_id = $1) AND" +
    "(date_trunc('month', sync_timestamp) = $2::timestamp)";
}
```
The value needs to be coalesced to a timestamp.

The `stepsOnMonth` method is shown in the next listing. It performs the SQL query based on the year and month path parameters.

> **Listing 10.26 Handling monthly steps requests**

```
private void stepsOnMonth(RoutingContext ctx) {
  try {
    String deviceId = ctx.pathParam("deviceId");
    LocalDateTime dateTime = LocalDateTime.of(
      Integer.parseInt(ctx.pathParam("year")),
      Integer.parseInt(ctx.pathParam("month")),
      1, 0, 0);
    Tuple params = Tuple.of(deviceId, dateTime);
    pgPool.preparedQuery(SqlQueries.monthlyStepsCount())
      .rxExecute(params)
      .map(rs -> rs.iterator().next())
      .subscribe(
        row -> sendCount(ctx, row),
        err -> handleError(ctx, err));
  } catch (DateTimeException | NumberFormatException e) {
    sendBadRequest(ctx);
  }
}
```
Query arguments tuple
JSON response based on the row data
Sends an HTTP 400 error
When a URL parameter is not a number or does not result in a valid date

The query result is again a `RowSet`, and we know from the SQL query that only one row can be returned, so we use the `map` operator to extract it. The `sendCount` method sends the data as a JSON document, while the `handleError` method produces an HTTP 500 error. When a year or month URL parameter is not a number or does not result in a valid date, `sendBadRequest` produces an HTTP 400 response to let the request know of the mistake.

It is now time to move on to integration testing strategies. I'll also show you some other data client methods, such as SQL batch queries, when we have to prepopulate a PostgreSQL database.

10.4 *Integration tests*

Testing the user profile service involves issuing HTTP requests to the corresponding API. The activity service has two facets: one that involves the HTTP API, and one that involves crafting Kafka events and observing the effects in terms of persisted state and produced events.

10.4.1   *Testing the user profile service*

The user profile tests rely on issuing HTTP requests that impact the service state and the database (e.g., creating a user) and then issuing further HTTP requests to perform some assertions, as illustrated in figure 10.3.

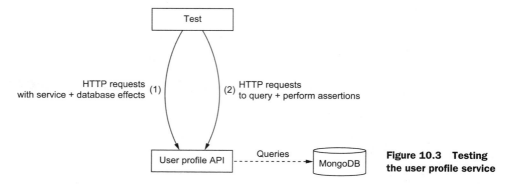

Figure 10.3   Testing the user profile service

The integration tests rely again on Testcontainers, as we need to have a MongoDB instance running. Once we have the container running, we need to prepare the MongoDB database to be in a clean state before we run any tests. This is important to ensure that a test is not affected by data left by a previous test's execution.

The `setup` method of the `IntegrationTest` class performs the test preparation.

Listing 10.27   User profile integration test setup

```
@BeforeEach
void setup(Vertx vertx, VertxTestContext testContext) {
  JsonObject mongoConfig = new JsonObject()
    .put("host", "localhost")
    .put("port", 27017)
    .put("db_name", "profiles");
  mongoClient = MongoClient.createShared(vertx, mongoConfig);

  mongoClient
    .rxCreateIndexWithOptions("user", new JsonObject().put("username", 1),      ⟵  Ensure we have an index on username.
      new IndexOptions().unique(true))
    .andThen(mongoClient.rxCreateIndexWithOptions("user",
      new JsonObject().put("deviceId", 1), new IndexOptions().unique(true)))    ⟵
    .andThen(dropAllUsers())                                                    Drop all users.
    .flatMapSingle(res ->
      vertx.rxDeployVerticle(new UserProfileApiVerticle()))
    .subscribe(
      ok -> testContext.completeNow(),                                          Ensure we have an index on deviceId.
      testContext::failNow);
}
```

We first connect to the MongoDB database and then ensure we have two indexes for the `username` and `deviceId` fields. We then remove all existing documents from the profiles database (see listing 10.28), and deploy an instance of the User-ProfileApiVerticle verticle before successfully completing the initialization phase.

```
private Maybe<MongoClientDeleteResult> dropAllUsers() {
  return mongoClient.rxRemoveDocuments("user", new JsonObject());   ◁─┐
}
```
Match unconditionally with an empty JSON query document.

The IntegrationTest class provides different test cases of operations that are expected to succeed, as well as operations that are expected to fail. RestAssured is used to write the test specifications of the HTTP requests, as in the following listing.

```
@Test
@DisplayName("Failing at authenticating an unknown user")
void authenticateMissingUser() {
  JsonObject request = new JsonObject()        ◁─┐  This user does
    .put("username", "Bean")                      │  not exist.
    .put("password", "abc");

  with()
    .spec(requestSpecification)
    .contentType(ContentType.JSON)
    .body(request.encode())
    .post("/authenticate")
    .then()
    .assertThat()                    We expect an HTTP
    .statusCode(401);   ◁─┘          401 status code.
}
```

The authenticateMissingUser method checks that authenticating against invalid credentials results in an HTTP 401 status code.

Another example is the following test, where we check what happens when we attempt to register a user twice.

```
given()
  .spec(requestSpecification)
  .contentType(ContentType.JSON)
  .accept(ContentType.JSON)              This method returns a predefined
  .body(basicUser().encode()))   ◁─┘     JSON object for a user.
  .when()
  .post("/register")
  .then()
  .assertThat()
  .statusCode(200);   ◁─── The first attempt is ok.
```

```
given()
  .spec(requestSpecification)
  .contentType(ContentType.JSON)
  .accept(ContentType.JSON)
  .body(basicUser().encode())
  .when()
  .post("/register")
  .then()
  .assertThat()
  .statusCode(409);    ◁——— The second attempt is not ok!
```

We could also peek into the database and check the data that is being stored after each action. Since we need to cover all functional cases of the HTTP API, it is more straightforward to focus on just the HTTP API in the integration tests. However, there are cases where an API on top of a database may not expose you to some important effects on the stored data, and in these cases, you will need to connect to the database to make some further assertions.

10.4.2 *Testing the activity service API*

Testing the activity service API is quite similar to testing the user profile service, except that we use PostgreSQL instead of MongoDB.

We first need to ensure that the data schema is defined as in listing 10.17. To do that, the SQL script in init/postgres/setup.sql is run automatically when the PostgreSQL container starts. This works because the container image specifies that any SQL script found in /docker-entrypoint-initdb.d/ will be run when it starts, and the Docker Compose file that we use mounts init/postgres to /docker-entrypoint-initdb.d/, so the SQL file is available in the container.

Once the database has been prepared with some predefined data, we issue HTTP requests to perform assertions, as shown in figure 10.4.

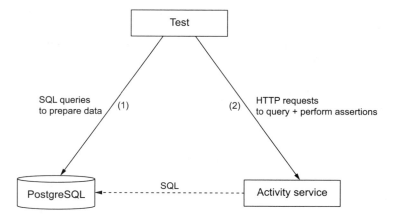

Figure 10.4   Testing the activity service API

We again rely on Testcontainers to start a PostgreSQL server, and then we rely on the test setup method to prepare the data as follows.

Listing 10.31   Preparing the activity service API test

Query to insert data

```
String insertQuery = "INSERT INTO stepevent
   VALUES($1, $2, $3::timestamp, $4)";
LocalDateTime now = LocalDateTime.now();              A set of entries
List<Tuple> data = Arrays.asList(                     for the database
  Tuple.of("123", 1, LocalDateTime.of(2019, 4, 1, 23, 0), 6541),
  Tuple.of("123", 2, LocalDateTime.of(2019, 5, 20, 10, 0), 200),
  Tuple.of("123", 3, LocalDateTime.of(2019, 5, 21, 10, 10), 100),
  Tuple.of("456", 1, LocalDateTime.of(2019, 5, 21, 10, 15), 123),
  Tuple.of("123", 4, LocalDateTime.of(2019, 5, 21, 11, 0), 320),
  Tuple.of("abc", 1, now.minus(1, ChronoUnit.HOURS), 1000),
  Tuple.of("def", 1, now.minus(2, ChronoUnit.HOURS), 100),
  Tuple.of("def", 2, now.minus(30, ChronoUnit.MINUTES), 900),
  Tuple.of("abc", 2, now, 1500)
);
PgPool pgPool = PgPool.pool(vertx, PgConfig.pgConnectOpts(),
   new PoolOptions());

pgPool.query("DELETE FROM stepevent")    <----  Ensure no event is left.
  .rxExecute()
  .flatMap(rows ->
   gPool.preparedQuery(insertQuery).rxExecuteBatch(data)  <---- Insert our data.
  .ignoreElement()
  .andThen(vertx.rxDeployVerticle(new ActivityApiVerticle()))  <----  Deploy the
  .ignoreElement()                                                    API verticle.
  .andThen(Completable.fromAction(pgPool::close))
  .subscribe(testContext::completeNow, testContext::failNow);
```
Close the connection pool.

Here we want a database with a data set that we control, with activities for devices 123, 456, abc, and def at various points in time. For instance, device 123 recorded 320 steps on 2019/05/21 at 11:00, and that was the fourth time the device made a successful synchronization with the backend. We can then perform checks against the HTTP API, as in the following listing, where we check the number of steps for device 123 in May 2019.

Listing 10.32   Checking steps for device 123 on a given month
---

```
JsonPath jsonPath = given()
  .spec(requestSpecification)
  .accept(ContentType.JSON)
  .get("/123/2019/05")    <----  URL of the query
  .then()
  .assertThat()
```

```
.statusCode(200)
.extract()
.jsonPath();

assertThat(jsonPath.getInt("count")).isEqualTo(620);   ⟵——— Check the JSON result.
```

The activity HTTP API is the read-only part of the service, so let's now look at the other part of the service.

10.4.3 *Testing the activity service's event handling*

The technique for testing the Kafka event processing part of `EventsVerticle` is very similar to what we did in the previous chapter: we'll send some Kafka records and then observe what Kafka records the service produces.

By sending multiple step updates for a given device, we should observe that the service produces updates that accumulate the steps on the current day. Since the service both consumes and produces Kakfa records that reflect the current state of the database, we won't need to perform SQL queries—observing that correct Kafka records are being produced is sufficient. Figure 10.5 provides an overview of how the testing is done.

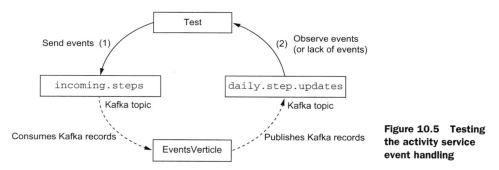

Figure 10.5   Testing the activity service event handling

The integration test class (`EventProcessingTest`) again uses TestContainers to start the required services: PostgreSQL, Apache Kafka, and Apache ZooKeeper. Before any test is run, we must start from a clean state by using the test preparation code in the following listing.

Listing 10.33   Preparation code for the event-processing integration tests

```
consumer = KafkaConsumer.create(vertx,
⟹ KafkaConfig.consumer("activity-service-test-" +
⟹ System.currentTimeMillis()));
producer = KafkaProducer.create(vertx, KafkaConfig.producer());
KafkaAdminClient adminClient = KafkaAdminClient.create(vertx,
⟹ KafkaConfig.producer());
PgPool pgPool = PgPool.pool(vertx, PgConfig.pgConnectOpts(),
⟹ new PoolOptions());

pgPool.query("DELETE FROM stepevent")   ⟵——┐ Delete data from
                                             the database.
```

```
.rxExecute()
.flatMapCompletable(rs ->
  adminClient.rxDeleteTopics(Arrays.asList("incoming.steps",
  "daily.step.updates")))
.andThen(Completable.fromAction(pgPool::close))
.onErrorComplete()
.subscribe(
  testContext::completeNow,
  testContext::failNow);
```

Delete Kafka topics.

Close the database connection pool.

We need to ensure that the PostgreSQL database is empty, and that the Kafka topics we use to receive and send events are deleted. We can then focus on the test method, where we will send two step updates for device 123.

Before that, we must first subscribe to the `daily.step.updates` Kafka topic, where the `EventsVerticle` class will send Kafka records. The following listing shows the first part of the test case.

Listing 10.34 First part of the events verticle test case

```
consumer.subscribe("daily.step.updates")
  .toFlowable()
  .skip(1)                                          Skip the first update.
  .subscribe(record -> {                            Get the second update.
    JsonObject json = record.value();
    testContext.verify(() -> {
      assertThat(json.getString("deviceId")).isEqualTo("123");
      assertThat(json.containsKey("timestamp")).isTrue();
      assertThat(json.getInteger("stepsCount")).isEqualTo(250);
    });
    testContext.completeNow();
  }, testContext::failNow);
```

Perform some assertions.

Since we send two updates, we skip the emitted record and only perform assertions on the second one, as it should reflect the sum of the steps from the two updates. The preceding code is waiting for events to be produced, so we now need to deploy `EventsVerticle` and send the two updates as follows.

Listing 10.35 Second part of the events verticle test case

```
vertx
  .rxDeployVerticle(new EventsVerticle())           Deploy EventsVerticle.
  .flatMap(id -> {                                  First update
    JsonObject steps = new JsonObject()
      .put("deviceId", "123")
      .put("deviceSync", 1L)
      .put("stepsCount", 200);
    return producer.rxSend(KafkaProducerRecord.create("incoming.steps",
      "123", steps));
  })
  .flatMap(id -> {                                  Second update
    JsonObject steps = new JsonObject()
```

```
      .put("deviceId", "123")
      .put("deviceSync", 2L)
      .put("stepsCount", 50);
    return producer.rxSend(KafkaProducerRecord.create("incoming.steps",
      ➥ "123", steps));
  })
  .subscribe(ok -> {
  }, testContext::failNow);
```

The test completes as `EventsVerticle` properly sends correct updates to the `daily.step.updates` Kafka topic. We can again note how RxJava allows us to compose asynchronous operations in a declarative fashion and ensure the error processing is clearly identified. We have essentially two RxJava pipelines here, and any error causes the test context to fail.

> **NOTE** There is a tiny vulnerability window for this test to fail if the first update is sent before midnight and the second right after midnight. In that case, the second event will not be a sum of the steps in the two events. This is very unlikely to happen, since the two events will be emitted a few milliseconds apart, but still, it could happen.

Speaking of event streams, the next chapter will focus on advanced event processing services with Vert.x.

Summary

- The Vert.x MongoDB client allows you to store and query documents.
- Vert.x can also use MongoDB to perform authentication and safely store user credentials, roles, and permissions.
- Vert.x offers an efficient reactive driver for PostgreSQL.
- You do not always need an object-relational mapper. Working directly with SQL and relational data can be simple and efficient.
- It is important to ensure clean state in databases before executing integration tests.

11

End-to-end real-time reactive event processing

This chapter covers

- Combining RxJava operators and Vert.x clients to support advanced processing
- Using RxJava operators to perform content enrichment and aggregate data processing on top of event streams
- Extending the Vert.x event bus to web applications to unify backend and frontend communication models
- Managing state in a stream-processing setting

In this chapter we'll explore advanced reactive stream processing, where application state is subject to live changes based on events. By performing transformations and aggregations on events, we will compute live statistics about what is happening in the larger 10k steps application. You will also see how event streams can impact real-time web applications by unifying Java and JavaScript code under the Vert.x event-bus umbrella.

This chapter starts by looking at advanced stream processing with RxJava operators and Vert.x clients. We'll then discuss the topic of real-time web applications connected over the event bus, and we'll finish with techniques for properly dealing with state (and especially *initial* state) in a context of continuous events.

11.1 *Advanced stream data processing with Kafka and RxJava*

In previous chapters we used RxJava operators to process events of all kinds: HTTP requests, AMQP messages, and Kafka records. RxJava is a versatile library for reactive programming, and it is especially well suited for processing event streams with the Flowable type for back-pressured streams. Kafka provides solid middleware for event streaming, while Vert.x provides a rich ecosystem of reactive clients that connect to other services, databases, or messaging systems.

The *event stats* service is an event-driven reactive service that consumes Kafka records and produces some statistics as other Kafka records. We will look at how we can use RxJava operators to efficiently address three common operations on event streams:

- Enriching data
- Aggregating data over time windows
- Aggregating data by grouping elements using a key or a function

11.1.1 *Enriching daily device updates to generate user updates*

The daily.step.updates Kafka topic is populated with records sent from the activity service. The records contain three entries: the device identifier, a timestamp of when the record was produced, and a number of steps.

Whenever a device update is processed by the activity service, it stores the update to a PostgreSQL database and then produces a Kafka record with the number of steps on the current day for the corresponding device. For instance, when device abc receives an update of, say, 300 steps recorded at 11:25, it sends a Kafka record to daily.step .updates with the number of steps for the day corresponding to device abc.

The event stats service consumes these events to enrich them with user data, so other services can be updated in real time about the number of steps recorded on the current day for any user. To do that, we take the records from the daily.step.updates Kafka topic, and add the data from the user API: user name, email, city, and whether the data shall be public. The enriched data is then sent as records to the event-stats.user-activity.updates topic. The steps for enriching data are illustrated in figure 11.1.

> **TIP** This is an implementation technique for the *content enricher* messaging pattern in the seminal *Enterprise Integration Patterns* book by Gregor Hohpe and Bobby Woolf (Addison-Wesley Professional, 2003).

For each incoming Kafka record, we do the following:

1 Make a request to the user profile API to determine who the device belongs to.
2 Make another request to the user profile API to get all the data from the user, and merge it with the incoming record data.
3 Write the enriched record to the event-stats.user-activity.updates Kafka topic, and commit it.

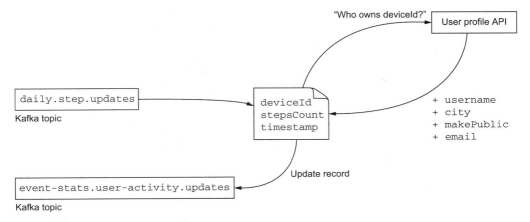

Figure 11.1 Enriching device updates with user data

The following listing shows the corresponding RxJava pipeline.

Listing 11.1 RxJava pipeline for generating user updates

**Subscribe to the
source Kafka topic.**

**Get who owns
the device from
the record.**

```
KafkaConsumer.<String, JsonObject>create(vertx,
    KafkaConfig.consumer("event-stats-user-activity-updates"))
  .subscribe("daily.step.updates")
  .toFlowable()
  .flatMapSingle(this::addDeviceOwner)
  .flatMapSingle(this::addOwnerData)
  .flatMapCompletable(this::publishUserActivityUpdate)
  .doOnError(err -> logger.error("Woops", err))
  .retryWhen(this::retryLater)
  .subscribe();
```

**Fetch the user
data and merge it
with the record.**

**Commit to the
target Kafka topic.**

The RxJava pipeline composes asynchronous operations with `flatMapSingle` and `flatMapCompletable`. This is because doing an HTTP request produces a (single) result, whereas committing a Kafka record is an operation with no return value (hence it is completable). You can also see the common error handling logic from earlier chapters with a delayed re-subscription.

The next listing shows the implementation of the `addDeviceOwner` method.

Listing 11.2 Adding a device owner

This is the incoming Kafka record.

```
private Single<JsonObject> addDeviceOwner(KafkaConsumerRecord<String,
    JsonObject> record) {
  JsonObject data = record.value();
  return webClient
    .get(3000, "localhost", "/owns/" + data.getString("deviceId"))
```

**Make an HTTP request
to the user profile API.**

```
    .as(BodyCodec.jsonObject())
    .rxSend()
    .map(HttpResponse::body)      ◁─────┐
    .map(data::mergeIn);          ◁──┐
}
```
> **Extract the HTTP response body (a JsonObject).**

> **Return the JSON data merge.**

This method makes an HTTP request whose result is a JSON object, and it returns the merge of the source Kafka record's JSON data with the request result data.

Once this is done, we know who the device of the record belongs to, so we can chain with another request to get the user data from the user profile API, as shown next.

> **Listing 11.3   Adding owner data**

```
private Single<JsonObject> addOwnerData(JsonObject data) {      ◁─┐
    String username = data.getString("username");              ◁─┘
    return webClient
        .get(3000, "localhost", "/" + username)      ◁───── Make the HTTP request.
        .as(BodyCodec.jsonObject())
        .rxSend()
        .map(HttpResponse::body)
        .map(data::mergeIn);        ◁───── Merge the data.
}
```
> **This is the data returned by addDeviceOwner.**

This method follows the same pattern as addDeviceOwner, as it takes the result from the previous operation as a parameter, makes an HTTP request to the user profile API, and then returns merged data.

The last operation is that of the publishActivityUpdate method, shown in the following listing.

> **Listing 11.4   Publishing a user activity update Kafka record**

Write the Kafka record.
```
   private CompletableSource publishUserActivityUpdate(JsonObject data) {
└─▷   return producer.rxWrite(
         KafkaProducerRecord.create("event-stats.user-activity.updates",
      ➡   data.getString("username"), data));
   }
```

The implementation writes the Kafka record to the target event-stats.user-activity .updates topic.

11.1.2 *Computing device-update ingestion throughput using time-window aggregates*

The ingestion service receives the incoming device updates from HTTP and AMQP, and then publishes them to the incoming.steps Kafka topic. The ingestion throughput is typical of a dashboard metric, where the value is frequently updated with the number of device updates ingested per second. This is a good indicator of the stress level on the larger application, as every update triggers further events that are processed by other microservices.

To compute the ingestion throughput, we need to listen for records on the `incoming.steps` topic, aggregate records over a fixed time window, and count how many records have been received. This is illustrated in figure 11.2.

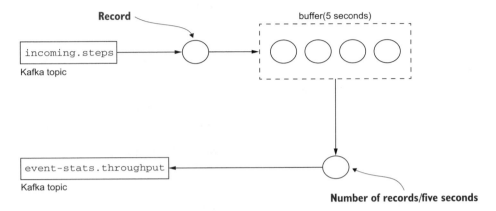

Figure 11.2   Throughput computation from ingestion records

The following listing shows the RxJava pipeline for computing the throughput and publishing the results to the `event-stats.throughput` Kafka topic.

Listing 11.5   RxJava pipeline for computing ingestion throughput

Subscribe to the source Kafka topic.

```
KafkaConsumer.<String, JsonObject>create(vertx,
    KafkaConfig.consumer("event-stats-throughput"))
  .subscribe("incoming.steps")
  .toFlowable()
  .buffer(5, TimeUnit.SECONDS, RxHelper.scheduler(vertx))
  .flatMapCompletable(this::publishThroughput)
  .doOnError(err -> logger.error("Woops", err))
  .retryWhen(this::retryLater)
  .subscribe();
```

Buffer records in windows of five seconds

Compute and publish the throughput.

The `buffer` operator is one of several aggregation operators that you can use in RxJava. It aggregates events for a time period and then passes the result as a `List`. You can see that we pass a Vert.x scheduler from the `RxHelper` class; this is because `buffer` delays event processing and by default will call the next operators on an RxJava-specific thread. The Vert.x scheduler ensures that operators are instead called from the original Vert.x context so as to preserve the Vert.x threading model.

Once `buffer` has aggregated all Kafka records over the last five seconds, the `publishThroughput` method computes and publishes the throughput as shown next.

Listing 11.6   Publish the ingestion throughput

```
private CompletableSource publishThroughput(List<KafkaConsumerRecord<String,
➥ JsonObject>> records) {
  KafkaProducerRecord<String, JsonObject> record =
➥ KafkaProducerRecord.create("event-stats.throughput",
    new JsonObject()
      .put("seconds", 5)
      .put("count", records.size())
      .put("throughput", (((double) records.size()) / 5.0d)));
  return producer.rxWrite(record);
}
```

Payload as a JSON object

Compute the throughput.

Write the Kafka record.

Given the `records` list, we can easily compute a throughput and publish a new record. We take care to indicate the number of records and time window size in seconds, so that event consumers have all the information and not just the raw result.

11.1.3 Computing per-city trends using aggregation discriminants and time windows

Let's now look at another form of data aggregation based on RxJava operators by computing per-city trends. More specifically, we'll compute periodically how many steps have been recorded in each city on the current day. To do that, we can reuse the events published to the `event-stats.user-activity.updates` Kafka topic by the very same event stats service, since they contain the number of steps a user has recorded today, along with other data, including the city.

We could reuse the `buffer` operator, as in listing 11.5, and then iterate over the list of records. For each record, we could update a hash table entry where the key would be the city and the value would be the number of steps. We could then publish an update for each city based on the values in the hash table.

We can, however, write a more idiomatic RxJava processing pipeline thanks to the `groupBy` operator, as shown in the following listing and figure 11.3.

Listing 11.7   RxJava pipeline to compute per-city trends

```
KafkaConsumer.<String, JsonObject>create(vertx,
➥ KafkaConfig.consumer("event-stats-city-trends"))
  .subscribe("event-stats.user-activity.updates")
  .toFlowable()
  .groupBy(this::city)    ← Group by city.
  .flatMap(group ->
➥   group.buffer(5, TimeUnit.SECONDS, RxHelper.scheduler(vertx)))
  .flatMapCompletable(this::publishCityTrendUpdate)
  .doOnError(err -> logger.error("Woops", err))
  .retryWhen(this::retryLater)
  .subscribe();
```

Buffer by windows of five seconds.

Publish a Kafka record.

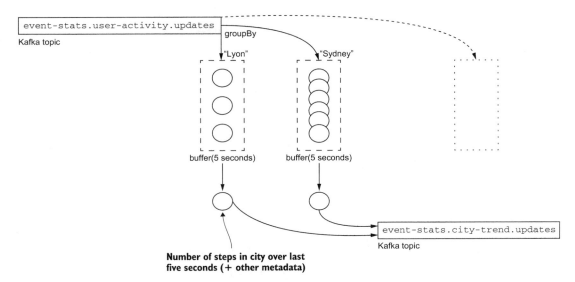

Figure 11.3   Computing per-city trends from user activity records

As events enter the pipeline, the `groupBy` operator dispatches them to groups based on the city values found in the records (the *discriminant*). You can think of `groupBy` as the equivalent of `GROUP BY` in an SQL statement. The filtering function `city` is shown in the next listing and extracts the city value from the Kafka record.

Listing 11.8   Filter based on the city value

```
private String city(KafkaConsumerRecord<String, JsonObject> record) {
  return record.value().getString("city");
}
```

The `groupBy` operator in listing 11.7 returns a `Flowable` of `GroupedFlowable` of Kafka records. Each `GroupedFlowable` is a flowable that is dedicated to the grouped records of a city, as dispatched by `groupBy` using the `city` function. For each group, the `flatMap` operator is then used to group events in time windows of five seconds, meaning that per-city steps are updated every five seconds.

Finally, the `publishCityTrendUpdate` method prepares a new record with updated stats for each city, as shown in the following listing.

Listing 11.9   Publishing per-city stats

Check if records have been received in the time window.

```
private CompletableSource
  publishCityTrendUpdate(List<KafkaConsumerRecord<String,
  JsonObject>> records) {
  if (records.size() > 0) {
    String city = city(records.get(0));
```

All records have the same city, so the first one identifies it.

```
Long stepsCount = records.stream()
  .map(record -> record.value().getLong("stepsCount"))    ◁──┐   Extract the
  .reduce(0L, Long::sum);                                     │   step counts.
KafkaProducerRecord<String, JsonObject> record =
  KafkaProducerRecord.create("event-stats.city-trend.updates",
  city, new JsonObject()
  .put("timestamp", LocalDateTime.now().toString())
  .put("seconds", 5)
  .put("city", city)
  .put("stepsCount", stepsCount)
  .put("updates", records.size()));
  return producer.rxWrite(record);          ┌─────────────────────
} else {                                     │ If there was no record,
  return Completable.complete();    ◁────────┤ just report a completed
}                                            │ operation.
}
```

Compute the sum. (label for `.reduce(0L, Long::sum);`)

Write the Kafka record. (label for `return producer.rxWrite(record);`)

The `publishCityTrendUpdate` method receives a list of Kafka records for a given city and from a time window. We first have to check if there is a record, because otherwise there is nothing to do. With records, we can use Java streams to compute the sum with a `reduce` operator and then prepare a Kafka record with several entries: a timestamp, the time window duration in seconds, the city, how many steps have been recorded, and how many updates were observed during the time window. Once this is done, we write the record to the `event-stats.city-trend.updates` Kafka topic.

Now that we've looked at performing advanced event-streaming processing with RxJava and Vert.x, let's see how we can propagate events to reactive web applications.

11.2 Real-time reactive web applications

As specified in chapter 7, the dashboard web application consumes events from the stats service and displays the following:

- Ingestion throughput
- Rankings of public users
- Per-city trends

This application is updated live, as soon as new data is received, which makes for a nice case of end-to-end integration between backend services and web browsers. The application is a microservice, as illustrated in figure 11.4.

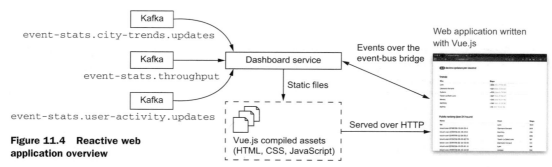

Figure 11.4   Reactive web application overview

The dashboard service is made of two parts:

- A Vue.js application
- A Vert.x service that does the following:
  - Serves the Vue.js resources
  - Connects to Kafka and forwards updates to the Vert.x event bus
  - Bridges between the connected web browsers and the Vert.x event bus

Let's start with the forwarding from Kafka to the event bus.

11.2.1 *Forwarding Kafka records to the Vert.x event bus*

Both throughput and city trend updates are directly forwarded to the Vue.js application code. These are the records received on the `event-stats.throughput` and `event-stats.city-trend.updates` Kafka topics.

In `DashboardWebAppVerticle`, we put in place the RxJava pipelines, as follows.

Listing 11.10 RxJava pipelines to forward throughput and city trend updates

```
KafkaConsumer.<String, JsonObject>create(vertx,
  KafkaConfig.consumerConfig("dashboard-webapp-throughput"))
  .subscribe("event-stats.throughput")          ◁────── Subscribe to the Kafka topic.
  .toFlowable()
  .subscribe(record ->
    forwardKafkaRecord(record, "client.updates.throughput"));     ◁──────

KafkaConsumer.<String, JsonObject>create(vertx,                    Forward to
  KafkaConfig.consumerConfig("dashboard-webapp-city-trend"))       the event bus.
  .subscribe("event-stats.city-trend.updates")
  .toFlowable()
  .subscribe(record -> forwardKafkaRecord(record,
    "client.updates.city-trend"));
```

These two RxJava pipelines have no complicated logic, as they forward to the `client.updates.throughput` and `client.updates.city-trend` event bus destinations.

The next listing shows the implementation of the `forwardKafkaRecord` method.

Listing 11.11 Forwarding a Kafka record to the event bus

```
private void forwardKafkaRecord(KafkaConsumerRecord<String, JsonObject>
  record, String destination) {
  vertx.eventBus().publish(destination, record.value());     ◁────── Publish to the
}                                                                     event bus.
```

Since the Kafka record values are of type `JsonObject`, there is no data conversion to perform to publish them to the Vert.x event bus.

11.2.2   Bridging the event bus and web applications

The dashboard web application starts an HTTP server, as shown in the following excerpt.

Listing 11.12   Dashboard service HTTP server

```
Router router = Router.router(vertx);                          ◁──  A Vert.x web router to
// (...) RxJava pipelines to forward Kafka records                  dispatch HTTP requests

// (...) Event bus bridge setup   ◁──  See listing 11.13.

router.route().handler(StaticHandler.create("webroot/assets"));  ◁──  Serve static
router.get("/*").handler(ctx -> ctx.reroute("/index.html"));  ◁──       files from the
                                                                         webroot/assets
return vertx.createHttpServer()                  Redirect traffic on     resource folder.
    .requestHandler(router)                      /* to /index.html.
    .rxListen(HTTP_PORT)
    .ignoreElement();
```

Start the HTTP server.

Listing 11.12 shows an HTTP server for serving static files. This is only an excerpt: we now need to see how the Vert.x event bus can be connected to web applications.

Vert.x offers an event-bus integration using the SockJS library (https://github.com/sockjs). SockJS is an emulation library for the WebSocket protocol (https://tools.ietf.org/html/rfc6455), which allows browsers and servers to communicate in both directions on top of a persistent connection. The Vert.x core APIs offer support for WebSockets, but SockJS is interesting because not every browser in the market properly supports WebSockets, and some HTTP proxies and load balancers may reject WebSocket connections. SockJS uses WebSockets whenever it can, and it falls back to other mechanisms such as long polling over HTTP, AJAX, JSONP, or iframe.

The Vert.x web module offers a handler for SockJS connections that bridge the event bus, so the same programming model can be used from the server side (in Vert.x) and the client side (in JavaScript). The following listing shows how to configure it.

Listing 11.13   Configuring the SockJS event-bus bridge

SockJS handler

```
SockJSHandler sockJSHandler = SockJSHandler.create(vertx);
SockJSBridgeOptions bridgeOptions = new SockJSBridgeOptions()
    .addInboundPermitted(new PermittedOptions()
    .setAddressRegex("client.updates.*"))        ◁──
    .addOutboundPermitted(new PermittedOptions()
    .setAddressRegex("client.updates.*"));        ◁──
sockJSHandler.bridge(bridgeOptions);
router.route("/eventbus/*").handler(sockJSHandler);   ◁──
```

Install the bridge.

Accept inbound event-bus messages from destinations that start with client.updates.

Accept outbound event-bus messages to destinations that start with client.updates.

SockJS clients endpoint

The bridge relies on a handler for SockJS client connections, with a set of permissions to allow only certain event-bus destinations to be bridged. It is indeed important to limit the events that flow between the connected web applications and backend, both for security and performance reasons. In this case, I decided that only the destinations starting with `client.updates` will be available.

On the web application side, the Vert.x project offers the `vertx3-eventbus-client` library, which can be downloaded manually or by using a tool like npm (the Node package manager). With this library we can connect to the event bus, as outlined in the following listing.

Listing 11.14 Using the JavaScript SockJS event-bus client

```javascript
import EventBus from 'vertx3-eventbus-client'

const eventBus = new EventBus("/eventbus")
eventBus.enableReconnect(true)

eventBus.onopen = () => {
  eventBus.registerHandler("a.b.c", (err, message) => {
    console.log(`Received: ${message.body}`)
  })

  eventBus.publish("d.e.f", {
    book: "Vert.x in Action",
    comment: "A great book!"
  })
}
```

- Import the JavaScript module. (`import EventBus from 'vertx3-eventbus-client'`)
- Connect to the event-bus endpoint. (`const eventBus = new EventBus("/eventbus")`)
- Automatically reconnect when the connection is lost. (`eventBus.enableReconnect(true)`)
- Called when the connection to the event bus has been established (`eventBus.onopen`)
- Register an event-bus destination handler. (`eventBus.registerHandler`)
- Publish a message to the event bus. (`eventBus.publish`)

The full code for using the Vert.x event bus in a Vue.js component is in the part2-steps-challenge/dashboard-webapp/src/App.vue file from the source code repository. As you can see, we have the same programming model in the JavaScript code; we can register event-bus handlers and publish messages, just like we would in Vert.x code.

11.2.3 *From Kafka to live web application updates*

The dashboard uses Vue.js, just like the public web application service that you saw earlier. The whole application essentially fits in the App.vue component, which can be found in the project source code. The component data model is made of three entries, as follows.

Listing 11.15 Data model of the Vue.js component

```javascript
data() {
  return {
    throughput: 0,
    cityTrendData: {},
    publicRanking: []
  }
},
```

- Current throughput (`throughput: 0`)
- City trend data (`cityTrendData: {}`)
- Public rankings (`publicRanking: []`)

These entries are updated when events are received from the Vert.x event bus. To do that, we use the Vue.js `mounted` life-cycle callback to connect to the event bus, and then register handlers as follows.

Listing 11.16   Event-bus handlers in the Vue.js component

```
mounted() {                                              Subscribe to throughput updates.
  eventBus.onopen = () => {
    eventBus.registerHandler("client.updates.throughput", (err, message) => {
      this.throughput = message.body.throughput
    })
    eventBus.registerHandler("client.updates.city-trend", (err, message) => {
      const data = message.body
      data.moment = moment(data.timestamp)
      this.$set(this.cityTrendData, message.body.city, data)
    })
    eventBus.registerHandler("client.updates.publicRanking", (err, message)
      => {
      this.publicRanking = message.body
    })
  }
},
```

Update the model. (annotation pointing to the city-trend handler lines)

The handlers update the model based on what is received from the event bus. Since Vue.js is a reactive web application framework, the interface is updated when the data model changes. For instance, when the value of `throughput` changes, so does the value displayed by the HTML template in the following listing.

Listing 11.17   Throughput Vue.js HTML template

```
(...)
<h4>
  <span class="badge badge-pill badge-dark">{{ throughput }}</span>     Binds to the
  device updates per second                                            throughput data value
</h4>
(...)
```

The city-trends view rendering is a more elaborated template.

Listing 11.18   City trends vue.js HTML template

```
<h4>Trends</h4>
<table class="table table-sm table-hover">
  <thead>
  <tr>
    <th scope="col">City</th>
    <th scope="col">Steps</th>
  </tr>
  </thead>
  <transition-group name="city-trends" tag="tbody">                Iterate over all
    <tr v-for="item in cityTrendRanking" v-bind:key="item.city">    city entries.
```

```
                <td scope="row">{{ item.city }}</td>        ⟵─── City name
Step  ┌         <td>
count └─⟶         +{{ item.stepsCount }}
                  <span class="text-secondary font-weight-lighter">
                  ({{ item.moment.format("ddd    hh:mm:ss") }})   ⟵─┐ Format the
                  </span>                                           │ timestamp with the
                </td>                                               │ Moment.js library.
              </tr>
          </transition-group>
    </table>
```

The template iterates over all city data and renders a table row for each city. When a city has an update, the city row is updated thanks to the `item.city` binding, which ensures uniqueness in the rows generated by the `v-for` loop. The `transition-group` tag is specific to Vue.js and is used for animation purposes: when the data order changes, the row order changes with an animation. The loop iterates over `cityTrendRanking`, which is a computed property shown in the following listing.

Listing 11.19 Computed ranking property

```
computed: {
  cityTrendRanking: function () {
    const values = Object.values(this.cityTrendData).slice(0)      ⟵─┐ Order by
    values.sort((a, b) => b.stepsCount - a.stepsCount)    ⟵──────────┘ step count.
    return values
  }
},
```

The `cityTrendRanking` computed property ranks entries by their number of steps, so the dashboard shows cities with the most steps on top.

The throughput and city trends are updated every five seconds, with updates coming from Kafka records and JSON payloads being forwarded to the dashboard web application. This works well because updates are frequent and cover aggregated data, but as you'll see next, things are more complicated for the users' ranking.

11.3   Streams and state

The dashboard web application shows a live ranking of users based on the number of steps they have taken over the last 24 hours. Users can be ranked based on the updates produced by the event stats service and sent to the `event-stats.user-activity .updates` Kafka topic.

11.3.1 A stream of updates

Each record sent to `event-stats.user-activity.updates` contains the latest number of steps for a given user. The dashboard service can observe these events, update its state to keep track of how many steps a given user has taken, and update the global ranking accordingly. The problem here is that we need some state to start with, because when it starts (or restarts!), the dashboard service doesn't know about the earlier updates.

We could configure the Kafka subscriber to restart from the beginning of the stream, but it could potentially span several days' or even weeks' worth of data. Replaying all records when the dashboard service starts would in theory allow us to compute an accurate ranking, but this would be a costly operation. Also, we would need to wait until all the records have been processed before sending updates to the connected web applications, because this would create a lot of traffic on the event bus.

Another solution is to start by asking the activity service what the current day rankings are, which is a straightforward SQL query built into the service. We'll call this the *hydration* phase. We can then update the rankings as we receive updates from the `event-stats.user-activity.updates` Kafka topic.

11.3.2 *Hydrating the ranking state*

The dashboard service maintains a `publicRanking` field, which is a map where keys are user names and values are the latest user update entries as JSON data. When the service starts, this collection is empty, so the first step is to fill it with data.

To do that, the `hydrate` method is called from the `DashboardWebAppVerticle` initialization method (`rxStart`), right after the Kafka consumers have been set, as in listing 11.10. This method assembles ranking data by calling the activity and user profile services, as shown in the following listing.

> **Listing 11.20   Implementation of the `hydrate` method**

```
WebClient webClient = WebClient.create(vertx);
webClient
  .get(3001, "localhost", "/ranking-last-24-hours")      ← Activity service ranking endpoint
  .as(BodyCodec.jsonArray())
  .rxSend()
  .delay(5, TimeUnit.SECONDS, RxHelper.scheduler(vertx))  ← Allow a delay when the service starts.
  .retry(5)
  .map(HttpResponse::body)                                 ← Allow five retries if the activity service is not available.
  .flattenAsFlowable(Functions.identity())
  .cast(JsonObject.class)
  .flatMapSingle(json -> whoOwnsDevice(webClient, json))   ← For each device ranking entry, find the owner.
  .flatMapSingle(json -> fillWithUserProfile(webClient, json)) ← Fill with the user details.
  .subscribe(
    this::hydrateEntryIfPublic,                            ← Track only the users who've opted to be public.
    err -> logger.error("Hydration error", err),
    () -> logger.info("Hydration completed"));
```

The implementation of the `hydrate` method relies on getting a ranking of the devices over the last 24 hours. The service returns a JSON array ordered by the number of steps. We allow an arbitrary five-second delay before making the request, and allow five retries in case the activity service is not available. Once we have ranking data, the `whoOwnsDevice` method (listing 11.21) and `fillWithUserProfile` method (listing 11.22) correlate the pedometer-centric data with a user. Finally, the `hydrateEntryIfPublic` method in listing 11.23 fills the `publicRanking` collection with data from users who opted to be in public rankings.

Listing 11.21 Finding who owns a device

```
private Single<JsonObject> whoOwnsDevice(WebClient webClient,
➥ JsonObject json) {
  return webClient
    .get(3000, "localhost", "/owns/" + json.getString("deviceId"))   ◀─┐
    .as(BodyCodec.jsonObject())
    .rxSend()                                                      Request to find a
    .retry(5)                                                       device owner.
    .map(HttpResponse::body)
    .map(resp -> resp.mergeIn(json));   ◀──── Merge JSON data.
}
```

The `whoOwnsDevice` method performs an HTTP request to determine who owns a device, and then merges the resulting JSON data. At this point, we need to fill the remaining user data, which is done via the `fillWithUserProfile` method, shown next.

Listing 11.22 Adding user data to the ranking data

```
private Single<JsonObject> fillWithUserProfile(WebClient webClient,
➥ JsonObject json) {
  return webClient
    .get(3000, "localhost", "/" + json.getString("username"))   ◀─┐
    .as(BodyCodec.jsonObject())                                  Get user
    .rxSend()                                                     data.
    .retry(5)
    .map(HttpResponse::body)
    .map(resp -> resp.mergeIn(json));   ◀──── Merge JSON data.
}
```

This code is very similar to that of the `whoOwnsDevice` method.

Last but not least, the `hydrateEntryIfPublic` method in the following listing adds data to the `publicRanking` collection.

Listing 11.23 Hydration of public user data

Only store public users.
```
 private void hydrateEntryIfPublic(JsonObject data) {                  Insert a local
└─▷  if (data.getBoolean("makePublic")) {                             timestamp for
       data.put("timestamp", Instant.now().toString());   ◀─┘        the update.
       publicRanking.put(data.getString("username"), data);  ◀─┐
    }                                                          Store the
  }                                                            user data.
```

Hydration is a process that's started asynchronously when the verticle starts, and eventually the `publicRanking` collection holds accurate data. Note that at this stage we have not pushed any ranking data to the dashboard web application clients. Let's now see what happens next.

11.3.3 *Periodically updating rankings from the updates stream*

The user ranking is updated every five seconds. To do so, we collect updates from users for five seconds, update the public ranking data, and push the result to the dashboard web application. We batch data over spans of five seconds to pace the dashboard refresh, but you can reduce the time window or even get rid of it if you want a more lively dashboard. The following listing shows the RxJava pipeline to manage this process.

Listing 11.24   RxJava pipeline to update user rankings

```
KafkaConsumer.<String, JsonObject>create(vertx,        Subscribe to
    KafkaConfig.consumerConfig("dashboard-webapp-ranking"))   the updates.
  .subscribe("event-stats.user-activity.updates")      ◁
  .toFlowable()                                              Keep only the
  .filter(record -> record.value().getBoolean("makePublic"))   ◁   public users.
  .buffer(5, TimeUnit.SECONDS, RxHelper.scheduler(vertx))   ◁
  .subscribe(this::updatePublicRanking);   ◁          Group events over
                                        Update rankings   five seconds.
                                        and push data.
```

The `filter` operator is used to keep only Kafka records where the user data is public, and the `buffer` operator makes five-second windows of events.

The following listing shows the implementation of the `updatePublicRanking` method that processes these event batches.

Listing 11.25   Public ranking maintenance process

```
private void updatePublicRanking(List<KafkaConsumerRecord<String,
    JsonObject>> records) {
  copyBetterScores(records);     ◁——— Merge the data.
  pruneOldEntries();
  vertx.eventBus().publish("client.updates.publicRanking", computeRanking());   ◁
}
                                        Compute ranking and
                                        send to the event bus
```

Discard older data.

The method describes the process in three steps:

1 Use the collected data to update ranking data.
2 Discard older entries.
3 Compute a new ranking and send it to the connected web applications over the event bus.

The next listing shows the implementation of the `copyBetterScores` method.

Listing 11.26 Updating ranking data

**Get the proposed
update number of steps.**

```
private void copyBetterScores(List<KafkaConsumerRecord<String, JsonObject>>
   records) {
  for (KafkaConsumerRecord<String, JsonObject> record : records) {
    JsonObject json = record.value();
    long stepsCount = json.getLong("stepsCount");
    JsonObject previousData = publicRanking.get(json.getString("username"));
    if (previousData == null || previousData.getLong("stepsCount") <
      stepsCount) {
      publicRanking.put(json.getString("username"), json);
    }
  }
}
```

**Update only when
there are more steps.**

The preceding method updates the `publicRanking` collection when a collected entry
has a higher step count than the previous one, because there could potentially be a
conflict between a hydration process and a user update.

The next listing shows the `pruneOldEntries` method.

Listing 11.27 Pruning older data

```
private void pruneOldEntries() {
  Instant now = Instant.now();
  Iterator<Map.Entry<String, JsonObject>> iterator =
    publicRanking.entrySet().iterator();
  while (iterator.hasNext()) {
    Map.Entry<String, JsonObject> entry = iterator.next();
    Instant timestamp =
      Instant.parse(entry.getValue().getString("timestamp"));
    if (timestamp.until(now, ChronoUnit.DAYS) >= 1L) {
      iterator.remove();
    }
  }
}
```

Get the current time.

Iterate over all ranking data.

**Remove entries
after a day.**

This method simply iterates over all ranking data entries in the `publicRanking` collection and removes entries older than one day.

The ranking is produced by the `computeRanking` method, shown next.

Listing 11.28 Computing the ranking

**Extract values in
publicRanking.**

```
private JsonArray computeRanking() {
  List<JsonObject> ranking = publicRanking.entrySet()
    .stream()
    .map(Map.Entry::getValue)
    .sorted(this::compareStepsCountInReverseOrder)
```

**Sort by decreasing
step count.**

```
    .map(json -> new JsonObject()              ◁──── Copy values.
      .put("username", json.getString("username"))
      .put("stepsCount", json.getLong("stepsCount"))
      .put("city", json.getString("city")))
    .collect(Collectors.toList());
  return new JsonArray(ranking);               ◁──── Wrap as a JSON array.
}
```

The method sorts public ranking data and produces a JSON array, where entries are ranked in reverse order (the first value is the user with most steps over the last 24 hours, and so on).

The compareStepsCountInReverseOrder method used to compare and sort entries is shown in the following listing.

Listing 11.29   Comparing user data against their step count

```
private int compareStepsCountInReverseOrder(JsonObject a, JsonObject b) {
  Long first = a.getLong("stepsCount");
  Long second = b.getLong("stepsCount");          Delegates to compareTo in
  return second.compareTo(first);      ◁─┘        the java.lang.Long class
}
```

The comparison returns -1 when b has fewer steps than a, 0 when they are equal, and 1 when b has more steps than a.

The Vue.js template for rendering the user ranking table is shown in the next listing.

Listing 11.30   User ranking template in Vue.js

```
<h4>Public ranking (last 24 hours)</h4>
<table class="table table-sm table-hover">
  <thead>
  <tr>
    <th scope="col">Name</th>
    <th scope="col">From</th>
    <th scope="col">Steps</th>
  </tr>
  </thead>
  <transition-group name="public-ranking" tag="tbody">          Iterate over
  <tr v-for="item in publicRanking" v-bind:key="item.username">  ◁─┘  the data.
    <td scope="row">{{ item.username }}</td>
    <td>{{ item.city }}</td>
    <td>{{ item.stepsCount }}</td>
  </tr>
  </transition-group>
</table>
```

The Vue.js code for the web application receives the ranking array over the event bus and updates the publicRanking data entry. Whenever this happens, the display is updated to reflect the changes. Just like the city trends table, entries move using an animation as their order changes.

This concludes the end-to-end stream processing, from Kafka records to reactive web applications. The next chapter focuses on resilience and fault-tolerance in reactive systems.

Summary

- RxJava offers advanced operators like `buffer` and `groupBy` that can be composed to perform aggregate data processing.
- A microservice does not have to expose an HTTP API. The event stats service only consumes and produces Kafka records.
- There are stream-processing works that can start at any point of a stream, like computing a throughput, while other works require some initial state, like maintaining a live ranking of users over the last 24 hours.
- The Vert.x event bus can be extended to web applications using the SockJS protocol, offering the same communication model across service and web code bases.
- Vert.x allows you to build end-to-end reactive systems, where events trigger computations in services and impact user-facing web applications.

12

Toward responsiveness with load and chaos testing

This chapter covers

- Simulating users with Locust
- Load testing HTTP endpoints with Hey
- Chaos testing with Pumba
- Mitigating failures with explicit timeouts, circuit breakers, and caches

We have now covered all the important technical parts of the 10k steps challenge application: how to build web APIs, web applications, and edge services, and how to use databases and perform event-stream processing. By using Vert.x's asynchronous and reactive programming, we can expect the set of services that form the application to be *reactive*: scalable as workloads grow and resilient as failures happen.

Are the services that we built actually reactive? Let's discover that now through testing and experimentation, and see where we can make improvements toward being reactive.

To do that, we will use load testing tools to stress services and measure latencies. We will then add failures using chaos testing tools to see how this impacts the service behaviors, and we will discuss several options for fixing the problems that we identify. You will be able to apply this methodology in your own projects too.

Software versions

The chapter was written and tested with the following tool versions:

- Locust 1.0.3
- Python 3.8.2
- Hey 0.1.3
- Pumba 0.7.2

12.1 *Initial experiments: Is the performance any good?*

This chapter is extensively based on experiments, so we need to generate some workloads to assess how the application copes with demanding workloads and failures. There are many load testing tools, and it is not always easy to pick one. Some tools are very good at stressing a service with a specific request (e.g., "What is the latency when issuing 500 requests per second to /api/hello"). Some tools provide more flexibility by offering scripting capabilities (e.g., "Simulate a user that logs in, then adds items to a cart, then perform a purchase"). And finally, some tools do all of that, but the reported metrics may be inaccurate due to how such tools are implemented.

I have chosen two popular and easy-to-use tools to use in this chapter:

- *Locust*—A versatile load testing tool that simulates users through scripts written in Python (https://locust.io/)
- *Hey*—A reliable HTTP load generator (https://github.com/rakyll/hey)

These two tools can be used together, or not. Locust allows us to simulate a representative workload of users interacting with the application, while Hey give us precise metrics of how specific HTTP endpoints behave under stress.

TIP Both Locust and Hey work on Linux, macOS, and Windows. As usual, if you are a Windows user, I recommend that you use the Windows Subsystem for Linux (WSL).

12.1.1 *Some considerations before load testing*

Before we run a load testing tool, I'd like to discuss a few points that have to be considered to get representative results. Most importantly, we need to interpret them with care.

First, when you run the 10k steps application as outlined in chapter 7, all services are running locally, while the third-party middleware and services are running in Docker containers. This means that everything is actually running on the same machine, avoiding real network communications. For instance, when the user profile service talks to MongoDB, it goes through virtual network interfaces, but it never reaches an actual network interface, so there is no fluctuating latency or data loss. We will use other tools later in this chapter to simulate network problems and get a more precise understanding of how our services behave.

Next, there is a good chance that you will be performing these experiments on your laptop or desktop. Keep in mind that a real server is different from your workstation, both in terms of hardware and software configurations, so you will likely perform tests with lower workloads than the services could actually cope with in a production setting. For instance, when we use PostgreSQL directly from a container, we won't have done any tuning, which we would do in a production setting. More generally, running the middleware services from containers is convenient for development purposes, but we would run them differently in production, with or without containers. Also note that we will be running the Vert.x-based services without any JVM tuning. In a production setting, you'd need to at least adjust memory settings and tune the garbage collector.

Also, each service will run as a single instance, and verticles will also be single instances. They have all been designed to work with multiple instances, but deploying, say, two instances of the ingestion service would also require deploying an HTTP reverse proxy to distribute traffic between the two instances.

Last but not least, it is preferable that you run load tests with two machines: one to run the application, and one to run a load testing tool. You can perform the tests on a single machine if that is more convenient for you, but keep these points in mind:

- You will not go through the network, which affects results.
- Both the services under test and the load testing tool will compete for operating system resources (CPU time, networking, open file descriptors, etc.), which also affects the results.

The results that I present in this chapter are based on experiments conducted with two Apple MacBook laptops, which hardly qualify as production-grade servers. I am also using a domestic WiFi network, which is not as good as an Ethernet wired connection, especially when it comes to having a stable latency. Finally, macOS has very low limits on the number of file descriptors that a process can open (256), so I had to raise them with the `ulimit` command to run the services and the load testing tools— otherwise errors unrelated to the services' code can arise because too many connections have been opened. I will show you how to do that, and depending on your system, you will likely have to use this technique to run the experiments.

12.1.2 *Simulating users with Locust*

Locust is a tool for generating workloads by simulating users interacting with a service. You can use it for demonstrations, tests, and measuring performance.

You will need a recent version of Python on your machine. If you are new to Python, you can read Naomi Ceder's *Exploring Python Basics* (Manning, 2019) or look through one of the many tutorials online. At the time of writing, I am using Python 3.8.2.

You can install Locust by running `pip install locust` on the command line, where `pip` is the standard Python package manager.

The Locust file that we will use is locustfile.py, and it can be found in the part2-steps-challenge/load-testing folder of the book's Git repository. We will be simulating the user behaviors illustrated in figure 12.1:

1 Each new user is generated from random data and a set of predefined cities.
2 A newly created user registers itself through the public API.
3 A user fetches a JWT token on the first request after having been registered, and then periodically makes requests:
    – The user sends step updates (80% of its requests).
    – The user fetches its profile data (5% of its requests).
    – The user fetches its total steps count (5% of its requests).
    – The user fetches its steps count for the current day (10% of its requests).

This activity covers most of the services: ingesting triggers event exchanges between most services, and API queries trigger calls to the activity and user profile services.

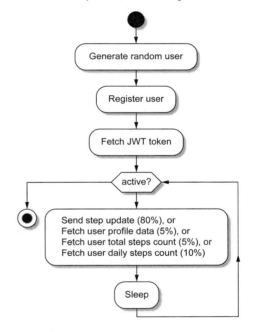

The locustfile.py file defines two classes. `UserBehavior` defines the tasks performed by a user, and `UserWithDevice` runs these tasks with a random delay between 0.5 and 2 seconds. This is a relatively short delay between requests to increase the overall number of requests per second.

There are two parameters for running a test with Locust:

■ The number of users to simulate
■ The hatch rate, which is the number of new users to create per second during the initial ramp-up phase

As described in chapter 7, you need to run the container services with Docker Compose from the part2-steps-challenge folder using `docker-compose up` in a terminal.

Figure 12.1 Activity of a simulated user in Locust

Then you can run all Vert.x-based services in another terminal. You can use `foreman start` if you have foreman installed, or you can run all services using the commands in the Procfile.

The following listing shows the command to perform an initial warm-up run.

Listing 12.1   Locust warm-up run

Raise the number of open file
descriptors to 10,000 per process.

```
$ cd part2-steps-challenge/load-testing
$ ulimit -n 10000
$ locust --headless \
    --host http://192.168.0.23 \
    --users 50 --hatch-rate 1 --run-time 3m
```

Do not start
the Locust
web interface.

Replace this with the IP
address of the machine
running the services (or
in the worst case, use
localhost).

50 clients, 1 new client per
second, 3 minutes of execution

It is important to do such a warm-up run because the JVM running the various services needs to have some workload before it can start to run code efficiently. After that, you can run a bigger workload to get a first estimation of how your services are going.

The following listing shows the command to run a test for 5 minutes with 150 clients and a hatch rate of 2 new users per second.

Listing 12.2   Locust run

```
$ mkdir data/
$ locust --headless \
    --host http://192.168.0.23 \
    --users 150 --hatch-rate 2 --run-time 5m \
    --csv data/locust-run
```

Output the result
to CSV files.

Let's run the experiment and collect results. We'll get various metrics on each type of request, such as the average response time, the minimum/maximum times, the median time, and so on. An interesting metric is the latency given a percentile.

Let's take the example of the latency at the 80th percentile. This is the maximum latency observed for 80% of the requests. If that latency is 100 ms, it means that 80% of the requests took less than 100 ms. Similarly, if the 95th percentile latency is 150 ms, it means that 95% of the requests took at most 150 ms. The 100th percentile reveals the worst case observed.

When measuring performance, we are often interested in the latencies between the 95th and 100th percentiles. Suppose that latency at the 90th percentile is 50 ms, but it's 3 s at the 95th percentile and 20 s at the 99th percentile. In such a case, we clearly have a performance problem, because we observe a large share of bad latencies. By contrast, observing a latency of 50 ms at the 90th percentile and 70 ms at the 99th percentile shows a service with very consistent behavior.

The latency distribution of a service's behavior under load tells more than the average latency. What we are actually interested in is not the best cases but those cases where we observed the worst results. Figure 12.2 shows the latency report for a run that I did with 150 users over 5 minutes.

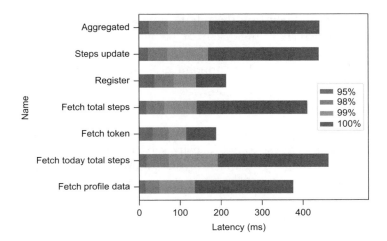

Figure 12.2 Latencies observed with Locust for 150 users over 5 minutes

The plot contains values at the 95th, 98th, 99th, and 100th percentiles. The reported latencies are under 200 ms at the 99th percentile for all requests, which sounds reasonable for a run with imperfect conditions and no tuning. The 100th percentile values show us the worst response times observed, and they are all under 500 ms.

We could increase the number of users to stress the application even more, but we are not going to do precise load testing with Locust. If you raise the number of users, you will quickly start seeing increasing latencies and errors being raised. This is not due to the application under test but due to a limitation of Locust at the time of writing:

- Locust's network stack is not very efficient, so we quickly reach limits in the number of concurrent users.
- Like many load testing tools, Locust suffers from *coordinated omission*, a problem where time measures are incorrect due to ignoring the wait time before the requests are actually made.[1]

For accurate load testing, we thus have to use another tool, and Hey is a good one.

> **TIP** Locust is still a great tool for producing a small workload and even automating a demo of the project. Once it is started and is simulating users, you can connect to the dashboard web application and see it updated live.

12.1.3 Load testing the API with Hey

Hey is a much simpler tool than Locust, as it cannot run scripts and it focuses on stressing an HTTP endpoint. It is, however, an excellent tool for getting accurate measures on an endpoint under stress.

---

[1] Gil Tene, "How NOT to Measure Latency," talk given at the Strange Loop conference, 2015; www.youtube.com/watch?v=lJ8ydIuPFeU.

We are still going to use Locust on the side to simulate a small number of users. This will generate some activity in the system across all services and middleware, so our measurements won't be made on a system that is idle.

We are going to stress the public API endpoint with two different requests:

- Get the total number of steps for a user.
- Authenticate and fetch a JWT token.

This is interesting, because to get the number of steps for a user, the public API service needs to make an HTTP request to the activity service, which in turn queries a PostgreSQL database. Fetching a JWT token involves more work, as the user profile service needs to be queried twice before doing some cryptography work and finally returning a JWT token. The overall latency for these requests is thus impacted by the work done in the HTTP API, in the user and activity services, and finally in the databases.

> **NOTE** The goal here is not to identify the limits of the services in terms of maximum throughput and best latency. We want to have a baseline to see how the service behaves under a sustained workload, and that will later help us to characterize the impact of various types of failures and mitigation strategies.

Since Hey cannot run scripts, we have to focus on one user and wrap calls to Hey in shell scripts. You will find helper scripts in the part2-steps-challenge/load-testing folder. The first script is create-user.sh, shown in the following listing.

Listing 12.3 Script to create a user

```bash
#!/bin/bash
http http://localhost:4000/api/v1/register \     ◁────┐ Register the
  username="loadtesting-user" \                        │ loadtesting-user user.
  password="13tm31n" \
  email="loadtester@my.tld" \
  deviceId="p-123456-abcdef" \
  city="Lyon" \
  makePublic:=true
                                          Publish 10 updates
for n in `seq 10`; do          ◁─────────  of 1,200 steps.
  http http://localhost:3002/ingest \
    deviceId="p-123456-abcdef" \
    deviceSync:=$n \
    stepsCount:=1200
done
```

This script ensures that user `loadtesting-user` is created and that a few updates have been recorded.

The run-hey-user-steps.sh script shown in the following listing uses Hey and fetches the total number of steps for user `loadtesting-user`.

Listing 12.4   Script to run Hey and load test for getting a user's total step count

```
#!/bin/bash
hey -z $2 \
    -o csv \
    -H 'Authorization: Bearer <TOKEN>' \
    http://$1:4000/api/v1/loadtesting-user/total \
    > data/hey-run-steps-z$2.csv
```

Duration of the run (10s, 5m, etc) — points to `hey -z $2`

Enable CSV output. — points to `-o csv`

Pass the JWT token for user loadtesting-user. — points to `-H 'Authorization...`

URL to the service, where the hostname is a variable — points to `http://$1:4000...`

Redirect the CSV output to a file. — points to `> data/hey-run-steps-z$2.csv`

The run-hey-token.sh script in the following listing is similar and performs an authentication request to get a JWT token.

Listing 12.5   Script to run Hey and load test getting a JWT token

```
#!/bin/bash
hey -z $2 \
    -m POST \
    -D auth.json \
    -T application/json \
    -o csv \
    http://$1:4000/api/v1/token \
    > data/hey-run-token-z$2.csv
```

Send the content of the auth.json file, which has the credentials of the loadtesting-user user.

Specify that this is an HTTP POST request.

Specify that the payload is some JSON data.

We are now ready to perform a run on the user total steps count endpoint. In my case, I'm doing the experiment with a second laptop, while my main laptop runs the services and had IP address 192.168.0.23 when I ran the tests. First off, we'll get some light background workload with Locust, again to make sure the system is not exactly idle:

```
$ locust --headless --host http://192.168.0.23 --users 20 --hatch-rate 2
```

In another terminal, we'll launch the test with Hey for five minutes:

```
./run-hey-user-steps.sh 192.168.0.23 5m
```

Once we have collected the results, the best way to analyze them is to process the data and plot it. You will find Python scripts to do that in the part2-steps-challenge/load-testing folder. Figure 12.3 shows the plot for this experiment.

The figure contains three subplots:

- A scattered plot of the request latencies over time
- A throughput plot that shares the same scale as the requests latencies plot
- A latency distribution over the 95th to 100th percentiles

The 99.99th percentile latency is very good while the throughput is high. We get better results with Hey compared to a 100-user workload with Locust. We can see a few short throughput drops correlated with higher latency responses, but there is nothing to worry about in these conditions. These drops could have been caused by various factors, including PostgreSQL, the WiFi network, or a JVM garbage collector run. It is easy to get better results with better hardware running Linux, a wired network, some JVM tuning, and a properly configured PostgreSQL database server.

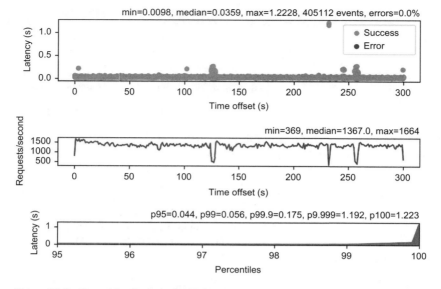

Figure 12.3 Report for the user total steps count load test

We can run another load testing experiment, fetching JWT tokens:

```
./run-hey-token.sh 192.168.0.23 5m
```

The results are shown in figure 12.4.

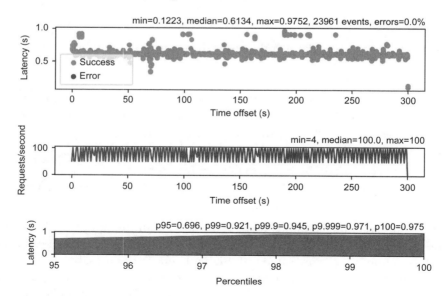

Figure 12.4 JWT token load test report

These results again show consistent behavior, albeit with a higher latency and lower throughput than the step count endpoint could achieve. This is easy to explain, as there are two HTTP requests to the user profile service, and then the token has to be generated and signed. The HTTP requests are mostly I/O-bound, while token signing requires CPU-bound work to be done on the event loop. The results are consistent over the five-minute run.

It is safe to conclude that the tested service implementations deliver solid performance under load. You could try to increase the number of workers for Hey and see what happens with bigger workloads (see the -c flag of the hey tool). You could also perform latency measures with increasing request rates (see the -q flag), but note that by default Hey does not do rate limiting, so in the previous runs Hey did the best it could with 50 workers (the default).

Scalability is only half of being reactive, so let's now see how our services behave with the same workloads in the presence of failures.

12.2 *Let's do some chaos engineering*

Strictly speaking, *chaos engineering* is the practice of voluntarily introducing failures in production systems to see how they react to unexpected application, network, and infrastructure failures. For instance, you can try to shut down a database, take down a service, introduce network delays, or even interrupt traffic between networks. Instead of waiting for failures to happen in production and waking up on-duty site reliability engineers at 4 a.m. on a Sunday, you decide to be proactive by periodically introducing failures yourself.

You can also do chaos engineering before software hits production, as the core principle remains the same: run the software with some workload, introduce some form of failure, and see how the software behaves.

12.2.1 *Test plan*

We need a reproducible scenario to evaluate the services, as they will alternate between nominal and failure phases. We will introduce failures according to the plan in figure 12.5.

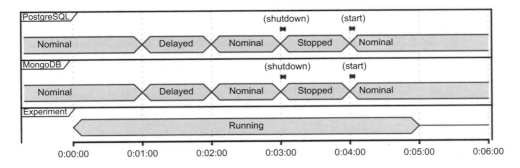

Figure 12.5 Test plan

We will run the same load testing experiments as we did in previous sections over periods of five minutes. What will change is that we're going to split it into five phases of one minute each:

1 The databases work nominally for the first minute.
2 We will introduce network delays of three seconds (+/− 500 ms) for all database traffic for the second minute.
3 We will get back to nominal performance for the third minute.
4 We will stop the two databases for the forth minute.
5 We will get back to nominal performance for the fifth and final minute.

Network delays increase latency, but they also simulate an overloaded database or service that starts to become unresponsive. With extreme delay values, they can also simulate an unreachable host, where establishing TCP connections takes a long time to fail. On the other hand, stopping the databases simulates services being down while their hosts remain up, which should lead to quick TCP connection errors.

How are we going to introduce these failures?

12.2.2 *Chaos testing with Pumba*

Pumba is a chaos testing tool for introducing failures in Docker containers (https://github.com/alexei-led/pumba). It can be used to do the following:

- Kill, remove, and stop containers
- Pause processes in containers
- Stress container resources (e.g., CPU, memory, or filesystem)
- Emulate network problems (packet delays, loss, duplication, corruption, etc.)

Pumba is a very convenient tool that you can download and run on your machine. The only dependency is having Docker running.

We are focusing on two types of failures in our test plan because they are the most relevant to us. You can play with other types of failures just as easily.

With the 10k steps application running locally, let's play with Pumba and add some delay to the MongoDB database traffic. Let's fetch a JWT token with the load-testing/fetch-token.sh script, as follows.

Listing 12.6   Fetching a JWT token

```
$ load-testing/fetch-token.sh                  ◁┐  Found in the part2-
HTTP/1.1 200 OK                                 │  steps-challenge folder
Content-Type: application/jwt
content-length: 528

<VALUE OF THE TOKEN>
```

In another terminal, let's introduce the delays with the following command.

Listing 12.7 Introducing some network delays with Pumba

netem is the subcommand for
network problem emulation.

There will be delays
for one minute.

```
$ pumba netem \
    --duration 1m \
    --tc-image gaiadocker/iproute2 \
    delay --time 3000 --jitter 500 \
    part2-steps-challenge_mongo_1
```

A helper Docker image

Three-second delays +/– 500 ms

Name of the target container (you can have regular
expressions to target multiple containers, etc)

Pumba should now be running for one minute. Try fetching a JWT token again; the
command should clearly take more time than before, as shown in the following listing.

Listing 12.8 Fetching a token with network delays

```
$ time ./fetch-token.sh
HTTP/1.1 200 OK
Content-Type: application/jwt
content-length: 528

<TOKEN VALUE>

./fetch-token.sh  0.27s user 0.08s system 5% cpu 6.157 total
```

Use time to measure a
process execution time.

The process took 6.157 seconds to fetch a token, due to waiting for I/O. Similarly, you
can stop a container with the following command.

Listing 12.9 Stopping a container with Pumba

```
$ pumba stop --restart \
    --duration 1m \
    part2-steps-challenge_mongo_1
```

Stop, then restart
the container.

If you run the script to fetch a token again, you will be waiting, while in the logs you
will see some errors due to the MongoDB container being down, as follows.

Listing 12.10 Fetching a token with a stopped database server

```
time ./fetch-token.sh
HTTP/1.1 200 OK
Content-Type: application/jwt
content-length: 528

<TOKEN VALUE>

./fetch-token.sh  0.25s user 0.07s system 0% cpu 57.315 total
```

It took a
long time!

The service is now unresponsive. My request took 57.315 seconds to complete because
it had to wait for the database to be back.

Let's get a clearer understanding by running the test plan, and we'll see what happens when these failures happen and the system is under load testing.

12.2.3 We are not resilient (yet)

To run these experiments you will use the same shell scripts to launch Hey as we did earlier in this chapter. You will preferably use two machines. The part2-steps-challenge/load-testing folder contains a run-chaos.sh shell script to automate the test plan by calling Pumba at the right time. The key is to start both the run-chaos.sh and Hey scripts (e.g., run-hey-token.sh) at the same time.

Figure 12.6 shows the behavior of the service on getting a user's total steps count. The results show a clear lack of responsiveness when Pumba runs.

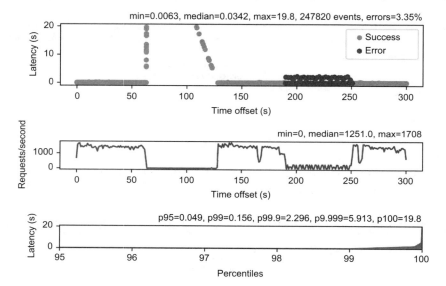

Figure 12.6   Total step count load test with failures

In the phase of network delays, we see a rapid latency increase spike to nearly 20 seconds, after which the throughput implodes. What happens here is that requests are enqueued, waiting for a response in both the public API and user profile services, up to the point where the system is at a halt. The database delays are between 2.5 s and 3.5 s, which can temporarily happen in practice. Of course, the issue is vastly amplified here due to load testing, but any service with some sustained traffic can show this kind of behavior even with smaller delays.

In the phase where databases are down we see errors for the whole simulated outage duration. While it is hard to be surprised about errors, we can see that the system has not come to a halt either. This is far from perfect, though, since the reduced throughput is a sign that requests need *some* time to be given an error, while other requests are waiting until they time out, or they eventually complete when the databases restart.

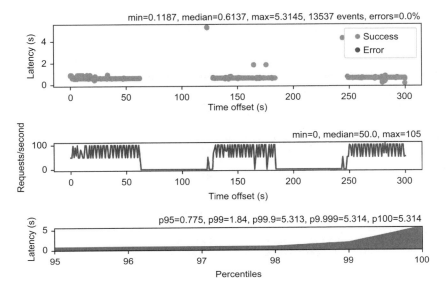

Figure 12.7 JWT token load test with failures

Let's now look at figure 12.7 and see how fetching JWT tokens goes.

Network delays also cause the system to come to a halt, but we do not observe the same shape in the scatter plot. This is due to the inherently lower throughput of the service for this type of request, and also the fact that two HTTP requests are needed. Requests pile up, waiting for responses to arrive, and once the delays stop, the system gets going again. More interestingly, we do not observe errors in the phase where databases have been stopped. There are just no requests being served anymore as the system is waiting for databases.

From these two experiments, we can see that the services become unresponsive in the presence of failures, so they are not reactive. The good news is that there are ways to fix this, so let's see how we can become reactive, again using the public API as a reference. You will then be able to extrapolate the techniques to the other services.

12.3   *From "scalable" to "scalable and resilient"*

To make our application resilient, we have to make changes to the public API and make sure that it responds *quickly* when a failure has been detected. We will explore two approaches: enforcing timeouts, and then using a circuit breaker.

12.3.1 *Enforcing timeouts*

Observations in the preceding experiments showed that requests piled up while waiting for either the databases to get back to nominal conditions, or for TCP errors to arise. A first approach could be to enforce short timeouts in the HTTP client requests, so that they fail fast when the user profile or activity services take too long to respond.

The changes are very simple: we just need to add timeouts to the HTTP requests made by the Vert.x web client, as shown in listing 12.11.

> **TIP** You can find the corresponding code changes in the chapter12/public-api-with-timeouts branch of the Git repository.

Listing 12.11   Implementation of the `totalSteps` method with timeouts

```
private void totalSteps(RoutingContext ctx) {
  String deviceId = ctx.user().principal().getString("deviceId");
  webClient
    .get(3001, "localhost", "/" + deviceId + "/total")
    .timeout(5000)                        ⟵  Times out after
    .as(BodyCodec.jsonObject())                five seconds
    .rxSend()
    .subscribe(
      resp -> forwardJsonOrStatusCode(ctx, resp),
      err -> sendBadGateway(ctx, err));
}
```

The changes are the same in the `fetchUserDetails` and `token` methods. A timeout of five seconds is relatively short and ensures a quick notification of an error.

Intuitively, this should improve the responsiveness of the public API services and avoid throughput coming to a halt. Let's see what happens by running the chaos testing experiments again, as shown in figure 12.8.

Compared to the experiment in figure 12.6, we still have drastically reduced throughputs during failures, but at least we see errors being reported, thanks to the

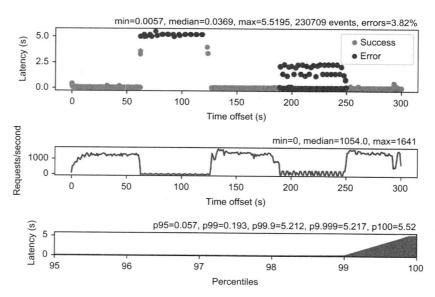

Figure 12.8   Total steps count load test with failures and timeouts

timeout enforcements. We also see that the maximum latency is below six seconds, which is in line with the five-second timeouts.

Let's now see how the JWT token load test behaves, as shown in figure 12.9. This run confirms what we have observed: timeouts get enforced, ensuring that some requests are still served during the failures. However, the worst-case latencies are worse than without the timeouts: network delays stretch the time for doing two HTTP requests to the user profile service, so the higher values correspond to those requests where the second request timed out.

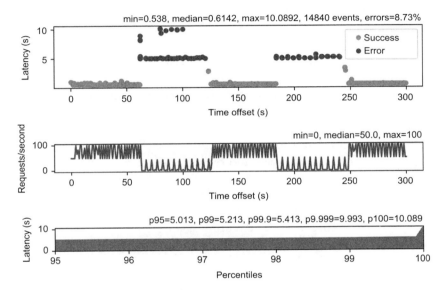

Figure 12.9   JWT token load test with failures and timeouts

Timeouts are better than no timeouts when it comes to improving responsiveness, but we cannot qualify our public API service as being resilient. What we need is a way for the service to *know* that there is a failure happening, so it fails fast rather than waiting for a timeout to happen. This is exactly what a circuit breaker is for!

12.3.2 *Using a circuit breaker*

The goal of a circuit breaker is to prevent the problems observed in the previous section, where requests to unresponsive systems pile up, causing cascading errors between distributed services. A circuit breaker acts as a form of proxy between the code that makes a (networked) request, such as an RPC call, HTTP request, or database call, and the service to be invoked.

Figure 12.10 shows how a circuit breaker works as a finite state machine. The idea is quite simple. The circuit breaker starts in the closed state, and for each request, it observes whether the request succeeded or not. Failing can be because an error has

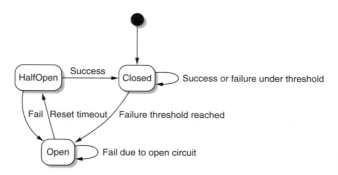

Figure 12.10   Circuit breaker state machine

been reported (for example, a TCP timeout or TCP connection error), or because an operation took too long to complete.

Once a certain number of errors have been reported, the circuit breaker goes to the open state. From here, all operations are notified of a failure due to the circuit being open. This avoids further requests being issued to an unresponsive service, which allows for fast error responses, trying alternative recovery strategies, and reducing the pressure on both the service and requester ends.

The circuit breaker leaves the open state and goes to the half-open state after some reset timeout. The first request in the half-open state determines whether the service has recovered. Unlike the open state, the half-open state is where we start doing a real operation again. If it succeeds, the circuit breaker goes back to the closed state and resumes normal servicing. If not, another reset period starts before it goes back to the half-open state and checks if the service is back.

TIP You can find the code changes discussed here in the chapter12/public-api-with-circuit-breaker branch of the Git repository.

Vert.x provides the `vertx-circuit-breaker` module that needs to be added to the public API project. We will use two circuit breakers: one for token generation requests, and one for calls to the activity service (such as getting the total steps count for a user). The following listing shows the code to create a circuit breaker in the `PublicApiVerticlerxStart` method.

Listing 12.12   Creating a circuit breaker

**Create a circuit breaker
with a name and options.**

```
String tokenCircuitBreakerName = "token-circuit-breaker";
tokenCircuitBreaker = CircuitBreaker.create(
  tokenCircuitBreakerName, vertx, circuitBreakerOptions());

tokenCircuitBreaker
  .openHandler(v -> this.logBreakerUpdate("open", tokenCircuitBreakerName));
tokenCircuitBreaker
```

**Callback when
entering the
open state**

```
    .halfOpenHandler(v -> this.logBreakerUpdate("half open",
      tokenCircuitBreakerName));
tokenCircuitBreaker
    .closeHandler(v ->
      this.logBreakerUpdate("closed", tokenCircuitBreakerName));
```

◁──── **Callback when entering the half-open state**

◁──── **Callback when entering the closed state**

The `tokenCircuitBreakerName` reference is a field of type `CircuitBreaker`. There is another field called `activityCircuitBreaker` for the activity service circuit breaker, and the code is identical. The callbacks on state change can be optionally set. It is a good idea to log these state changes for diagnosis purposes.

The following listing shows a circuit breaker configuration.

Listing 12.13 Configuring a circuit breaker

Open after five failures.

```
private CircuitBreakerOptions circuitBreakerOptions() {
  return new CircuitBreakerOptions()
    .setMaxFailures(5)
    .setMaxRetries(0)          ◁────── Do not retry a failed operation.
    .setTimeout(5000)          ◁──────
    .setResetTimeout(10_000);         Report timeout failures
  }                                    after five seconds.
```

Reset timeout to 10 seconds.

We are going to open the circuit breaker after five failures, including operations timing out after five seconds (to be consistent with the previous experiments). The reset timeout is set to 10 seconds, which will let us frequently check how the service goes. How long this value should be depends on your context, but you can anticipate that long timeouts will increase the time a service operates in degraded mode or reports errors, whereas short values may diminish the effectiveness of using a circuit breaker.

The following listing shows the modified `token` method with the code wrapped into a circuit breaker call.

Listing 12.14 Implementation of the token method with a circuit breaker

```
private void token(RoutingContext ctx) {
  tokenCircuitBreaker.<String>rxExecute(promise -> {
    JsonObject payload = ctx.getBodyAsJson();
    String username = payload.getString("username");
    webClient
      .post(3000, "localhost", "/authenticate")
// (...)
      .subscribe(promise::complete, err -> {
        if (err instanceof NoStackTraceThrowable) {
          promise.complete("");
        } else {
          promise.fail(err);    ◁────── Fail due to some other error.
```

Execute an operation that provides a String.

Regular web client call

Complete with a successful token.

Web client and RxJava operators, as in the previous code

Check if the service returned a non-200 status code and complete.

```
        }
      });
  }).subscribe(                        ←————   Send the token or manage
    token -> sendToken(ctx, token),             the authentication error.
    err -> handleAuthError(ctx, err));
}
```

The circuit breaker executes an operation, which here is making two HTTP requests to the user profile service and then making a JWT token. The operation's result is a `Single<String>` of the JWT token value. The execution method passes a promise to the wrapped code, so it can notify if the operation succeeded or not.

The `handleAuthError` method had to be modified as in the following listing to check the source of any error.

Listing 12.15   Handling authentication errors

The circuit breaker is open.

```
  private void handleAuthError(RoutingContext ctx, Throwable err) {
 ┌─➤  if (err instanceof OpenCircuitException) {
        logger.error("Circuit breaker is open: {}", tokenCircuitBreaker.name());
        ctx.fail(504);
      } else if (err instanceof TimeoutException) {   ←———  The operation timed out.
        logger.error("Circuit breaker timeout: {}", tokenCircuitBreaker.name());
        ctx.fail(504);                     ┌────  Regular authentication error
      } else {                          ←──┘
        logger.error("Authentication error", err);
        ctx.fail(401);
      }
  }
```

The circuit breaker reports open circuit conditions and operation timeouts with dedicated exceptions. In these cases, we report an HTTP 500 status code or a classic 401 so the requester knows if a failure is due to bad credentials or not.

This is great, but what is the actual effect of the circuit breaker on our system? Let's see by running the experiment on the JWT token generation. The results are shown in figure 12.11.

The impact of the circuit breaker is striking: the service is now highly responsive during failure periods! We get a high throughput during failures, as the service now fails fast when the circuit breaker is open. Interestingly, we can spot when the circuit breaker tries to make requests when in the half-open state: these are the high-latency error points at regular intervals. We can also see that the 99.99th percentile is back to a lower latency compared to the previous runs.

This is all good, but what about fetching the total steps count for a user?

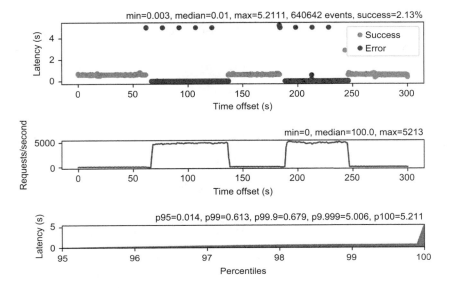

Figure 12.11   JTW token load testing with failures and a circuit breaker

12.3.3 *Resiliency and fallback strategies*

The circuit breaker made JWT token generation responsive even with failures, so the endpoint is now fully reactive. That being said, it did not offer much in the way of fallback strategies: if we can't talk to the user profile service, there is no way we can authenticate a user and then generate a JWT token. This is why the circuit breaker always reports errors.

We could adopt the same strategy when issuing requests to the activity service, and simply report errors. That being said, we could provide further resiliency by caching data and provide an older value to a requester. Fallback strategies depend on the functional requirements: we cannot generate a JWT token without authentication working, but we can certainly serve some older step count data if we have it in a cache.

We will use the efficient in-memory Caffeine caching library (https://github.com/ben-manes/caffeine). This library provides configurable strategies for managing cached data, including count, access, and time-based eviction policies. We could cache data in a Java `HashMap`, but that would quickly expose us to memory exhaustion problems if we didn't put a proper eviction policy in place.

The following listing shows how to create a cache of at most 10,000 entries, where keys are strings and values are long integers.

Listing 12.16   Creating a cache

```
private Cache<String, Long> stepsCache = Caffeine.newBuilder()
    .maximumSize(10_000)          ◁          Cache at most 10,000 entries.
    .build();
```

We add entries to the cache with the `cacheTotalSteps` method in the following list-ing, and Caffeine evicts older entries when the 10,000 entries limit has been reached.

Listing 12.17   Caching total steps

```
private void cacheTotalSteps(String deviceId, HttpResponse<JsonObject> resp) {
  if (resp.statusCode() == 200) {
    stepsCache.put("total:" + deviceId, resp.body().getLong("count"));   ◁
  }
}
```
Store data just like in a regular Java map.

The preceding method is used in the `totalSteps` method, shown next, where the code has been wrapped using a circuit breaker call.

Listing 12.18   Implementation of the `totalSteps` method with a circuit breaker

```
private void totalSteps(RoutingContext ctx) {
  String deviceId = ctx.user().principal().getString("deviceId");
  activityCircuitBreaker.<Void>executeWithFallback(promise -> {   ◁  Variant of
    webClient                                                          execute that
      .get(3001, "localhost", "/" + deviceId + "/total")              takes a fallback
      .expect(ResponsePredicate.SC_OK)
      .as(BodyCodec.jsonObject())
      .rxSend()
      .subscribe(resp -> {
        cacheTotalSteps(deviceId, resp);      ◁——  Cache total steps.
        forwardJsonOrStatusCode(ctx, resp);
        promise.complete();
      }, err -> {
        tryToRecoverFromCache(ctx, deviceId);      ◁  Try to recover
        promise.fail(err);                             from the cache.
      });
  }, err -> {                   ◁   Fall back.
    tryToRecoverFromCache(ctx, deviceId);
    return null;
  });
}
```

We now use a circuit breaker that does not return any value, hence the `Void` paramet-ric type. The `executeWithFallback` method allows us to provide a fallback when the circuit is open, so we can try to recover a value from the cache. This is done in the `tryToRecoverFromCache` method in the following listing.

Listing 12.19   Implementation of the recovery from cache

Send an error because we don't have any data.
```
private void tryToRecoverFromCache(RoutingContext ctx, String deviceId) {
  Long steps = stepsCache.getIfPresent("total:" + deviceId);
  if (steps == null) {
```

```
      logger.error("No cached data for the total steps of device {}", deviceId);
      ctx.fail(502);
    } else {
      JsonObject payload = new JsonObject()          Send cached data as a
        .put("count", steps);                         successful response.
      ctx.response()
        .putHeader("Content-Type", "application/json")
        .end(payload.encode());
    }
}
```

By recovering from a cache in the `tryToRecoverFromCache` method, we don't always send errors. If we have data in the cache, we can still provide a response, albeit with a possibly outdated value.

> **NOTE** Caching step counts and recovering from older values with a circuit breaker fallback could also be done directly in the activity service.

It is now time to check the behavior of the service when fetching step counts. First, let's have a cold-start run where the database is initially down and the service has just started. Figure 12.12 shows a two-minute run where the database starts after a minute.

The service immediately starts with a few errors, and then the circuit breaker opens, at which point the service consistently provides errors with a very low latency. Remember that the service hasn't cached any data yet.

When the database starts, we can see a latency spike as errors turn into successes, and then the service is able to respond nominally. Note that in the first success seconds,

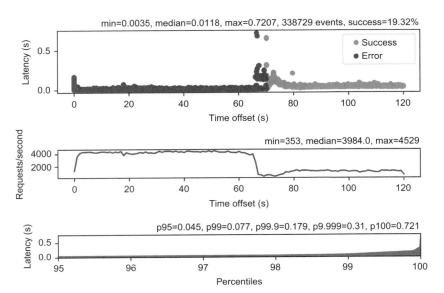

Figure 12.12 Total step count load test with failures, a circuit breaker, and a cold start

the JVM will start optimizing the code that talks to the database, so there is an improved throughput.

Figure 12.13 shows the service behavior over the full five-minute test plan. Since the test plan starts with databases running nominally, the service manages to cache data for the test user. This is why we get no errors across the whole run. We see a few successes with higher latency when the network delays appear, which actually impact the last few percentiles above 99.99th. These are due to the circuit breaker reporting timeouts on making HTTP requests, but note that the circuit breaker cannot cancel the HTTP requests. Hence, we have a few HTTP requests waiting for an unresponsive activity service, while the circuit breaker meanwhile completes the corresponding HTTP responses with some cached data.

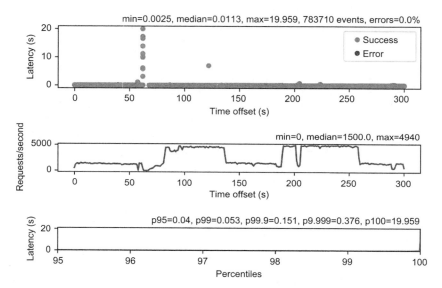

Figure 12.13   Total step count load test with failures and a circuit breaker

Figure 12.14 shows the effect of combining the circuit breaker with a five-second time-out on the web client HTTP requests (see the chapter12/public-api-with-circuit-breaker-and-timeouts branch of the Git repository).

This clearly improves the result, as we don't have any worst-case latency around 20 seconds anymore. Other than that, the latency and throughputs are consistent over the rest of the run, and they're barely impacted by the databases being stopped around minute 4.

NOTE   A circuit breaker is a very useful tool for avoiding cascading failures, but you don't have to wrap every operation over the network in a circuit breaker. Every abstraction has a cost, and circuit breakers do add a level of indirection. Instead, it is best to use chaos testing and identify where they are most likely to have a positive effect on the overall system behavior.

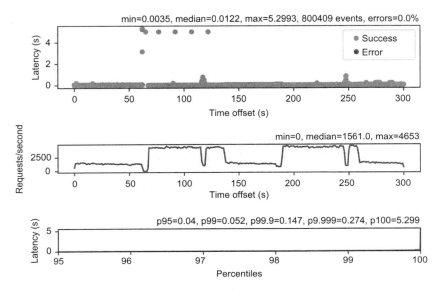

Figure 12.14 Total step count load test with failures, timeouts, and a circuit breaker

We now have a reactive service: it is not just resource-efficient and scalable, but is also resilient to failures. The service keeps responding in all situations, and the latency is kept under control.

The next and final chapter discusses running Vert.x applications in container environments.

Summary

- A reactive service is not just scalable; it has to be resilient and responsive.
- Load testing and chaos testing tools are key to analyzing service behavior both when operating in nominal conditions, and when surrounded by failures from the network and services it relies on.
- Circuit breakers are the most efficient tool for shielding a service from unresponsive services and network failures.
- A resilient service is not just responsive when it can quickly notify of an error; it may still be able to respond successfully, such as by using cached data if the application domain allows it.

13
Final notes:
Container-native Vert.x

This chapter covers

- Efficiently building container images with Jib
- Configuring Vert.x clustering to work in a Kubernetes cluster
- Deploying Vert.x services to a Kubernetes cluster
- Using Skaffold and Minikube for local development
- Exposing health checks and metrics

By now you should have a solid understanding of what a reactive application is, and how Vert.x can help you build scalable, resource-efficient, and resilient services. In this chapter we'll discuss some of the main concerns related to deploying and operating a Vert.x application in a Kubernetes cluster container environment. You will learn how to prepare Vert.x services to work well in Kubernetes and how to use efficient tools to package container images and run them locally. You will also learn how to expose health checks and metrics to better integrate services in a container environment.

268

This chapter is optional, given that the core objectives of the book are about teaching yourself reactive concepts and practices. Still, Kubernetes is a popular deployment target, and it is worth learning how to make Vert.x applications first-class citizens in such environments.

In this chapter I'll assume you have a basic understanding of containers, Docker, and Kubernetes, which are covered in depth in other books such as Marko Lukša's *Kubernetes in Action*, second edition (Manning, 2020) and *Docker in Action*, second edition, by Jeff Nickoloff and Stephen Kuenzli (Manning, 2019). If you don't know much about those topics, you should still be able to understand and run the examples in this chapter, and you'll learn some Kubernetes basics along the way, but I won't spend time explaining the core concepts of Kubernetes, such as *pods* and *services*, or describe the subtleties of the `kubectl` command-line tool.

Tool versions

The chapter was written and tested with the following tool versions:

- Minikube 1.11.0
- Skaffold 1.11.0
- k9s 0.20.5 (optional)
- Dive 0.9.2 (optional)

13.1 *Heat sensors in a cloud*

In this final chapter, we'll go back to a use case based on heat sensors, as it will be simpler than working with the 10k steps challenge application.

In this scenario, heat sensors regularly publish temperature updates, and an API can be used to retrieve the latest temperatures from all sensors, and also to identify sensors where the temperature is abnormal. The application is based on three microservices that you can find in the source code Git repository and that are illustrated in figure 13.1.

Here is what each services does:

- `heat-sensor-service`—Represents a heat sensor that publishes temperature updates over the Vert.x event bus. It exposes an HTTP API to fetch the current temperature.
- `sensor-gateway`—Collects temperature updates from all heat sensor services over the Vert.x event bus. It exposes an HTTP API for retrieving the latest temperature values.
- `heat-api`—An HTTP API for retrieving the latest temperature values and for detecting the sensors where temperatures are not within expected bounds.

The heat sensor service needs to be scaled to simulate multiple sensors, whereas the sensor gateway and API services work fine with just one instance of each. That being

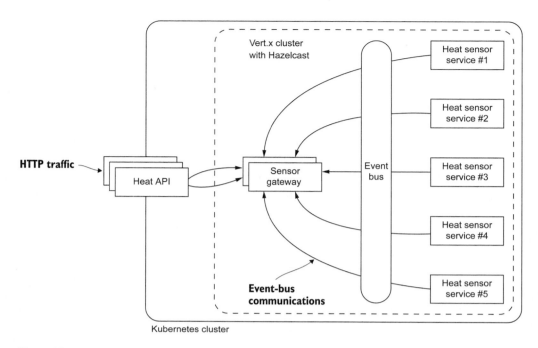

Kubernetes cluster

Figure 13.1   Use case overview

said, the latter two do not share state, so they can also be scaled to multiple instances if the workload requires it.

The heat API is the only service meant to be exposed outside the cluster. The sensor gateway is a cluster-internal service. The heat sensor services should just be deployed as instances inside the cluster, but they do not require a load balancer. The Vert.x cluster manager uses Hazelcast.

Let's quickly see the noteworthy code portions in these service implementations.

13.1.1 *Heat sensor service*

The heat sensor service is based on the code found in the early chapters of this book, especially that of chapter 3. The `update` method called from a timer set in the `scheduleNextUpdate` method has been updated as follows.

Listing 13.1   The new `update` method

```
private void update(long tid) {
  temp = temp + (delta() / 10);
  vertx.eventBus().publish(targetDestination, makeJsonPayload());   ◁─┐ Publish to
  logger.info("{} new temperature is {}", id, temp);                  │ the event
  scheduleNextUpdate();                                               │ bus.
}
```

```
private JsonObject makeJsonPayload() {        <──────┐  Prepare a JSON temperature
  return new JsonObject()                             │  update payload.
    .put("id", id)
    .put("timestamp", System.currentTimeMillis())
    .put("temp", temp);
}
```

We still have the same logic, and we publish a JSON temperature update document to the event bus. We've also introduced the makeJsonPayload method, as it is also used for the HTTP endpoint, as shown next.

Listing 13.2 Getting heat sensor data over HTTP

```
private void handleRequest(RoutingContext ctx) {
  ctx.response()
    .putHeader("Content-Type", "application/json")
    .end(makeJsonPayload().encode());          <────── Send JSON data
}
```

Finally we get the service configuration from environment variables in the HeatSensor verticle's start method, as follows.

Listing 13.3 Getting the sensor configuration from environment variables

Access the environment variables.   **Get the HTTP port.**

```
┌─▷ Map<String, String> env = System.getenv();
    int httpPort = Integer.parseInt(env.getOrDefault("HTTP_PORT", "8080"));   <─┘
    targetDestination = env.getOrDefault("EB_UPDATE_DESTINATION",
➡  "heatsensor.updates");                 <──────┐ Get the event-bus destination.
```

Environment variables are great because they are easy to override when running the service. Since they are exposed as a Java Map, we can take advantage of the getOrDefault method to have default values.

Vert.x also provides the vertx-config module (not covered in this book) if you need more advanced configuration, like combining files, environment variables, and distributed registries. You can learn more about it in the Vert.x website documentation (https://vertx.io/docs/). For most cases, however, parsing a few environment variables using the Java System class is much simpler.

13.1.2 Sensor gateway

The sensor gateway collects temperature updates from the heat sensor services over Vert.x event-bus communications. First, it fetches configuration from environment variables, as shown in listing 13.3, because it needs an HTTP port number and an event bus destination to listen to. The start method sets an event-bus consumer, as in the following listing.

Listing 13.4   Gateway event-bus consumer

```
vertx.eventBus().<JsonObject>consumer(targetDestination, message -> {     ◁─┐
  JsonObject json = message.body();                                         │
  String id = json.getString("id");                          Register a handler.
  data.put(id, json);
  logger.info("Received an update from sensor {}", id);
});
```

Put it in a map.

Each incoming JSON update is put in a `data` field, which is a `HashMap<String, JsonObject>`, to store the last update of each sensor.

The HTTP API exposes the collected sensor data over the `/data` endpoint, which is handled by the following code.

Listing 13.5   Gateway data requests HTTP handler

```
private void handleRequest(RoutingContext ctx) {
  JsonArray entries = new JsonArray();                  Collect entries
  for (String key : data.keySet()) {          ◁─        in a JSON array.
    entries.add(data.get(key));
  }
  JsonObject payload = new JsonObject().put("data", entries);  ◁─┐
  ctx.response()                                               Put the array
    .putHeader("Content-Type", "application/json")             in a JSON
    .end(payload.encode());                                    document
}                                                              and send it.
```

This method prepares a JSON response by assembling all collected data into an array, which is then wrapped in a JSON document.

13.1.3 Heat API

This service provides all sensor data, or just the data for services where temperatures are outside an expected correct value range. To do so, it makes HTTP requests to the sensor gateway.

The configuration is again provided through environment variables, as follows.

Listing 13.6   Heat API configuration environment variables

The sensor gateway address   **The sensor gateway port number**

```
Map<String, String> env = System.getenv();
int httpPort = Integer.parseInt(env.getOrDefault("HTTP_PORT", "8080"));
String gatewayHost = env.getOrDefault("GATEWAY_HOST", "sensor-gateway");
int gatewayPort = Integer.parseInt(env.getOrDefault("GATEWAY_PORT", "8080"));  ◁─
lowLimit = Double.parseDouble(env.getOrDefault("LOW_TEMP", "10.0"));
highLimit = Double.parseDouble(env.getOrDefault("HIGH_TEMP", "30.0"));    ◁─
```

The correct temperature lower bound   **The correct temperature higher bound**

The service resolves the sensor gateway address as well as the correct temperature range using environment variables. As you will see later, we can override the values when deploying the service to a cluster.

The start method configures the web client to make HTTP requests to the sensor gateway, and it also uses a Vert.x web router to expose API endpoints.

Listing 13.7 Heat API web client and routes

Prebind the web client host and port for requests.

```
webClient = WebClient.create(vertx, new WebClientOptions()
    .setDefaultHost(gatewayHost)
    .setDefaultPort(gatewayPort));

Router router = Router.router(vertx);              The router that exposes
router.get("/all").handler(this::fetchAllData);     the API endpoints
router.get("/warnings").handler(this::sensorsOverLimits);
```

Data is fetched from the sensor gateway with HTTP GET requests, as shown in the following listing.

Listing 13.8 Fetching sensor data

```
private void fetchData(RoutingContext routingContext,
    Consumer<HttpResponse<JsonObject>> action) {
  webClient.get("/data")                        Make a request to /data.
    .as(BodyCodec.jsonObject())
    .expect(ResponsePredicate.SC_OK)
    .timeout(5000)
    .send(ar -> {
      if (ar.succeeded()) {
        action.accept(ar.result());             Call the action handler.
      } else {
        routingContext.fail(500);               Handle errors.
        logger.error("Could not fetch data", ar.cause());
      }
    });
}
```

The fetchData method is generic, with a custom action given as the second parameter, so the two HTTP endpoints that we are exposing can reuse the request logic.

The implementation of the fetchAllData method is shown next.

Listing 13.9 Fetching all sensor data

```
private void fetchAllData(RoutingContext routingContext) {
  fetchData(routingContext, resp -> {
    routingContext.response()
      .putHeader("Content-Type", "application/json")
      .end(resp.body().encode());
  });
}
```

This method doesn't do anything special besides completing the HTTP request with the JSON data.

The `sensorsOverLimits` method shown next is more interesting, as it filters the data.

> **Listing 13.10   Filtering out-of-range sensor data**

```
private void sensorsOverLimits(RoutingContext routingContext) {
    Predicate<JsonObject> abnormalValue = json -> {
        Double temperature = json.getDouble("temp");
        return (temperature <= lowLimit) || (highLimit <= temperature);
    };
    fetchData(routingContext, resp -> {                        An array to collect over-limit data
        JsonObject data = resp.body();
        JsonArray warnings = new JsonArray();    <───        Use a Java stream to filter entries.
        data.getJsonArray("data").stream()       <───
            .map(JsonObject.class::cast)                       Filter based on temperature values.
            .filter(abnormalValue)               <───
            .forEach(warnings::add);             <───  Add to the array.
        data.put("data", warnings);
        routingContext.response()
            .putHeader("Content-Type", "application/json")
            .end(data.encode());
    });
}
```

Cast from Object to JsonObject.

Assemble the final JSON response.

The `sensorsOverLimits` method keeps only the entries where the temperature is not within the expected range. To do so, we take a functional processing approach using Java collection streams, and then return the response. Note that the `data` array in the response JSON document may be empty if all sensor values are correct.

Now that you have seen the main interesting points in the three service implementations, we can move on to the topic of actually deploying them in a Kubernetes cluster.

13.1.4 *Deploying to a local cluster*

There are many ways to run a local Kubernetes cluster. Docker Desktop embeds Kubernetes, so it may be all you need to run Kubernetes, if you have it running on your machine.

Minikube is another reliable option offered by the Kubernetes project (https://minikube.sigs.k8s.io/docs/). It deploys a small virtual machine on Windows, macOS, or Linux, which makes it perfect for creating disposable clusters for development. If anything goes wrong, you can easily destroy a cluster and start anew.

Another benefit of Minikube is that it offers environment variables for Docker daemons, so you can have your locally built container images available right inside the cluster. In other Kubernetes configurations, you would have to push images to private or public registries, which can slow the development feedback loop, especially when pushing a few hundred megabytes to public registries over a slow internet connection.

I am assuming that you will use Minikube here, but feel free to use any other option.

TIP If you have never used Kubernetes before, welcome! Although you will not become a Kubernetes expert by reading this section, running the commands should still give you an idea of what it is all about. The main concepts behind Kubernetes are quite simple, once you go beyond the vast ecosystem and terminology.

The following listing shows how to create a cluster with four CPUs and 8 GB of memory.

Listing 13.11 Creating a Minikube cluster

```
$ minikube start --cpus=4 --memory=8G --addons ingress    ◁── Enable the
  minikube v1.9.2 on Darwin 10.15.4                             ingress add-on.
  MINIKUBE_ACTIVE_DOCKERD=minikube
  Automatically selected the hyperkit driver. Other choices:
➥ docker, virtualbox
  Starting control plane node m01 in cluster minikube
  Creating hyperkit VM (CPUs=4, Memory=8192MB, Disk=20000MB) ...
  Preparing Kubernetes v1.14.0 on Docker 19.03.8 ...
  Enabling addons: default-storageclass, ingress, storage-provisioner
  Done! kubectl is now configured to use "minikube"
```

The flags and the output will differ based on your operating system and software versions. You may need to adjust these by looking at the current Minikube documentation (which may have been updated by the time you read this chapter). I allocated four CPUs and 8 GB of memory because this is comfortable on my laptop, but you could be fine with one CPU and less RAM.

You can access a web dashboard by running the minikube dashboard command. Using the Minikube dashboard, you can look at the various Kubernetes resources and even perform some (limited) operations, such as scaling a service up and down or looking into logs.

There is another dashboard that I find particularly efficient and can recommend that you try: K9s (https://k9scli.io). It works as a command-line tool, and it can very quickly move between Kubernetes resources, access pod logs, update replica counts, and so on.

Kubernetes has a command-line tool called kubectl that you can use to perform any actions: deploying services, collecting logs, configuring DNS, and more. kubectl is the Swiss army knife of Kubernetes. We could use kubectl to apply the Kubernetes resource definitions found in each service's k8s/ folder. I will later describe the resources in the k8s/ folders. If you are new to Kubernetes, all you need to know right now is that these files tell Kubernetes how to deploy the three services in this chapter.

There is a better tool for improving your local Kubernetes development experience called Skaffold (https://skaffold.dev). Instead of using Gradle (or Maven) to build the services and package them, and then using kubectl to deploy to Kubernetes, Skaffold is able to do it all for us, avoiding unnecessary builds using caching, performing deployments, aggregating all logs, and cleaning everything on exit.

You first need to download and install Skaffold on your machine. Skaffold works out of the box with Minikube, so no additional configuration is needed. All it needs is a skaffold.yaml resource descriptor, as shown in the following listing (and is included at the root of the chapter13 folder in the Git repository).

Listing 13.12   Skaffold configuration

```
apiVersion: skaffold/v1
kind: Config
metadata:
  name: chapter13
build:
  artifacts:
    - image: vertx-in-action/heat-sensor-service      ◁──┐  Name of a container
      jib:                                                │  image to produce
        type: gradle
        project: heat-sensor-service     ◁────────┐
      context: .                                   │  Project containing
    - image: vertx-in-action/sensor-gateway        │  the source code
      jib:
        type: gradle
        project: sensor-gateway
      context: .
    - image: vertx-in-action/heat-api
      jib:
        type: gradle
        project: heat-api
      context: .
deploy:
  kubectl:
    manifests:
      - "**/k8s/*.yaml"     ◁──────  Also apply YAML files.
```

From the chapter13 folder, you can run `skaffold dev`, and it will build the projects, deploy container images, expose logs, and watch for file changes. Figure 13.2 shows a screenshot of Skaffold running.

Congratulations, you now have the services running in your (local) cluster!

You don't have to use Skaffold, but for a good local development experience, this is a tool you can rely on. It hides some of the complexity of the `kubectl` command-line interface, and it bridges the gap between project build tools (such as Gradle or Maven) and the Kubernetes environment.

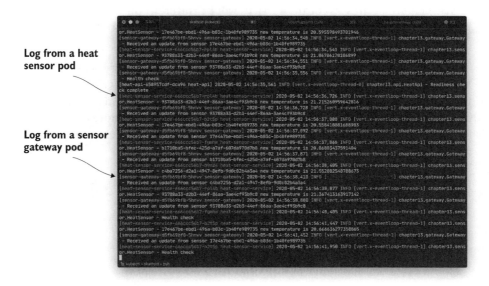

Log from a heat sensor pod

Log from a sensor gateway pod

Figure 13.2   Screenshot of Skaffold running services

The following listing shows a few commands that check on the services deployed in a cluster.

Listing 13.13   Checking the exposed services

Network tunnel, run in a separate terminal

```
$ minikube tunnel        ◁
$ kubectl get services        ◁───── Get the services.
NAME                 TYPE          CLUSTER-IP      EXTERNAL-IP     PORT(S)               AGE
heat-api             LoadBalancer  10.103.127.60   10.103.127.60   8080:31673/TCP        102s
heat-sensor-service  ClusterIP     None            <none>          8080/TCP,5701/TCP     102s
kubernetes           ClusterIP     10.96.0.1       <none>          443/TCP               42m
sensor-gateway       ClusterIP     10.108.31.235   <none>          8080/TCP,5701/TCP     102s
```

The `minikube tunnel` command is important for accessing `LoadBalancer` services, and it should be run in a separate terminal. Note that it will likely require you to enter your password, as the command needs to adjust your current network settings.

You can alternatively use the following Minikube command to obtain a URL for a `LoadBalancer` service without `minikube tunnel`:

```
$ minikube service heat-api --url
http://192.168.64.12:31673
```

TIP   The IP addresses for the services will be different on your machine. They will also change as you delete and create new services, so don't make any assumptions about IP addresses in Kubernetes.

This works because Minikube also exposes `LoadBalancer` services as `NodePort` on the Minikube instance IP address. Both methods are equivalent when using Minikube, but the one using `minikube tunnel` is closer to what you would get with a production cluster, since the service is accessed via a cluster-external IP address.

Now that you have a way to access the heat API service, you can make a few requests.

Listing 13.14   Interacting with the heat API service

```
$ http 10.103.127.60:8080/all      ◁───── Get all data.
HTTP/1.1 200 OK
Content-Type: application/json
content-length: 402

<JSON DATA>
                                              Get out-of-range
$ http 10.103.127.60:8080/warnings    ◁───┐ sensor data.
HTTP/1.1 200 OK
Content-Type: application/json
content-length: 11

<JSON DATA>
```

You can also access the sensor gateway using port forwarding, as shown next.

Listing 13.15   Interacting with the sensor gateway

```
$ kubectl port-forward services/sensor-gateway 8080   ◁─┐
$ http :8080/data                    ◁───┐              Port forward from a
HTTP/1.1 200 OK                          │ Call the      service to a local port (run
Content-Type: application/json           │ service.      in a separate terminal).
content-length: 400

<JSON data>
```

The `kubectl port-forward` command must be run in another terminal, and as long as it is running, the local port 8080 forwards to the sensor gateway service inside the cluster. This is very convenient for accessing anything that is running in the cluster without being exposed as a `LoadBalancer` service.

Finally, we can make a DNS query to see how the heat sensor headless services are resolved. The following listing uses a third-party image that contains the `dig` tool, which can be used to make DNS requests.

Listing 13.16 DNS query to discover the headless heat sensor services

An image with dig installed

```
$ kubectl run --image tutum/dnsutils dns -it --rm -- bash
root@dns:/# dig +short heat-sensor-service.default.svc.cluster.local      ◁
172.17.0.8
172.17.0.12                                                        Run a DNS query.
172.17.0.11
172.17.0.9
root@dns:/#
```

Now if we increase the number of replicas, as in the following listing, we can see that the DNS reflects the change.

Listing 13.17 Increasing the number of heat sensor service replicas

```
$ kubectl scale deployment/heat-sensor-service --replicas 5         ◁
$ kubectl run --image tutum/dnsutils dns -it --rm -- bash
root@dns:/# dig +short heat-sensor-service.default.svc.cluster.local
172.17.0.11
172.17.0.12                                                    Scale to five replicas.
172.17.0.8
172.17.0.13
172.17.0.9
root@dns:/#
```

Also, if we make HTTP requests like in listing 13.14, we can see that we have data from five sensors.

Now that we have deployed the services and interacted with them, let's look at how deployment in Kubernetes works for Vert.x services.

13.2 *Making the services work in Kubernetes*

Making a service work in Kubernetes is fairly transparent for the most part, especially when it has been designed to be agnostic of the target runtime environment. Whether it runs in a container, in a virtual machine, or on bare-metal should never be an issue. Still, there are some aspects where adaptation and configuration need to be done due to how Kubernetes works.

In our case, the only major adaptation that has to be made is configuring the cluster manager so instances can discover themselves and messages can be sent across the distributed event bus. The rest is just a matter of building container images of the services and writing Kubernetes resource descriptors to deploy the services.

Let's start by talking about building container images.

13.2.1 *Building container images*

There are many ways to build a container image, which technically is based on the *OCI Image Format* (OCIIF; https://github.com/opencontainers/image-spec). The most basic way to build such an image is to write a `Dockerfile` and use the `docker build` command to build an image. Note that `Dockerfile` descriptors can be used by other tools such as Podman (https://podman.io/) or Buildah (https://github.com/containers/buildah), so you don't actually need Docker to build container images.

You could thus choose a base image with Java, and then copy a self-contained executable Jar file to be run. While this approach is simple and works just fine, it means that for every change in the source code, you need to build a new image layer of the size of the Jar file that includes all dependencies such as Vert.x, Netty, and more. The compiled classes of a service typically weigh a few kilobytes, while a self-contained Jar file weighs a few megabytes.

Alternatively, you can either craft a `Dockerfile` with multiple stages and layers, or you can use a tool like Jib to automatically do the equivalent for you (https://github.com/GoogleContainerTools/jib). As shown in figure 13.3, Jib assembles different layers to make a container image.

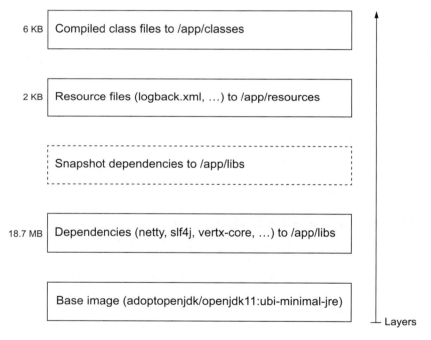

Figure 13.3   Container image layers with Jib

Project dependencies are put just above the base image; they are typically bigger than the application code and resources, and they also tend not to change very often, except when upgrading versions and adding new dependencies. When a project has snapshot dependencies, they appear as a layer on top of the fixed-version dependencies, because newer snapshots appear frequently. The resources and class files change more often, and they are typically light on disk use, so they end up on top. This clever layering approach does not just save disk space; it also improves build time, since layers can often be reused.

Jib offers Maven and Gradle plugins, and it builds container images by deriving information from a project. Jib is also great because it is purely written in Java and it does not need Docker to build images, so you can produce container images without any third-party tools. It can also publish container images to registries and Docker daemons, which is useful in development.

Once the Jib plugin has been applied, all you need is a few configuration elements, as in the following listing for a Gradle build (the Maven version is equivalent, albeit done in XML).

Listing 13.18   Configuring the Jib Gradle plugin

```
jib {
  from {
    image = "adoptopenjdk/openjdk11:ubi-minimal-jre"    ⟵—— Base image
  }
  to {
    image = "vertx-in-action/heat-sensor"        ⟵—— Image name
    tags = setOf("v1", "latest")    ⟵┐
  }                                               Image tags
  container {
    mainClass = "chapter13.sensor.HeatSensor"    ⟵—— Main class to run
    jvmFlags = listOf("-noverify",
    ➥  "-Djava.security.egd=file:/dev/./urandom")   ⟵—— JVM tuning flags
    ports = listOf("8080", "5701")    ⟵┐
    user = "nobody:nobody"              Ports to be exposed by the container
  }
}
```

Run as this user. points to `user = "nobody:nobody"`

The base image comes from the AdoptOpenJDK project, which publishes many builds of OpenJDK (https://adoptopenjdk.net). Here we are using OpenJDK 11 as a *Java Runtime Environment* (JRE) rather than a full *Java Development Kit* (JDK). This saves disk space, as we just need a runtime, and a JDK image is bigger than a JRE image. The `ubi-minimal` part is because we use an AdoptOpenJDK build variant based on the Red Hat Universal Base Image, where the "minimal" variant minimizes the embedded dependencies.

Jib needs to know the main class to execute as well as the ports to be exposed outside the container. In the case of the heat sensor and sensor gateway services, we need to expose port 8080 for the HTTP service and port 5701 for the Vert.x clustering with Hazelcast. The JVM tuning is limited to disabling the JVM bytecode verifier so it boots marginally faster, and also using /dev/urandom for random number generation (the default /dev/random pseudo-file may block when a container starts and there isn't enough entropy). Finally, we run as user `nobody` in group `nobody` to ensure the process runs as an unprivileged user inside the container.

You can build an image and inspect it as shown next.

Listing 13.19   Building a service container image to a Docker daemon

```
$ ./gradlew :heat-sensor-service:jibDockerBuild   ⊲┐   Build a container image for the
(...)                                                  heat sensor service and push it
                                                       to a local Docker daemon.

$ docker image inspect vertx-in-action/heat-sensor:latest   ⊲┐   Inspect the
(...)                                                            container image.
```

All three services' container images build the same way. The only configuration difference is that the heat API service only exposes port 8080, since it does not need a cluster manager.

> **TIP** You can use a tool like Dive (https://github.com/wagoodman/dive) if you are curious about the content of the different layers produced to prepare the container images of the three services.

Speaking of clustering, there is configuration work to be done!

13.2.2 Clustering and Kubernetes

Both Hazelcast and Infinispan, which you used in chapter 3, by default use multicast communications to discover nodes. This is great for local testing and many bare-metal server deployments, but multicast communications are not possible in a Kubernetes cluster. If you run the containers as is on Kubernetes, the heat sensor services and sensor gateway instances will not be able to communicate over the event bus.

These cluster managers can, of course, be configured to perform service discovery in Kubernetes. We will briefly cover the case of Hazelcast, where two discovery modes are possible:

- Hazelcast can connect to the Kubernetes API to listen for and discover pods matching a request, such as a desired label and value.
- Hazelcast can periodically make DNS queries to discover all pods for a given Kubernetes (headless) service.

The DNS approach is more limited.

Instead, let's use the Kubernetes API and configure Hazelcast to use it. By default, the Hazelcast Vert.x cluster manager reads configuration from a cluster.xml resource. The following listing shows the relevant configuration excerpt of the heat-sensor-service/src/main/resource/cluster.xml file.

Listing 13.20   Kubernetes configuration for Hazelcast discovery

```
(...)
<join>
  <multicast enabled="false"/>        ⊲┐  Disable multicast communications.
  <tcp-ip enabled="false" />
  <discovery-strategies>                   Enable the Kubernetes
    <discovery-strategy enabled="true"     discovery strategy.
     class="com.hazelcast.kubernetes.HazelcastKubernetesDiscoveryStrategy">  ⊲┘
```

```
        <properties>
          <property name="service-label-name">vertx-in-action</property>
          <property name="service-label-value">chapter13</property>
        </properties>
      </discovery-strategy>
    </discovery-strategies>
  </join>
(...)
```

Match services with the value chapter13 for label vertx-in-action.

Match services with the label vertx-in-action.

We disable the default discovery mechanism and enable the Kubernetes ones. Here Hazelcast forms clusters of pods that belong to a service where a `vertx-in-action` label is defined with the value `chapter13`. Since we opened port 5701, the pods will be able to connect. Note that the configuration is the same for the sensor gateway.

Since Hazelcast needs to read from the Kubernetes API, we need to ensure that we have permissions using the Kubernetes role-based access control (RBAC). To do so, we need to apply the `ClusterRoleBinding` resource of the following listing and the k8s/rbac.yaml file.

Listing 13.21 RBAC to grant view access to the Kubernetes API

```
apiVersion: rbac.authorization.k8s.io/v1
kind: ClusterRoleBinding          <--- Resource type
metadata:
  name: default-cluster
roleRef:
  apiGroup: rbac.authorization.k8s.io   <--- View role reference
  kind: ClusterRole
  name: view
subjects:
- kind: ServiceAccount
  name: default
  namespace: default
```

The last thing we need to do is ensure that the heat sensor and gateway services run with clustering enabled. In both cases the code is similar. The following listing shows the main method for the heat sensor service.

Listing 13.22 Enabling clustering for the heat sensor service

Get the IPv4 address of the host.

```
public static void main(String[] args) throws UnknownHostException {
  String ipv4 = InetAddress.getLocalHost().getHostAddress();
  VertxOptions options = new VertxOptions()
    .setEventBusOptions(new EventBusOptions()   <--- Customize the event-bus options.
    .setHost(ipv4)
    .setClusterPublicHost(ipv4));         <--- Set the host that other nodes need to talk to.
  Vertx.clusteredVertx(options, ar -> {   <--- Start Vert.x in cluster mode.
    if (ar.succeeded()) {
```

Set the host address.

```
        ar.result().deployVerticle(new HeatSensor());
      } else {
        logger.error("Could not start", ar.cause());
      }
    });
}
```

We start a clustered Vert.x context and pass options to customize the event-bus configuration. In most cases you don't need to do any extra tuning here, but in the context of Kubernetes, clustering will likely resolve to `localhost` rather the actual host IPv4 address. This is why we first resolve the IPv4 address and then set the event-bus configuration host to that address, so the other nodes can talk to it.

> **TIP**   The event-bus network configuration performed in listing 13.22 will be done automatically in future Vert.x releases. I show it here because it can help you troubleshoot distributed event-bus configuration issues in contexts other than Kubernetes.

13.2.3 *Kubernetes deployment and service resources*

Now that you know how to put your services into containers and how to make sure Vert.x clustering works in Kubernetes, we need to discuss resource descriptors. Indeed, Kubernetes needs some descriptors to deploy container images to pods and expose services.

Let's start with the heat sensor service's deployment descriptor, shown in the following listing.

Listing 13.23   Heat sensor service deployment descriptor

```
apiVersion: apps/v1
kind: Deployment          ⊲──── This is a deployment resource.
metadata:
  labels:
    app: heat-sensor-service
  name: heat-sensor-service    ⊲──── Name of the deployment
spec:
  selector:
    matchLabels:
      app: heat-sensor-service
  replicas: 4               ⊲──── Deploy four instances by default.
  strategy:
    type: RollingUpdate
    rollingUpdate:          ⊲──── Rolling update configuration for Hazelcast
      maxSurge: 1
      maxUnavailable: 1
  template:
    metadata:
      labels:
        app: heat-sensor-service
```

```
spec:
  containers:
    - image: vertx-in-action/heat-sensor-service:latest     ◁──┐  Container image
      name: heat-sensor-service                                 │  to deploy
```

This deployment descriptor by default deploys four pods of the `vertx-in-action/heat-sensor-service` container image. Deploying pods is a good first step, but we also need a service definition that maps to these pods. This is especially important for Hazelcast: remember that these instances discover themselves through Kubernetes services with the label `vertx-in-action` and value `chapter13`.

Kubernetes performs rolling updates when a deployment is updated by progressively replacing pods of the older configuration with pods of the newer configuration. It is best to set the values of `maxSurge` and `maxUnavailable` to 1. When you do so, Kubernetes replaces pods one after the other, so the cluster state is smoothly transferred to the new pods. You can avoid this configuration and let Kubernetes be more aggressive when rolling updates, but the cluster state may be inconsistent for some time.

The following listing shows the service resource definition.

Listing 13.24 Heat sensor service definition

```
apiVersion: v1
kind: Service
metadata:
  labels:
    app: heat-sensor-service
    vertx-in-action: chapter13       ◁──┐  Label used for
  name: heat-sensor-service              │  Hazelcast discovery
spec:
  clusterIP: None                    ◁──┐  We want a
  selector:                             │  "headless" service.
    app: heat-sensor-service         ◁──┐  Matches pods with
  ports:                                │  this label/value pair
    - name: http
      port: 8080
    - name: hazelcast
      port: 5701
```

The ports to expose

The service descriptor exposes a *headless* service, which is to say that there is no load balancing among the pods. Because each service is a sensor, they cannot be taken one for the other. Headless services can instead be discovered using DNS queries that return the list of all pods. You saw in listing 13.16 how headless services could be discovered using DNS queries.

The deployment descriptor for the sensor gateway is nearly identical to that of the heat sensor service, as you can see in the next listing.

Listing 13.25   Sensor gateway deployment descriptor

```
apiVersion: apps/v1
kind: Deployment
metadata:
  labels:
    app: sensor-gateway
  name: sensor-gateway
spec:
  selector:
    matchLabels:
      app: sensor-gateway
  strategy:
    type: RollingUpdate
    rollingUpdate:
      maxSurge: 1
      maxUnavailable: 1
  template:
    metadata:
      labels:
        app: sensor-gateway
    spec:
      containers:
        - image: vertx-in-action/sensor-gateway:latest    <──── Container image
          name: sensor-gateway
```

Aside from the names, you can note that we did not specify the replica count, which by default is 1. The service definition is shown in the following listing.

Listing 13.26   Sensor gateway service definition

```
apiVersion: v1
kind: Service
metadata:
  labels:
    app: sensor-gateway
    vertx-in-action: chapter13
  name: sensor-gateway
spec:
  type: ClusterIP    <────┐  Cluster-internal
  selector:               │  load balancing
    app: sensor-gateway
  ports:
    - name: http
      port: 8080
    - name: hazelcast
      port: 5701
```

Now we expose a service that does load balancing. If we start further pods, the traffic will be load balanced between them. A `ClusterIP` service is load balanced, but it is not exposed outside the cluster.

The heat API deployment is very similar to the deployments we've already done, except that there is configuration to pass through environment variables. The following listing shows the interesting portion of the descriptor in the `spec.template.spec.containers` section.

Listing 13.27 Heat API deployment excerpt

```
spec:
  containers:
    - image: vertx-in-action/heat-api:latest
      name: heat-api
      env:
        - name: LOW_TEMP
          value: "12.0"
        - name: HIGH_TEMP
          value: "32.0"
        - name: GATEWAY_HOST
          valueFrom:
            configMapKeyRef:
              name: sensor-gateway-config
              key: gateway_hostname
        - name: GATEWAY_PORT
          valueFrom:
            configMapKeyRef:
              name: sensor-gateway-config
              key: gateway_port
```

Define environment variables.

Override the LOW_TEMP environment value.

Get a value from a ConfigMap resource.

Environment variables can be either passed directly by value, as for `LOW_TEMP`, or passed through the indirection of a `ConfigMap` resource, as in the following listing.

Listing 13.28 Configuration map example

```
apiVersion: v1
kind: ConfigMap
metadata:
  name: sensor-gateway-config
data:
  gateway_hostname: sensor-gateway.default.svc.cluster.local
  gateway_port: "8080"
```

Name of the ConfigMap resource

Value for the gateway_hostname key

By passing environment variables through a `ConfigMap`, we can change configuration without having to update the heat API deployment descriptor. Note the value of `gateway_hostname`: this is the name used to resolve the service with DNS inside the Kubernetes cluster. Here `default` is the Kubernetes namespace, `svc` designates a service resource, and `cluster.local` resolves to the `cluster.local` domain name (remember that we are using a local development cluster).

Finally, the following listing shows how to expose the heat sensor API as an externally load-balanced service.

Listing 13.29   Heat API service definition

```
apiVersion: v1
kind: Service
metadata:
  labels:
    app: heat-api
  name: heat-api
spec:
  type: LoadBalancer        ⟵——  Load balance
  selector:                        externally.
    app: heat-api
  ports:
    - name: http
      port: 8080
```

A LoadBalancer service is exposed outside the cluster. It can also be mapped to a host name using an Ingress, but this is not something that we will cover.[1]

We have now covered deploying the services to Kubernetes, so you may think that we are done. Sure, the services work great in Kubernetes as-is, but we can make the integration even better!

13.3   *First-class Kubernetes citizens*

As you have seen, the services that we deployed work fine in Kubernetes. That being said, we can make them first-class Kubernetes citizens by doing two things:

- Exposing health and readiness checks
- Exposing metrics

This is important to ensure that a cluster knows how services behave, so that it can restart services or scale them up and down.

13.3.1   *Health checks*

When Kubernetes starts a pod, it assumes that it can serve requests on the exposed ports, and that the application is running fine as long as the process is running. If a process crashes, Kubernetes will restart its pod. Also, if a process consumes too much memory, Kubernetes will kill it and restart its pod.

We can do better by having a process *inform* Kubernetes about how it is doing. There are two important concepts in health checking:

- *Liveness checks* allow a service to report if it is working correctly, or if it is failing and needs to be restarted.
- *Readiness checks* allow a service to report that it is ready to accept traffic.

Liveness checks are important because a process may be working, yet be stuck with a fatal error, or be stuck in, say, an infinite loop. Liveness probes can be based on files,

---

[1]For more on Ingresses and other Kubernetes topics, see Marko Lukša's *Kubernetes in Action*, second edition (Manning, 2020).

TCP ports, and HTTP endpoints. When probes fail beyond a threshold, Kubernetes restarts the pod.

The heat sensor service and sensor gateway can provide simple health-check reporting using HTTP. As long as the HTTP endpoint is responding, that means the service is operating. The following listing shows how to add health-check capability to these services.

Listing 13.30 Simple HTTP health-check probe

```
// In the verticle start method:
router.get("/health").handler(this::healthCheck);      ⟵  Add a route for
                                                           a health check.
// (...)
private final JsonObject okStatus = new JsonObject().put("status", "UP");   ⟵

                                                       JSON payload to say
                                                         the service is up
private void healthCheck(RoutingContext ctx) {   ⟵
  logger.info("Health check");
  ctx.response()
    .putHeader("Content-Type", "application/json")    Vert.x web handler
    .end(okStatus.encode());                          for health checks
}
```

With HTTP probes, Kubernetes is interested in the HTTP status code of the response: 200 means the check succeeded, and anything else means that there is a problem. It is a loose convention to return a JSON document with a `status` field and the value `UP` or `DOWN`. Additional data can be in the document, such as messages from various checks being done. This data is mostly useful when logged for diagnosis purposes.

We then have to let Kubernetes know about the probe, as in the following listing.

Listing 13.31 Heat sensor service liveness probe

```
# (...)
spec:
  containers:
    - image: vertx-in-action/heat-sensor-service:latest
      name: heat-sensor-service
      livenessProbe:        ⟵——  Define a liveness probe.
        httpGet:
          path: /health
          port: 8080                          Initial delay before
          initialDelaySeconds: 15   ⟵——┘      doing checks
          periodSeconds: 15      ⟵
          timeoutSeconds: 5            Interval between checks
```

Specify the HTTP endpoint.

Check timeout

Here the liveness checks start after 15 seconds, happen every 15 seconds, and time out after 5 seconds. We can check this by looking at the logs of one of the heat sensor service pods.

Listing 13.32   Health checks in logs

```
$ kubectl logs -f heat-sensor-service-6944f78b84-2tpnx | grep
⇒ 'Health check'
2020-05-02 17:27:54,218 INFO [vert.x-eventloop-thread-1]        ◁——    The pod
⇒ chapter13.sensor.HeatSensor - Health check                              name will
2020-05-02 17:28:09,182 INFO [vert.x-eventloop-thread-1]                 be different
⇒ chapter13.sensor.HeatSensor - Health check                             on your
2020-05-02 17:28:24,181 INFO [vert.x-eventloop-thread-1]                 machine.
⇒ chapter13.sensor.HeatSensor - Health check
2020-05-02 17:28:39,182 INFO [vert.x-eventloop-thread-1]
⇒ chapter13.sensor.HeatSensor - Health check
```

To get a pod name and check the logs, you can look at the output of `kubectl logs`. Here we see that the checks indeed happen every 15 seconds.

The case of the heat API is more interesting, as we can define both liveness and readiness checks. The API needs the sensor gateway, so its readiness depends on that of the gateway. First, we have to define two routes for liveness and readiness checks, as shown in the next listing.

Listing 13.33   Health-check routes of the heat API service

```
    router.get("/health/ready").handler(this::readinessCheck);   ◁——   Readiness
┌─▷ router.get("/health/live").handler(this::livenessCheck);             check
│
Liveness check
```

The implementation of the `livenessCheck` method is identical to that of listing 13.30: if the service responds, it is alive. There is no condition under which the service would respond yet be in a state where a restart would be required. The service can, however, be unable to accept traffic because the sensor gateway is not available, which will be reported by the following readiness check.

Listing 13.34   Readiness check of the heat API service

```
private void readinessCheck(RoutingContext ctx) {
  webClient.get("/health")                        ◁——
    .expect(ResponsePredicate.SC_OK)                     Make a request to
    .timeout(5000)                                       the sensor gateway.
    .send(ar -> {
      if (ar.succeeded()) {
        logger.info("Readiness check complete");
        ctx.response().setStatusCode(200)          ◁———— Send a 200 status.
          .putHeader("Content-Type", "application/json")
          .end(okStatus.encode());
      } else {
        logger.error("Readiness check failed", ar.cause());
        ctx.response().setStatusCode(503)          ◁———— Report a failure.
          .putHeader("Content-Type", "application/json")
          .end(new JsonObject()
            .put("status", "DOWN")
```

```
                    .put("reason", ar.cause().getMessage().encode()); ◁─┐  Give the error
      }                                                                  │  message in
    });                                                                  │  the report.
}
```

To perform a readiness check, we make a request to the sensor gateway health-check endpoint. We could actually make any other request that allows us to know if the service is available. We then respond to the readiness check with either an HTTP 200 or 503.

The configuration in the deployment resource is shown in the following listing.

Listing 13.35 Configuring health checks for the heat API service

```
# (...)
spec:
  containers:
    - image: vertx-in-action/heat-api:latest
      name: heat-api
      # (...)
      livenessProbe:
        httpGet:
          path: /health/live
          port: 8080
        initialDelaySeconds: 1
        periodSeconds: 15
        timeoutSeconds: 5
      readinessProbe:        ◁─── Define a readiness probe.
        httpGet:
          path: /health/ready
          port: 8080
        initialDelaySeconds: 5
        periodSeconds: 10
        timeoutSeconds: 5
```

As you can see, a readiness probe is configured very much like a liveness probe. We have defined `initialDelaySeconds` to be five seconds; this is because the initial Hazelcast discovery takes a few seconds, so the sensor gateway hasn't deployed its verticle before this has been completed.

We can check the effect by taking down all instances of the sensor gateway, as shown next.

Listing 13.36 Scaling down the sensor gateway to 0 replicas

```
$ kubectl scale deployment/sensor-gateway --replicas 0   ◁─── Scale to 0.
deployment.extensions/sensor-gateway scaled
$ kubectl get pods                                ◁─────┐ List all pods in the default namespace.
NAME                                     READY   STATUS    RESTARTS   AGE
heat-api-5dbcc84795-ccb8d                0/1     Running   0          55m
heat-sensor-service-6946bc8f6f-2k7lv     1/1     Running   0          55m
heat-sensor-service-6946bc8f6f-d9hd8     1/1     Running   0          55m
heat-sensor-service-6946bc8f6f-rhdbg     1/1     Running   0          55m
heat-sensor-service-6946bc8f6f-xd28p     1/1     Running   0          55m
```

You should wait a few seconds before listing the pods, and observe that the heat API pod becomes marked as 0/1 ready. This is because the readiness checks have failed, so the pod will not receive traffic anymore. You can try running the following query and see an immediate error:

```
$ http $(minikube service heat-api --url)/warnings
```

Now if we scale back to one instance, we'll get back to a working state, as shown in the following listing.

Listing 13.37   Scaling up the sensor gateway to one replica

```
$ kubectl scale deployment/sensor-gateway --replicas 1   ⟵— Scale up to one instance.
deployment.extensions/sensor-gateway scaled
$ kubectl get pods
NAME                                      READY   STATUS    RESTARTS   AGE
heat-api-5dbcc84795-ccb8d                 1/1     Running   0          63m
heat-sensor-service-6946bc8f6f-2k7lv      1/1     Running   0          63m
heat-sensor-service-6946bc8f6f-d9hd8      1/1     Running   0          63m
heat-sensor-service-6946bc8f6f-rhdbg      1/1     Running   0          63m
heat-sensor-service-6946bc8f6f-xd28p      1/1     Running   0          63m
sensor-gateway-6b7cd8bbcb-bt14k           1/1     Running   0          2m18s
```

You can now make successful HTTP requests again.

NOTE The action you perform in a health or readiness check depends on what your service does. As a general rule, you should perform an action that has no side effect in the system. For instance, if your service needs to report a failed health check when a database connection is down, a safe action should be to perform a small SQL query. By contrast, doing a data insertion SQL query has side effects, and this is probably not how you want to check whether the database connection is working.

13.3.2 *Metrics*

Vert.x can be configured to report metrics on various items like event-bus communications, network communications, and more. Monitoring metrics is important, because they can be used to check how a service is doing and to trigger alerts. For instance, you can have an alert that causes Kubernetes to scale up a service when the throughput or latency of a given URL endpoint is above a threshold.

I will show you how to expose metrics from Vert.x, but the other topics, like visualization, alerting, and auto-scaling are vastly complex and are outside the scope of this book.

Vert.x exposes metrics over popular technologies such as JMX, Dropwizard, Jolokia, and Micrometer.

We will be using Micrometer and Prometheus. Micrometer (https://micrometer .io/) is interesting because it is an abstraction over metric-reporting backends such as

InfluxDB and Prometheus. Prometheus is a metrics and alerting project that is popular in the Kubernetes ecosystem (https://prometheus.io/). It also works in *pull* mode: Prometheus is configured to periodically collect metrics from services, so your services are not impacted by Prometheus being unavailable.

We will be adding metrics to the sensor gateway as it receives both event-bus and HTTP traffic; it is the most solicited service of the use case. To do that, we first have to add two dependencies as follows.

Listing 13.38   Adding metrics support

Vert.x Micrometer support
```
implementation("io.vertx:vertx-micrometer-metrics:$vertxVersion")
implementation("io.micrometer:micrometer-registry-prometheus:$mpromVersion")
```
Micrometer support for Prometheus

The sensor gateway needs clustering and metrics when starting Vert.x from the `main` method. We need to enable metrics as follows.

Listing 13.39   Enabling Micrometer/Prometheus metrics

```
VertxOptions options = new VertxOptions()                      Event-bus configuration,
  .setEventBusOptions(new EventBusOptions()         ⊲         just like before
    .setHost(ipv4)
    .setClusterPublicHost(ipv4))
  .setMetricsOptions(new MicrometerMetricsOptions()    ⊲       Enable Micrometer
    .setPrometheusOptions(new VertxPrometheusOptions()          metrics with
      .setPublishQuantiles(true)          ⊲                    Prometheus.
      .setEnabled(true))             Also publish
  .setEnabled(true));          metric quantiles.
```

We now have to define an HTTP endpoint for metrics to be available. The Vert.x Micrometer module offers a Vert.x web handler to make it easy, as shown in the following listing.

Listing 13.40   Exposing a metrics endpoint over HTTP

```
router.route("/metrics")       ⊲——— Expose at the /metrics path.
  .handler(ctx -> {
    logger.info("Collecting metrics");     ⊲——— Log requests.
    ctx.next();
  })
  .handler(PrometheusScrapingHandler.create());      ⊲——— Premade handler
```

It is a good idea to intercept metric requests and log them. This is useful when configuring Prometheus to check if it is collecting any metrics.

You can test the output using port forwarding.

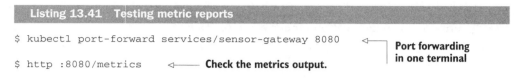

Prometheus metrics are exposed in a simple text format. As you can see when running the preceding commands, by default lots of interesting metrics are reported, like response times, open connections, and more. You can also define your own metrics using the Vert.x Micrometer module APIs and expose them just like the default ones.

You will find instructions and Kubernetes descriptors for configuring the Prometheus operator to consume metrics from the sensor gateway in the chapter13/ k8s-metrics folder of the book's Git repository. You will also find a pointer to make a dashboard with Grafana that looks like the one in figure 13.4.

Grafana is a popular dashboard tool that can consume data from many sources, including Prometheus databases (https://grafana.com/). All you need is to connect visualizations and queries. Fortunately, dashboards can be shared as JSON documents. Check the pointers in the Git repository if you want to reproduce the dashboard in figure 13.4.

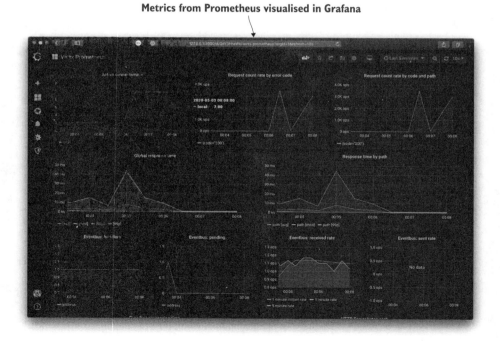

Figure 13.4   Metrics dashboard using Grafana

13.4 *The end of the beginning*

All good things come to an end, and this chapter concludes our journey toward reactive applications with Vert.x. We started this book with the fundamentals of asynchronous programming and Vert.x. Asynchronous programming is key to building scalable services, but it comes with challenges, and you saw how Vert.x helped in making this programming style simple and enjoyable. In the second part of this book we used a realistic application scenario to study the key Vert.x modules for databases, web, security, messaging, and event streaming. This allowed us to build an end-to-end reactive application made up of several microservices. By the end of the book, you saw a methodology based on a combination of load and chaos testing to ensure service resilience and responsiveness. This is important, as reactive is not just about scalability, but is also about writing services that can cope with failures. We concluded with notes on deploying Vert.x services in a Kubernetes cluster, something Vert.x is a natural fit for.

Of course, we did not cover all that's in Vert.x, but you will easily find your way through the project's website and documentation. The Vert.x community is welcoming, and you can get in touch over mailing lists and chat. Last but not least, most of the skills that you have learned by reading this book translate to technologies other than Vert.x. Reactive is not a technology that you pick off the shelf. A technology like Vert.x will only get you half of the way to reactive; there is a craft and mindset required in systems design to achieve solid scalability, fault resiliency, and ultimately responsiveness.

On a more personal note, I hope that you enjoyed reading this book as much as I enjoyed the experience of writing it. I'm looking forward to hearing from you in online discussions, and if we happen to attend an event together, I will be more than happy to meet you in person!

Have fun, and take care!

Summary

- Vert.x applications can easily be deployed to Kubernetes clusters with no need for Kubernetes-specific modules.
- The Vert.x distributed event bus works in Kubernetes by configuring the cluster manager discovery mode.
- It is possible to have a fast, local Kubernetes development experience using tools like Minikube, Skaffold, and Jib.
- Exposing health checks and metrics is a good practice for operating services in a cluster.

index

Modern Java in Action
by Raoul-Gabriel Urma, Mario Fusco,
and Alan Mycroft

ISBN 9781617293566
592 pages, $54.99
September 2018

The Java Module System
by Nicolai Parlog
Foreword by Kevlin Henney

ISBN 9781617294280
440 pages, $49.99
June 2019

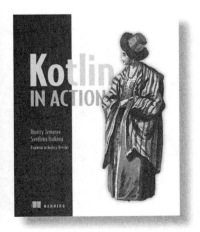

Kotlin in Action
by Dmitry Jemerov and Svetlana Isakova
Foreword by Andrey Breslav

ISBN 9781617293290
360 pages, $44.99
February 2017

For ordering information go to www.manning.com

RELATED MANNING TITLES

Reactive Design Patterns
by Roland Kuhn with Brian Hanafee and Jamie Allen
Foreword by Jonas Bonér

ISBN 9781617291807
392 pages, $49.99
February 2017

Microservices Patterns
by Chris Richardson

ISBN 9781617294549
520 pages, $34.99
October 2018

Microservices in Action
by Morgan Bruce and Paulo A. Pereira

ISBN 9781617294457
392 pages, $49.99
October 2018

For ordering information go to www.manning.com